A Student Handbook to the Plays of Arthur Miller

A Student Handbook to the Plays of Arthur Miller

All My Sons
Death of a Salesman
The Crucible
A View from the Bridge
Broken Glass

TOBY ZINMAN
ENOCH BRATER
SUSAN C. W. ABBOTSON
STEPHEN MARINO
ALAN ACKERMAN

Edited by
ENOCH BRATER

B L O O M S B U R Y
LONDON · NEW DELHI · NEW YORK · SYDNEY

Bloomsbury Methuen Drama

An imprint of Bloomsbury Publishing Plc

50 Bedford Square   1385 Broadway
London   New York
WC1B 3DP   NY 10018
UK   USA

www.bloomsbury.com

Bloomsbury is a registered trade mark of Bloomsbury Publishing Plc

Material from the present edition was previously published in the Methuen Drama
Student Edition series as follows: Chronology of Arthur Miller by Enoch Brater, with
grateful thanks to the Arthur Miller Society for permission to draw on their 'Brief
Chronology of Arthur Miller's Life and Works', published in All My Sons, Death of
a Salesman, The Crucible, A View from the Bridge and Broken Glass, 2010. Plot,
Commentary, Notes and Questions for Further Study previously published in
All My Sons, Death of a Salesman, The Crucible, A View from the Bridge,
Broken Glass. Notes copyright © 2010 by Bloomsbury Methuen Drama

British Library Cataloguing-in-Publication Data
A catalogue record for this book is available from the British Library.

ISBN: HB: 978-1-4725-1497-4
PB: 978-1-4081-8487-5
ePub: 978-1-4081-8568-1
ePDF: 978-1-4725-1437-0

Library of Congress Cataloging-in-Publication Data
A Student Handbook to the Plays of Arthur Miller : All My Sons, Death of a Salesman,
The Crucible, A View From the Bridge, Broken Glass / Toby Zinman, Enoch Brater,
Susan C. W. Abbotson, Stephen Marino, Alan Ackerman ; edited by Enoch Brater.
pages cm
Includes bibliographical references and index.
ISBN 978-1-4081-8487-5 (alk. paper) – ISBN 978-1-4725-1497-4 (alk. paper) –
ISBN 978-1-4081-8568-1 (print) – ISBN 978-1-4725-1437-0 (print)
1. Miller, Arthur, 1915-2005–Criticism and interpretation. 2. Miller, Arthur, 1915-2005–
Handbooks, manuals, etc. I. Zinman, Toby Silverman, 1942- II. Brater, Enoch. III. Abbotson,
Susan C. W., 1961- IV. Marino, Stephen A. V. Ackerman, Alan L. (Alan Louis)
PS3525.I5156Z897 2013
812'.52–dc23
2013025583

Typeset by Newgen Knowledge Works (P) Ltd., Chennai, India
Printed and bound in Great Britain

Contents

Introduction

'I could not imagine a theater worth my time that did not want to change the world', Arthur Miller wrote in *Timebends: A Life*, the luminous memoir he published in his seventy-fifth year as 'a Parthian shot' to ward off future biographers (they would come calling anyway). Although the nearly forty works he composed for the stage during his professional career as a playwright, not to mention the fiction and steady stream of essays and articles completed during the same years, did not exactly change the world (writing plays rarely does), they nonetheless continue to demonstrate the bold ambition that lies behind the very idea of theatre as a transformative art form in America. Miller's plays hold the stage with authority. They remind us time and again of the unique role drama plays in the national conversation any healthy society needs to have about itself. And in several of his most haunting scenes, nothing less than democracy itself is at stake.

The discussions of the five plays included in this volume are designed to give shape and meaning to the many questions students, audiences and theatre professionals bring to their initial encounters with a wide and ever-expansive Miller repertory. How Miller became 'Arthur Miller' tells us a great deal about the origin, the energy and the scope of this drama. The second of three children born to Augusta and Isidore Miller in an upper-middle-class Jewish family in Manhattan, his early years were shaped by the foundations set in place by a large urban minority community to celebrate its Eastern European roots as well as to counter the anti-Semitism experienced elsewhere in New York, a city where daily newspapers still printed job advertisements that ran 'No Jews or Irish need apply'. His family lived on the top floor of an apartment building on 110th Street; the front windows faced south onto Central Park. His father took a chauffeured-driven car to his office downtown in the garment district, where he ran a profitable coat manufacturing business. 'In my family the worker was always a huge pain in the ass.' His mother's prized possession was a baby grand piano, on which she played sheet music from the latest popular Broadway shows. The playwright's younger sister, the actress Joan Copeland, remembers her long-legged brothers Kermit and Arthur curled up, reading, underneath. Their secure childhood world seemed as though it would never end: ice-skating in the park, Hebrew school three times a week, P.S. 24 just around the corner (the same school their mother attended), and Barnett grandparents close by in the same Harlem neighbourhood.

Everything changed with the Crash of 1929. After the almost two years Izzy Miller tried to keep his Miltex Coat and Suit Company up and running, a business that once employed 800 workers finally went under. The family made a reverse migration: from upscale Manhattan to workaday Brooklyn, 'Willy Loman territory'. The 1930s meant hard times, but 'what my father lost most during those years', the playwright said, 'was hope'. There was still enough money to buy a house at 1350 East Third Street, on the same block where his mother's sisters, Annie Newman and Esther Balsam, lived. Miller was suddenly surrounded by cousins: 'All I knew about was family.' He explored his new neighbourhood on his Columbia Racer and planted a pear tree and an apple tree in the backyard (the latter was felled in a summer storm, prefiguring the opening scene of his 1947 play *All My Sons*). He read Gertrude Stein and remembered being 'mesmerised by Hemingway'. Obsessed with sports, he played football and stickball on a vacant lot on Avenue M and Gravesend Avenue and went to the ice-skating rink on Ocean Parkway. He woke up at 4:30 in the morning and used his bicycle to deliver freshly baked bread and bagels before going off to school; when his racer was stolen, he found part-time work in a local automobile supplies store.

Such biographical details, while intriguing, are by no means atypical of a city boy growing up in the early years of the Great Depression. In Miller's case such proletarian realities were to shadow him for the rest of his life; they had a profound and lasting effect on the kind of writer he wanted so much to become. His sister, half laughing, half crying, remembered him as the tall, lanky figure standing in the cold New York rain, in solidarity with shop workers on strike outside their own father's factory. His brother 'Kerm', a much better student and later a decorated war hero, went on to New York University after he left James Madison High School, but Miller was full of wanderlust and set his sights, unrealistically, on Stanford. 'I tried going to City College at night', Miller said. 'But I was working during the day and I kept falling asleep.' After a few weeks, he dropped out.

Miller's eventual enrolment at the University of Michigan was preceded by two letters of rejection. When he graduated from the new Abraham Lincoln High School in 1933, he needed four faculty members to write letters of recommendation; he could find only three. He had flunked algebra three times – shades of Biff Loman in *Death of a Salesman* here – and the rest of his academic record was unimpressive. He spent his first two years of high school at James Madison, mostly playing football, resulting in a serious leg injury that later kept him out of military service. When Michigan turned him down in 1933, he applied a year later, determined to gain admission at one 'of the few schools that took [creative] writing seriously'. When Miller received his second disappointing letter of rejection, he was emboldened to respond to the Dean of the College, telling him he had become a 'much more serious fellow'. The Dean wrote back, saying he would give Miller 'a try', but with the caveat that 'I had better make some grades. I could not conceive of a dean at Columbia or Harvard doing that'. Years later, looking back at this probationary period, he reflected that 'I still can't believe Michigan let me in.'

Miller's father was amazed to hear that any school would pay students money for writing. His son told him about the Hopwood Awards, built from a legacy given by a Michigan alumnus who had made a fortune on Broadway, mostly by writing popular bedroom farces. Impressed, his father nonetheless insisted that he make some money first – $500 for tuition fees and living expenses – before he tried his hand at the Hopwoods. Miller worked for almost two years making $15 a week at a gigantic warehouse for automobile parts on the site that would later become the Lincoln Center for the Performing Arts. The company, Chadwick-Delamater, had never hired anyone who was Jewish before, and only agreed to do so when Miller's former boss in Brooklyn intervened: 'This young guy knows more about parts than most of you guys, so if you don't give him a job there's only one reason.' After Miller saved enough money and left for Michigan, he found out that his replacement was an Italian: 'They hated him, too'.

Miller's first published writing in Ann Arbor was for the *Michigan Daily*, the student newspaper where he quickly moved from cub reporter to editorial board member. Initially run by 'the fraternity crowd', the *Daily* was in a period of transition in the 1930s as it witnessed the changing political climate on campus and elsewhere: lockouts in the nearby automobile factories, racism in the college football programme, the Japanese occupation of Manchuria, virulent anti-Semitic tirades broadcast by Father Coughlin from suburban Detroit, as well as the enthusiastic embrace by American corporations of the economic boom underway in Nazi Germany. Joined by fellow campus activists like Mary Slattery, who became his first wife in 1940, Miller was beginning to find his voice as an outspoken critic of repression and social injustice. He gave up writing for the student newspaper because he said he was 'tired of reporting the facts' on the ground. He might have a more lasting impact by rearranging them in some other, more imaginative form.

Miller found that form in the courses he took in playwriting and dramatic literature with Erich Walter and Kenneth Rowe in the English Department at the University of Michigan. He read a lot of Ibsen. 'Rowe, while I'm sure he wanted to teach me a lot, taught me really only one thing, and that was that I could hold the stage with dialogue.' He 'may not have created a playwright (no teacher ever did) but he surely read what we wrote with the urgency of one who actually had the power to produce the play'.

The aspiring playwright submitted three scripts to the Hopwood Awards Committee, *No Villain*, *Honors at Dawn*, and *The Great Disobedience*, winning prizes for the first two. His revision of *No Villain* under the new title of *They Too Arise* also received a major award of $1,250 from the Theatre Guild's Bureau of New Plays.

What we might now be tempted to call the Hopwood plays are important in the sense that they display many of the same tensions developed with much greater sophistication in the works discussed in this volume. *All My Sons*, Miller's first Broadway success in 1947, is their direct inheritor, reimagining as it does the psychological conflicts within a family in the context of a much wider field of economic reality and social responsibility. Tragedy embroils the common man in the guise of Fate, what the playwright liked to call 'chickens coming home to roost, one by one'. Miller's is a family play, but his focus turns on the proverbial 'family of man'; he noted, parenthetically, that *King Lear* and *Oedipus Rex* were also, 'among other things, family plays'.

Miller's maturity as a writer comes with his ability to locate the precise dramatic form that gives each work its unique volume and shape. It may come as a surprise to learn that before completing *All My Sons* he was experimenting, among other things, with writing dialogue in verse and even the epic dimensions of a story detailing the conquest of Montezuma's empire by conquistadores led by a wily Cortez. Both plans ended in frustration, although Miller was to revise and revisit such possibilities later in his career. *All My Sons*, as Toby Zinman discusses it here, is the playwright's most Ibsen-like play, relying as it does on the solid conventions of fourth-wall realism and the slow and steady revelation of an ominous backstory. All of the major choices these characters have made take place before the curtain goes up: you watch with increasing anxiety as their decisions come back to haunt and undo them. And you know for sure that when a character, in this case Joe Keller, makes a statement mid-way to the effect that 'if there's something' greater than one's family he'll take a gun to his head and blow his brains out, it's only a matter of (stage) time before a gun goes off. Despite the sudden revelation in a letter from the past – props, as in Papa Ibsen, can speak volumes – there's still something thrilling about watching how all of this so efficiently unfolds. You're crying in spite of yourself.

Miller's proletarian spirit is very much in evidence in his student plays, animated by such deliberate and pressing concerns as workers' rights, industrial action and corporate self-interest. Setting the drama within the contours of a familial conflict between father and son, the playwright's favourite trope, the young Miller found himself working in the same vein as the socially conscious playwrights of the period, established writers like Sidney Kingsley, Elmer Rice and most especially Clifford Odets, whose *Awake and Sing!*, with the legendary Stella Adler in the lead, was the Group Theatre's greatest triumph in the 1930s. Taking its title from the Book of Isaiah, Odets' trumpet call is now heard in the South Bronx, where Depression-era characters struggle for a chance 'to get to first base'. In his *Waiting for Lefty* taxi drivers go on strike; in *Golden Boy* a sensitive Italian-American boy abandons the poetry of his violin to become a prize-fighter. It's the unwritten law of such dramas that in each case the price has to be paid; the piper never gets stiffed. *All My Sons* positions its compelling narrative of war-profiteering in the following decade, soon after America's triumph in the Second World War. The social concerns of the previous decade, however, have still not been reconciled; they hover in the background of the Keller family saga, always threatening to overturn the surface texture of a world very much in peril. In Miller's next play, *Death of a Salesman*, such issues will take centre stage.

Willy Loman, the end-product of a new order that has passed him by without so much as a by-your-leave, is so commanding a stage figure, so representative of the tragic fate of a certain kind of common man, that we sometimes forget that this story is embedded in a dramatic form constantly defying the unforgiving strictures of fourth-wall realism. Unlike *All My Sons*, which precedes it by a mere two years, this work has the atmospheric quality of '*a dream rising out of reality*'. The play marks stage time in a series of counterpoints: scenes from the past vie with scenes from the so-called objective present; both vie with scenes staged as Willy wants to remember them. Sometimes there are even double journeys into the past; the sound of a flute, '*small and fine, telling of grass and trees and the horizon*', takes us there. Lyrical elements framed in this dimension are likely to be post-Ibsen (though not necessarily post-late Ibsen). They are certainly post-*All My Sons*. For Willy Loman there will be no golden handshake; there will, however, be a Requiem.

The discussion of *Death of a Salesman* that follows in this book traces the dramatic strategies Miller employs to make past and present interact on his stage in new and surprising ways. Miller also uses the past as prelude to the present in *The Crucible*, but there it is pursued for its metaphorical implications rather than as a stylisation of time and memory. The playwright was not really prepared for the reaction the first audiences had to Willy Loman's story. He thought he had written a hard-edged representation of the dark underside of the so-called American dream; the immediate response was raw and emotional, at times verging perilously on the sentimental. He was determined not to make the same 'mistake' again in his next play (although late in life he admitted that an audience must be made 'to feel before it can be made to think').

Miller's initial response to the Communist witch-hunts that began in the early 1950s was an adaptation of Ibsen's *An Enemy of the People*, which he wrote for his friends, the actors Florence Eldredge and Fredric March. 'I have made no secret of my early love for Ibsen's work', the playwright said, especially so for a drama that offered its audience a powerful depiction of social corruption, injustice and greed in light of a looming ecological disaster. Ibsen's theme, Miller reflected, 'concerns the crushing of the dissenting spirit by the majority, and the right and obligation of such a spirit to exist at all'. But it is *The Crucible* that most significantly captures the climate of fear, intimidation and the abuse of civil liberties set in motion by Senator Joseph McCarthy and other right-wing opportunists in the US Congress. 'I don't think I can adequately communicate the sheer density of the atmosphere of the time', he observed. 'For the outrageous had so suddenly become the accepted norm'. He told Christopher Bigsby that 'it was really a tremendous outburst of primitive human terror'.

In writing *The Crucible*, Miller tried hard to avoid the strong emotional undertow that had an uncanny way of overwhelming the argumentative texture of works like *All My Sons* and especially *Death of a Salesman*. Rather than situate the play in the contentious political climate of the McCarthyite present, he made the firm decision to look to the past not only for historical precedent but even more so for a controlling metaphor. In this landmark work Miller made what he called 'a living connection between myself and Salem, and between Salem and Washington . . . for whatever else they might be, I saw that the House Un-American Activities Committee hearings in Washington were profoundly and even avowedly ritualistic'.

Susan Abbotson makes clear in her commentary on *The Crucible* the many ways in which this work, at first glance so quintessential American, is both a play of its time and a play that travels far beyond it. Miller's most often produced stage play, it speaks with unsparing conviction to any society confronting the iron hand of political oppression, intolerance and unbending patriarchal authority. 'I have to admit', the playwright said, 'that it [feels] marvelous that McCarthy [is] what's-his-name while *The Crucible* is *The Crucible* still'. The play 'has outlived him'. When Miller refused to name names before HUAC three years after *The Crucible* was produced on Broadway, his testimony sounds as though it might very well be lifted from the monologue he provides for the defiant John Proctor at the end of his play. The update he offered at the time goes straight to the centre of the play's argument: 'A man doesn't have to be an informer in order to practice his profession in the United States.' Yet the great strength and range of *The Crucible* lies in the way it liberates its audience from the merely literal. Any threat to an entrenched authority at the moment when society is in transition, as Salem surely is in this work, will find its scapegoats. Miller reminds us that the outsider we fear most lies hidden deep within ourselves. The greatest threat of all is our potential to be so easily seduced not by the Devil, but by the lure of power in the crucible of tyranny. 'The longer I worked [on *The Crucible*]', Miller reflected, 'the more certain I felt that as impossible as it might seem, there were moments when an individual conscience was all that could keep a world from falling'.

The central drama of an individual's role in society is seen under a very different lens in *A View from the Bridge*, a play about betrayal, both personal and tribal. Eddie Carbone, Miller's uneasy protagonist, lies to himself, to his wife Beatrice and to the lawyer Alfieri long before he lets immigration authorities know about the 'submarine' status of Beatrice's cousins, the undocumented workers Marco and Rodolpho. The play is set in Red Hook, where longshoremen from a tightly knit Sicilian-American community ply their trade and look after one another in the highly unstable shadow of the Brooklyn Bridge. In the plays preceding this one, Miller looked for the essence of tragedy in the daily life of 'the common man'; he found it in the figure of Eddie Carbone. 'Modern drama', the playwright observed, 'has lost its ability to deal with the whole man. What is needed is a new social drama which will combine the approach of the Greek theater with modern discoveries in psychology and economics'. He had long been thinking about how to make this synthesis work on stage; in an early letter to his former professor, Kenneth Rowe, he had even wondered about the feasibility of writing plays in a 'Greek-like' mode. For *A View from the Bridge* he adapted a number of devices from the classical Greek theatre. Foremost among these is the ambiguous role he assigns to Alfieri, who serves as choral commentator, narrator as well as protagonist as the play's rising action leads to retribution and the finality of death. 'The secret of the Greek drama' for Miller 'is the vendetta'. As narrator, Alfieri's job is to frame the scene, nostalgically, in the full context of tragic inevitability. In another time and in another place the same story could have been told 'in Calabria perhaps, or on the cliff in Syracuse'. Miller's Red Hook is 'full of Greek tragedies'.

Miller's contribution to the genre is his uncanny ability for making even the most inarticulate characters eloquent. Eddie speaks the rough language of a dockworker; the playwright allows his subtext do the rest of the work: 'Once Eddie had been squarely placed in his social context, among his people, the myth-like feeling of the story emerged of itself.' This is a stunning psychological portrait, one conceived within the contours of a vibrant, colourful yet self-contained and even dangerous working-class world. An old-world Roman Catholicism is writ large, as is the Mediterranean code of honour. Marco challenges his betrayer; Eddie dies when the knife he holds in his hand is twisted into his own heart. When you betray 'the other' in your neighbour, you betray 'the other' in yourself. That is why Alfieri, in the closing lines of the play – an epilogue really – will always mourn Eddie 'with a certain . . . alarm'.

Miller did not come upon this dramatic solution easily. As Stephen Marino demonstrates, *A View from the Bridge* began its stage life as a one-act play, with several speeches originally written in verse. Expanding its scope and social milieu into a two-act drama, the revised script omitted Alfieri's poetic dialogue and, in order to bring more psychological depth to the inter-generational family conflict, greatly expanded the two major roles for women, especially that of Eddie's unacknowledged love interest, Beatrice's seventeen-year-old niece Catherine. Miller, however, had been thinking of writing a play about Sicilian-Americans as far back as the late 1940s. In the notebook he kept while working on the ideas and language he might use for the script that became *Death of a Salesman*, he jotted down a memo to himself to write 'the Italian play [about X] who ratted on the two immigrants'. Nor was the local setting for this play entirely new territory. In 1951 he abandoned a filmscript called *The Hook*, similarly set in the shadow of the Brooklyn Bridge amid a conspiracy of corrupt union leadership in league with the Mafia.

Miller moves to a different part of Brooklyn in his most substantial play of the 1990s, *Broken Glass,* a strange piece 'full of ambiguities'. The work also marks a return to the kind of fourth-wall realism associated with *All My Sons*, though in this case mediated by a number of disturbing textures based on elements drawn from a complex romantic triangle and the psychological thriller, both examined in the context of a horrifying political reality taking place elsewhere. Sylvia Gellberg suffers from a destabilising clinical depression after she reads about what is happening in Germany after Kristillnacht, the November 1938 night of broken glass when, in an organised pogrom, the Nazis torched and destroyed at least 7,500 shops, eleven synagogues, Jewish community centres and cemetery chapels, twenty-nine warehouses and 171 private homes. More than 30,000 Jewish men were rounded up and thrown into concentration camps. 'Where's Roosevelt?' she cries out in despair as she is suddenly struck down by a psychosomatic paralysis. 'Where's England?'

This is Miller's fourth Holocaust play, though, as Alan Ackerman argues, the shape he gives it here is decidedly different from those that come before. *Incident at Vichy*, loosely based on a real incident told to him by his wife Inge Morath, had the shape of a Socratic dialogue; its central thesis is masterfully pinpointed when Leduc intones, 'It's not your guilt I want, it's your responsibility'. *After the Fall* attempted to equate an individual's personal anxiety with the ominous shadows cast on stage by concentration camp towers; and *Playing for Time*, his adaptation of *The Musicians of Auschwitz*, Fania Fenelon's compelling memoir written with Marcelle Routier, cauterises its audience with a powerful ethical dilemma: 'We know a little something more about the human race that we didn't know before and it's not good news.' In *Broken Glass*, however, the ground is constantly shifting as the drama reveals the porous boundaries separating internal from outward catastrophes. 'What did I do with my life?' Sylvia wonders with pitch-perfect lucidity in what is, perhaps, the play's most arresting and intimate moment. 'I took better care of my shoes.' But it is her husband Gellberg, the man in black, who displays the real paralysis that informs both the background and the foreground of this work, the one 'that could destroy the world'. Miller's theatre aims to take 'us back to the time when the social contract was being torn up', when the road to indifference led to complicity, when, as Sylvia says, all the 'streets are covered with broken glass'. In each of the five plays discussed in this volume, Miller's conflation of personal doom and historical reality, even atrocity, may be shaky in its ability 'to change the world', yet his commitment to using stage time for provocation and serious thought is never, ever in doubt.

Enoch Brater

Chronology of Arthur Miller

Arthur Miller: 1915–2005

1915	17 October: Arthur Asher Miller born in New York City, the second of Isidore (Izzy) and Augusta (Gussie) Barnett Miller's three children. His brother Kermit born in 1912, sister Joan 1922.
1920–28	Attends PS 24 in Harlem, then an upper-middle-class Jewish neighbourhood, where his mother went to the same school. The family lives in an apartment overlooking Central Park on the top floor of a six-storey building at 45 West 110th Street, between Lenox and Fifth Avenues. Takes piano lessons, goes to Hebrew school and ice-skates in the park. His Barnett grandparents are nearby on West 118th Street. In summers the extended family rents a bungalow in Far Rockaway. Sees his first play in 1923, a melodrama at the Schubert Theatre.
1928	His father's successful manufacturing business in the Garment District, the Miltex Coat and Suit Company, with as many as 800 workers, begins to see hard times faced with the looming Depression. The family moves from Manhattan to rural Brooklyn, where they live at 1350 East 3rd Street, near Avenue M, in the same neighbourhood as his mother's two sisters, Annie Newman and Esther Balsam. Miller plants a pear tree in the backyard ('All I knew was cousins'). Celebrates his bar-mitzvah at the Avenue M Temple.
1930	Transfers from James Madison High School where he is reassigned to the newly built Abraham Lincoln High School on Ocean Parkway. Plays in the football team and injures his leg in a serious accident that will later excuse him from active military service. Academic record unimpressive, and he fails geometry twice.
1931	Early-morning delivery boy for a local bakery before going off to school; forced to stop when his bicycle is stolen. Works for his father during the summer vacation.
1933	Graduates from Abraham Lincoln High School and registers for night school at City College. He leaves after two weeks ('I just couldn't stay awake')

1933–34   Earns $ 15 a week as a clerk for Chadwick-Delamater,
           an automobile-parts warehouse in a run-down section of
           Manhattan that will later become the site for the Lincoln Center
           for the Performing Arts. He is the only Jewish employee, and
           experiences virulent anti-Semitism for the first time.

1934   Writes to the Dean of the University of Michigan to appeal
           against his second rejection and says he has become a 'much
           more serious fellow' ('I still can't believe they let me in').
           Travels by bus to Ann Arbor for the autumn semester, with
           plans to study journalism because 'Michigan was one of the
           few places that took writing seriously'. Lives in a rooming
           house on South Division Street and joins the *Michigan Daily*
           as reporter and night editor; takes a non-speaking part in a
           student production of Shakespeare's *King Henry VIII*. Moves
           to an attic room at 411 North State Street and works part-time
           in an off-campus laboratory feeding past-prime vegetables to
           thousands of mice.

1936   Writes his first play, *No Villain*, in six days during semester
           break and receives a Hopwood Award in Drama for $250 using
           the pseudonym 'Beyoum'. Changes his major to English.

1937   Enrols in Professor Kenneth T. Rowe's playwriting class.
           Rewrites *No Villain* as *They Too Arise* and receives a major
           award of $1,250 from the Theatre Guild's Bureau of New
           Plays (Thomas Lanier — later Tennessee – Williams was
           another winner in the same competition). *They Too Arise* is
           produced by the B'nai Brith Hillel Players in Detroit and at
           the Lydia Mendelssohn Theatre in Ann Arbor. Receives a
           second Hopwood Award for *Honors at Dawn* when Susan
           Glaspell is one of the judges. Contributes to *The Gargoyle*,
           the student humour magazine. Drives his college friend Ralph
           Neaphus east to join the Abraham Lincoln Brigade in the
           Spanish Civil War, but decides not to go with him. Months
           later Neaphus, twenty-three, was dead.

1938   Composes a prison play, *The Great Disobedience*, and revises
           They Too Arise as *The Grass Still Grows*. Graduates from
           the University of Michigan with a BA in English. Joins the
           Federal Theater Project in New York to write radio plays and
           scripts.

1939   The Federal Theater Project is shut down by conservative
           forces in Congress, and Miller goes on relief. Writes *Listen
           My Children* and *You're Next* with his friend and fellow

Michigan alumnus, Norman Rosten. *William Ireland's Confession* is broadcast on the Columbia Workshop.

1940   Marries Mary Grace Slattery, his college sweetheart at the University of Michigan. They move into a small apartment at 62 Montague Street in Brooklyn Heights. Writes *The Golden Years*, a play about Montezuma, Cortez, and the European conquest and corruption of Mexico. *The Pussycat and the Plumber Who Was a Man* airs on CBS Radio. Makes a trip to North Carolina to collect dialect speech for the Folk Division of the Library of Congress.

1941–43   Works as a shipfitter's helper on the night shift at the 43 Brooklyn Navy Yard repairing battle-scarred war vessels from the North Atlantic fleet. Finishes additional radio plays, including *The Eagle's Nest* and *The Four Freedom*. Completes *The Half-Bridge*. The one-act *That They May Win* is produced in New York.

1944   Daughter Jane is born. Prepares Ferenc Molnar's *The Guardsman* and Jane Austen's *Pride and Prejudice* for radio adaptation, and continues his own writing for the medium. Tours army camps in preparation for the draft of a screenplay called *The Story of G.I. Joe*, based on news reports written by the popular war correspondent Ernie Pyle (withdraws from the project when his role as author is compromised). Publishes *Situation Normal . . .*, a book about this experience that highlights the real challenges returning soldiers encountered on re-entering civilian life. Dedicates the book to his brother, 'Lieutenant Kermit Miller, United States Infantry', a war hero. *The Man Who Had All the Luck* opens on Broadway but closes after six performances, including two previews. The play receives the Theater Guild National Award.

1945   Publishes *Focus*, a novel about anti-Semitism and moral blindness set in and around New York. His article 'Should Ezra Pound Be Shot?' appears in *New Masses*.

1946   Adapts *Three Men on a Horse* by George Abbott and John C. Holm for radio.

1947   *All My Sons* opens in New York and receives the New York Drama Critics' Circle Award; the Donaldson Award and the first Tony Award for best author. His son Robert is born. Moves with his family to a house he purchases at 31 Grace Court in Brooklyn Heights. Also buys a new car, a

Studebaker, and a farmhouse in Roxbury, Connecticut. Writes the article 'Subsidized Theater' for the *New York Times*.

1948   Builds by himself a small studio on his Connecticut property where he writes *Death of a Salesman*. Edward G. Robinson and Burt Lancaster star in the film version of *All My Sons*.

1949   *Death of a Salesman*, starring Lee J. Cobb, Arthur Kennedy, Cameron Mitchell and Mildred Dunnock opens at the Morosco Theatre in New York on 10 February. Directed by Elia Kazan with designs by Jo Mielziner, it wins the New York Drama Critics' Circle Award, the Donaldson Prize, the Antoinette Perry Award, the Theatre Club Award and the Pulitzer Prize. His essay Tragedy and the Common Man' is printed in the *New York Times*. Attends the pro-Soviet Cultural and Scientific Conference for World Peace at the Waldorf-Astoria Hotel to chair a panel with Clifford Odets and Dimitri Shostakovich.

1950   Adaptation of Henrik Ibsen's *An Enemy of the People* produced on Broadway starring Fredric March and Florence Henderson ('I have made no secret of my early love for Ibsen's work'). First sound recording of *Death of a Salesman*. *The Hook*, a film script about graft and corruption in the closed world of longshoremen in the Red Hook section of Brooklyn, fails to reach production after backers yield to pressure from the House Committee on Un-American Activities. *On the Waterfront*, the Budd Schulberg–Elia Kazan collaboration featuring Marlon Brando, changes the setting to Hoboken, New Jersey, but is developed from the same concept, and is released four years later.

1951   Meets Marilyn Monroe. Fredric March in the role of Willy Loman for Columbia Pictures in the first film version of *Death of a Salesman*. Joseph Buloff translates the play into Yiddish; his production runs in New York and introduces Miller's play to Buenos Aires.

1952   Drives to Salem, Massachusetts, and visits the Historical Society, where he reads documents and researches the material he will use in *The Crucible*. Breaks with Kazan over the director's cooperation with HUAC.

1953   *The Crucible* wins the Donaldson Award and the Antoinette Perry Award when it opens in New York at the Martin Beck Theatre. Directs *All My Sons* in Arden, Delaware.

1954   US State Department denies Miller a passport to attend the Belgian premiere of *The Crucible* in Brussels ('I wasn't embarrassed for myself; I was embarrassed for my country'). NBC broadcasts the first radio production of *Death of a Salesman*. Mingei Theater stages first Japanese translation of *Salesman* in Tokyo, where the play is received as a cautionary tale about the 'salaryman'.

1955   The one-act version of *A View from the Bridge* opens in New York on a double-bill with *A Memory of Two Mondays*. HUAC pressurises city officials to withdraw permission for Miller to make a film about juvenile delinquency set in New York.

1956   Lives in Nevada for six weeks in order to divorce Mary Slattery. Marries Marilyn Monroe. Subpoenaed to appear before HUAC on 21 June, he refuses to name names. Accepts an honorary degree as Doctor of Humane Letters from his alma mater, the University of Michigan. Jean-Paul Sartre writes screenplay for French adaptation of *The Crucible*, called *Les Sorcieres de Salem*; the film stars Yves Montand and Simone Signoret. Travels with Monroe to England, where he meets Laurence Olivier, her co-star in *The Prince and the Showgirl*. Peter Brook directs revised two-act version of *A View from the Bridge* in London at the New Watergate Theatre Club, as censors determined it could not be performed in public. 'Once Eddie had been squarely placed in his social context, among his people,' Miller noted, 'the myth-like feeling of the story emerged of itself . . . Red Hook is full of Greek tragedies.'

1957   Cited for contempt of Congress for refusing to co-operate with HUAC. On the steps of the United States Congress, and with Monroe on his arm, he vows to appeal against the conviction. Monroe buys all members of Congress a year's subscription to *I.F. Stone's Weekly*. First television production of *Death of a Salesman* (ITA, UK). *Arthur Miller's Collected Plays* is published, and his short story, 'The Misfits', appears in *Esquire Magazine*.

1958–59   The US Court of Appeals overturns his conviction 59 for contempt of Congress. Elected to the National Institute of Arts and Letters and receives the Gold Medal for Drama.

1961   Miller and Monroe divorce (granted in Mexico on the grounds of 'incompatibility'). *The Misfits*, a black-and-white film directed by John Huston featuring the actress in her first serious dramatic role, is released for wide distribution. Miller calls his scenario 'an eastern western' and bases the plot on his short story of the same name. Co-stars include Clark Gable, Montgomery Clift, Eli Wallach and Thelma Ritter. *The Crucible: An Opera in Four Acts* by Robert Ward and Bernard Stambler is recorded. Sidney Lumet directs a movie version of *A View from the Bridge* with Raf Vallone and Carol Lawrence. Miller's mother, Augusta, dies.

1962   Marries Austrian-born Inge Morath, a photographer with Magnum, the agency founded in 1947 by Henri Cartier-Bresson. Marilyn Monroe, aged thirty-six, dies. His daughter, Rebecca Augusta, is born in September. NBC broadcasts an adaptation of *Focus* with James Whitmore and Colleen Dewhurst.

1963   Publishes a children's book, *Jane's Blanket*. Returns to Ann Arbor to deliver annual Hopwood Awards lecture, 'On Recognition'.

1964   Visits the Mauthausen death camp with Inge Morath and covers the Nazi trials in Frankfurt, Germany, for the *New York Herald Tribune*. Reconciles with Kazan. *Incident at Vichy*, whose through-line is 'It's not your guilt I want, it's your responsibility', opens in New York, as does *After the Fall*. The former is the first of the playwright's works to be banned in the Soviet Union. The latter Miller says 'is not about Marilyn' and that she is 'hardly the play's *raison d'etre*'.

1965   Elected president of PEN, the international organisation of writers dedicated to fighting all forms of censorship. American premiere of the two-act version of *A View from the Bridge* is performed Off-Broadway. Laurence Olivier's production of *The Crucible*, starring Colin Blakely and Joyce Redman, is staged in London at the Old Vic by the National Theatre. Returns to Ann Arbor, where his daughter Jane is now a student, to participate in the first teach-in in the US concerning the Vietnam conflict.

1966   First sound recording of *A View from the Bridge*. In Rome Marcello Mastroianni and Monica Vitti play the parts of

Quentin and Maggie in Franco Zeffirelli's Italian production of *After the Fall*. Miller's father, Isidore, dies.

1967   *I Don't Need You Any More*, a collection of short stories, is published. Sound recording of *Incident at Vichy*. Television production of *The Crucible* is broadcast on CBS. Visits Moscow and tries to persuade Soviet writers to join PEN. Playwright-in-Residence at the University of Michigan. His son, Daniel, is born in January.

1968   *The Price*, which the playwright called 'a quartet', 'the most specific play I've ever written', opens on Broadway. Sound recording *of After the Fall*. Attends the Democratic National Convention in Chicago as a delegate from Roxbury, Connecticut. Leads peace march against the war in South-East Asia with the Reverend Sloan Coffin, Jr, at Yale University in New Haven. *Death of a Salesman* sells its millionth copy.

1969   *In Russia*, a collaborative project with text by Miller and photography by Morath, is published. Visits Prague in a show of support for Czech writers; meets Vaclav Havel. Retires as president of PEN.

1970   Miller's works are banned in the Soviet Union, a result of his efforts to free dissident writers. *Fame* and *The Reason Why*, two one-act plays, are produced; the latter is filmed at his home in Connecticut.

1971   Television productions of *A Memory of Two Mondays* on PBS and *The Price* on NBC. Sound recording of *An Enemy of the People*. *The Portable Arthur Miller* is published.

1972   *The Creation of the World and Other Business* opens at the Schubert Theatre in New York on 30 November. Attends the Democratic National Convention in Miami as a delegate. First sound recording of *The Crucible*.

1973   PBS broadcasts Stacy Keach's television adaptation of *Incident at Vichy*, with Harris Yulin as Leduc. Champions the case of Peter Reilly, an eighteen-year-old falsely convicted of manslaughter for his mother's murder; four years later, all charges are dismissed. *After the Fall* with Faye Dunaway is televised on NBC. Teaches mini-course at the University of Michigan; students perform early drafts of scenes from *The American Clock*.

1974   *Up from Paradise*, musical version of *The Creation of the World and Other Business*, is staged at the Power Center

for the Performing Arts at the University of Michigan.
With music by Stanley Silverman and cover design by Al
Hirschfield, Miller calls it his 'heavenly cabaret'.

1977   A second collaborative project with Inge Morath, *In the
Country*, is published. Petitions the Czech government to halt
arrests of dissident writers. The *Archbishop's Ceiling* opens
at the Kennedy Center in Washington, DC. Miller said he
wanted to dramatise 'what happens . . . when people know
they are . . . at all times talking to Power, whether through a
bug or a friend who really is an informer'.

1978   *The Theater Essays of Arthur Miller* is published. NBC
broadcasts the film of *Fame* starring Richard Benjamin.
Belgian National Theatre mounts the twenty-fifth anniversary
production of *The Crucible*; this time Miller can attend.

1979   *Chinese Encounters*, with Inge Morath, is published. Michael
Rudman directs a major revival of *Death of a Salesman* at the
National Theatre in London, with Warren Mitchell as Willy
Loman.

1980   *Playing for Time*, the film based on Fania Fenelon's
autobiography *The Musicians of Auschwitz*, is broadcast
nationally on CBS, with Vanessa Redgrave and Jane Alexander.
('I tried to treat it as a story meaningful to the survivors, by
which I mean all of us. I didn't want it to be a mere horror
story.') *The American Clock* has its first performance at the
Spoleto Festival in South Carolina, then opens in New York
with the playwright's sister, Joan Copeland, as Rose Baum, a
role based on their mother. Miller sees his play as 'a mural', 'a
mosaic', 'a story of America talking to itself . . . There's never
been a society that hasn't had a clock running on it, and you
can't help wondering – How long?'

1981   Second volume of *Arthur Miller's Collected Plays*
is published. Delivers keynote address on the fiftieth
anniversary of the Hopwood Awards Program in Ann Arbor.

1982   Two one-act plays that represent 'the colors of memory',
Elegy for a Lady and *Some Kind of Love Story*, are produced
as a double-bill at the Long Wharf Theatre in Connecticut
under the title *2 by A.M.*

1983   Directs *Death of a Salesman* at the People's Art Theatre in
Beijing, part of a cultural exchange to mark the early stage of
the opening of diplomatic relations between the United States

and the People's Republic of China. Ying Ruocheng plays Willy Loman in his own Chinese translation. *I Think About You a Great Deal*, a monologue written as a tribture to Vaclav Havel, appears in *Cross Currents*, University of Michigan.

1984   '*Salesman' in Beijing* is published. The texts of *Elegy for a Lady* and *Some Kind of Love Story* are printed under a new title, *Two-Way Mirror*. Receives Kennedy Center Honors for lifetime achievement. Reworks the script of *The American Clock* for Peter Wood's London production at the National Theatre.

1985   Twenty-five million viewers see Dustin Hoffman play Willy Loman, with John Malkovich as Biff and Kate Reid as Linda in the production of *Death of a Salesman* shown on CBS. Goes to Turkey with Harold Pinter for PEN as an ambassador for freedom of speech. Serves as delegate at a meeting of Soviet and American writers in Vilnius, Lithuania, where he attacks Russian authorities for their continuing anti-Semitism and persecution of *samizdat* writers. *The Archbishop's Ceiling* is produced in the UK by the Bristol Old Vic. Completes adaptation of *Playing for Time* as a stage play.

1986   One of fifteen writers and scientists invited to meet Mikhail Gorbachev to discuss Soviet policies. The Royal Shakespeare Company uses a revised script of *The Archbishop's Ceiling* for its London production in the Barbican Pit.

1987   Miller publishes *Timebends: A Life*, his autobiography. Characterising it as 'a preemptive strike' against future chroniclers, he discusses his relationship with Marilyn Monroe in public for the first time. *Clara* and *I Can't Remember Anything* open as a double-bill at Lincoln Center in New York under the title *Danger: Memory!* Broadcasts of *The Golden Years* on BBC Radio and Jack O'Brien's television production of *All My Sons* on PBS. Michael Gambon stars as Eddie Carbone in Alan Ayckbourn's intimate production of *A View from the Bridge* at the National Theatre in London. University of East Anglia names its site for American Studies the Arthur Miller Centre.

1988   Publishes 'Waiting for the Teacher', a nineteen-stanza free-verse poem, in *Ha'aretz*, the Tel Aviv-based liberal newspaper, on the occasion of the fiftieth anniversary of the founding of the State of Israel.

1990   *Everybody Wins*, directed by Karel Reisz with Debra Winger
and Nick Nolte, is released: 'Through the evolution of the
story – a murder that took place before the story opens – we
will be put through an exercise in experiencing reality and
unreality.' Television production *of An Enemy of the People*
on PBS. Josette Simon plays Maggie as a sultry jazz singer
in Michael Blakemore's London revival *of After the Fall*
at the National Theatre, where *The Crucible* also joins the
season's repertory in Howard Davies's production starring
Zoë Wannamaker and Tom Wilkinson. Updated version of
The Man Who Had All the Luck is staged by Paul Unwin in a
joint production by the Bristol Old Vic and the Young Vic in
London.

1991   *The Last Yankee* premieres as a one-act play. *The Ride Down
Mount Morgan*, 'a moral farce', has its world premiere in
London: The play is really a kind of nightmare.' Television
adaptation of *Clara* on the Arts & Entertainment Network.
Receives Mellon Bank Award for lifetime achievement in the
humanities.

1992   *Homely Girl, A Life* is published with artwork by Louise
Bourgeois in a Peter Blum edition. Writes satirical op-
ed piece for the *New York Times* urging an end to capital
punishment in the US.

1993   Expanded version of *The Last Yankee* opens at the Manhattan
Theatre Club in New York. Television version of *The
American Clock* on TNT with the playwright's daughter,
Rebecca, in the role of Edie.

1994   *Broken Glass*, a work 'full of ambiguities' that takes 'us back
to the time when the social contract was being torn up', has a
pre-Broadway run at the Long Wharf Theatre in Connecticut;
opens at the Booth Theatre in New York on 24 April. David
Thacker's London production wins the Olivier Award for Best
Play.

1995   Tributes to the playwright on the occasion of his eightieth
birthday are held in England and the US. Receives William
Inge Festival Award for Distinguished Achievement in
American Theater. *Homely Girl, A Life and Other Stories*, is
published. In England the collection appears under the title
Plain Girl. Darryl V. Jones directs a production of *A View
from the Bridge* in Washington, DC, and resets the play in

a community of Domincan immigrants. The Arthur Miller
Society is founded by Steven R. Centola.

1996   Revised and expanded edition of *The Theater Essays of
Arthur Miller* is published. Receives the Edward Albee Last
Frontier Playwright Award. Rebecca Miller and Daniel Day-
Lewis are married.

1997   *The Crucible*, produced by the playwright's son, Robert A.
Miller, is released for wide distribution and is nominated
for an Academy Award. Revised version of *The Ride Down
Mount Morgan* performed at the Williamstown Playhouse in
Massachusetts. BBC airs television version of *Broken Glass*,
with Margot Leicester and Henry Goodman repeating their
roles from the award-winning London production.

1998   *Mr Peters' Connections* opens in New York with Peter Falk.
Revival of *A View from the Bridge* by the Roundabout Theatre
Company wins two Tony Awards. Revised version of *The
Ride Down Mount Morgan* on Broadway. Miller is named
Distinguished Inaugural Senior Fellow of the American
Academy in Berlin.

1999   Robert Falls's fiftieth anniversary production of *Death of
a Salesman*, featuring Brian Dennehy as Willy Loman,
moves from the Goodman Theater in Chicago and opens on
Broadway, where it wins the Tony Award for Best Revival
of a Play. Co-authors the libretto with Arnold Weinstein for
William Bolcom's opera of *A View from the Bridge*, which
has its world premiere at the Lyric Opera of Chicago.

2000   Patrick Stewart reprises his role as Lyman Felt in *The Ride
Down Mount Morgan* on Broadway, where *The Price* is
also revived (with Harris Yulin). Major eighty-fifth birthday
celebrations are organised by Christopher Bigsby at the
University of East Anglia and by Enoch Brater at the
University of Michigan, where plans are announced to build
a new theatre named in his honour; it opens officially on 29
March 2007 ('whoever thought when I was saving $500 to
come to the University of Michigan that it would come to
this'). 'Up to a certain point the human being is completely
unpredictable. That's what keeps me going . . . You live
long enough, you don't rust.' *Echoes Down the Corridor*, a
collection of essays from 1944 to 2000, is published. Miller
and Morath travel to Cuba with William and Rose Styron and

meet Fidel Castro and the Colombian writer Gabriel García Márquez.

2001   Williamstown Theater Festival revives *The Man Who Had All the Luck*. Laura Dern and William H. Macy star in a film based on the 1945 novel *Focus*. Miller is named the Jefferson Lecturer in the Humanities by NEH and receives the John H. Finley Award for Exemplary Service to New York City. His speech *On Politics and the Art of Acting* is published.

2002   Revivals in New York of *The Man Who Had All the Luck* and *The Crucible*, the latter with Liam Neeson as John Proctor. *Resurrection Blues* has its world premiere at the Guthrie Theatre in Minneapolis. Miller receives a major international award in Spain, the Premio Principe de Asturias de las Letras. Death of Inge Morath.

2003   Awarded the Jerusalem Prize. His brother, Kermit Miller, dies on 17 October. *The Price* is performed at the Tricycle Theatre in London.

2004   *Finishing the Picture* opens at the Goodman Theatre in Chicago. *After the Fall* revived in New York. Appears on a panel at the University of Michigan with Mark Lamos, who directs students in scenes from Miller's rarely performed plays.

2005   Miller dies of heart failure in his Connecticut home on 10 February. Public memorial service is held on 9 May at the Majestic Theatre in New York, with 1,500 in attendance. Asked what he wanted to be remembered for, the playwright said, 'A few good parts for actors.'

All My Sons

commentary and notes by
TOBY ZINMAN

Plot

Act One

The curtain rises on a summer Sunday morning in a suburban 'back yard', the garden at the back of the house. It is worth noting that this is the outskirts of a town, not a big city; these are small-town people in America's heartland – culturally, as well as geographically.

Joe Keller, the play's pivotal character, is sitting in a lawn chair reading the newspaper. His next-door neighbour, Jim Bayliss, a doctor, is staring at a tree that blew over in last night's storm. They are joined by another neighbour, Frank Lubey. Joe comments on the want ads, revealing both his interest in what people buy and his ignorance of the world, a lack of sophistication he is conscious of, although not embarrassed by. The conversation quickly turns to the fallen tree, a memorial for Larry, Joe's eldest son who was reported missing in action three years before during the Second World War. Frank remarks on the coincidence of the timing – the tree having fallen in the same month as Larry's birthday – revealing that, at Kate's request, he is creating a horoscope for Larry, part of Kate's attempt to 'prove' that Larry might still return home alive.

Joe reveals that Ann, Larry's former fiancée, arrived the night before for a visit. She and her family used to live in the house now occupied by the Bayliss family. Jim's wife Sue, a former nurse, interrupts their conversation by calling her husband to the phone, and their continuing squabble about Jim's professional life reveals her worries about money – she wants him to see any patient who will pay (this was still the era of doctors who made house calls) and Jim reveals his impatience with hypochondriacs. Next, Lydia, Frank's wife, arrives, complaining about a broken toaster; she wonders aloud if Ann has recovered from Larry's death, marvelling that in the few years that have passed since then, she herself has had three babies; Joe remarks that 'it [war] changed all the tallies', that he had two sons and now has one.

Enter Chris, the son he still has, with his morning coffee; he chooses the book-review section of the newspaper which establishes his interest in intellectual matters. Bert, a neighbourhood child, arrives, continuing the make-believe game Joe invented for the local boys: they are his 'policemen', inspecting the neighbourhood for signs of wrongdoing. This game, we will learn, is a result of Joe's return to the neighbourhood after the factory scandal: his partner, Steve, Ann's father, went to prison while Joe was exonerated. The game evolved from the neighbourhood boys' fascination with this brush with the law. Chris tells Joe that Kate was outside in the yard the previous night and saw the tree crack and fall. They discuss her need to believe that Larry is still alive and Chris explains that they should have made her confront the reality of his death that they have both accepted. Chris then tells his father that he plans to ask Ann to marry him, knowing that his parents feel she is still 'Larry's girl'. This leads to Chris's declaration that if his parents can't accept his marriage to Ann, he will leave them and the business and move away. Joe is thunderstruck by this, protesting that his years of work in the business have all been for Chris.

Kate comes out of the house, oddly preoccupied, complaining of a headache. Surprisingly, she is pleased that the tree blew down, reasoning that planting it as a memorial for Larry was premature, that this is a sign that Larry is still alive. She recounts her dream the night before in which Larry called to her from a low-flying plane. Kate insists that the timing of Ann's visit and the fact that Ann has remained unmarried support her belief, and she is clearly suspicious of Chris's interest in his brother's fiancée. As a way to change the subject and the mood, Chris suggests they all go out for dinner and dancing that night, although once Chris goes into the house, Kate's smile vanishes and she continues, with great urgency and distress, to tell her husband of her uneasiness about Ann's arrival. They seem to touch on what will become the central fact of the play – although we cannot know this yet – when she says 'You above all have got to believe . . .' and Joe replies, 'What does that mean, me above all?' Bert rushes into the yard and distracts them (and us) from this crucial conversation. Kate is distraught about the game Joe and Bert play, 'that whole jail business', and Joe asks, significantly, but apparently indignantly, 'What have I got to hide?'

Finally, Ann appears, looking lovely, with news of her family: this is where we get the first clue that her father, Joe's former business partner, is in prison. Ann tells Kate that she does not believe Larry is alive and is no longer waiting for him. Kate argues that she has to keep believing he is alive: 'That's why there's God.' Frank returns, borrows a ladder, sympathises with Ann about her father. Ann recalls the past, when the neighbours called Joe and her father Steve 'Murderers!', but Joe assures her that it is all forgotten, and that all those accusatory neighbours now play poker on Saturday nights in the Kellers' back yard.

Joe traces the events of the past when he walked down the street after he was released from prison, facing down his neighbours on their verandas, all of whom believed he was guilty despite the court's exoneration. 'Fourteen months later I had one of the best shops in the state again, a respected man again; bigger than ever.' Ann is amazed that Joe doesn't hold a grudge against her father who was found guilty of shipping damaged airplane parts to the US Army. Ann discloses that neither she nor her brother has seen or written to their father since the trial.

Joe then explains his version of how the signal event of the past happened: the cracks in the cylinder heads were discovered, the pressure from the Army to deliver the goods, Steve's decision to cover up the flaws and ship them out. Joe asserts that he was at home sick that day, and that it was simply a 'mistake' on Steve's part.

Ann and Chris confess their love for each other. Chris tells her about his painful experiences in the war. Many of his men were killed, though they displayed their loyalty to each other, a willingness to sacrifice themselves rather than be selfish, revealing to Chris the 'one new thing' made out of all the war's destruction: 'responsibility. Man for man.' He explains his disillusionment when he returned home to work in his father's factory, feeling 'ashamed' because the rat-race was still on. America seemed to have learned nothing from the war except how profitable it was.

Joe returns to the yard to find Chris and Ann in an embrace, and Chris tells him they are getting married. They decide to tell Kate later. He announces that Ann's brother, George, has telephoned. While she is in the house talking to George on the phone, Joe urges Chris to enjoy their factory's financial success, and tells him he wants to change the business's name to his son's. Chris deflects the offer. Ann returns to the yard to announce that George, who is now a lawyer, is arriving by train that evening, having just visited their father in prison. Kate, who has now come out of the house, is very frightened and warns Joe to 'be smart'.

Act Two

It is early evening of the same day, and Chris has been sawing apart the broken tree. Kate and Joe are both worried about George's imminent visit, suspicious that he – and perhaps Ann, too – hates the Kellers because Steve took all the blame and punishment. Sue and Ann discuss the prospect of Chris and Ann's marriage, and Sue reveals her bitterness about her own marriage. She hopes Ann and Chris will live elsewhere since Chris's nobility, what Sue calls his 'phony idealism', makes Jim feel trapped and dissatisfied. Sue further reveals that everyone knows 'Joe pulled a fast one to get out of jail', and casts doubt on Ann's certainty that Chris wouldn't work for a firm built on blood money.

When Joe appears after his nap, Chris and Ann gently mock his lack of education; he then cleverly suggests setting up George in legal practice locally, and proffers the possibility of Steve's return to the firm when he finishes his prison term, causing Chris to explode angrily.

Lydia arrives to fix Kate's hair for the planned night out. Jim arrives, having left George in the car, and warns Chris that George has 'blood in his eye'. George, who has just visited Steve in prison, tells Chris and Ann the truth of the events of that fateful day: Joe told him to ship the damaged cylinder heads. Chris becomes enraged, denying George's accusations.

But once Kate enters, George is disarmed by her affection and by nostalgia for the innocent pre-war past when they were all children. Joe, too, manipulates George, using George's contempt for his father to turn the argument around. But then Joe casually brags that he has never been sick – and suddenly they all freeze with the revelation that gives the lie to Joe's claim he was too ill to go into work the day Steve shipped the damaged goods.

Frank bursts into the scene, excited to announce that Larry's horoscope 'proves' that he should still be alive. George leaves; Kate tells Ann to leave, saying she is still 'Larry's girl'. In the ensuing argument, Kate tells Chris that unless he believes Larry is still alive, he condemns his father as his murderer. Chris confronts Joe with the truth. Joe admits wrongdoing, but insists it was all so that Chris would inherit a successful business. Chris is horrified.

Act Three

In the middle of the night, Kate is sitting outside waiting for Chris who has disappeared; Jim joins her and reveals that he has always known of Joe's guilt. Joe enters, desperate for advice about what to do. She suggests that Chris might be mollified by Joe's willingness to admit guilt and take his punishment by saying he will go to prison. Kate explains that to Chris there is 'something bigger than the family', and Joe replies, in a remark that foreshadows the end of the play, 'if there's something bigger than that I'll put a bullet in my head!'

Ann enters, and offers Kate a deal: she will not prosecute Joe in exchange for Kate's admission that Larry is dead and that Chris is free to marry her. When Kate refuses, Ann shows her Larry's last letter explaining that he had just read the news of the twenty-one pilots killed as a result of his father's faulty airplane parts, and announcing his suicide. Chris returns, saying that he is going away and Ann shows the letter to him. He reads it to Joe. Joe learns the play's lesson of moral responsibility for the family of man, not just one's own family. Chris demands more than 'sorry' from his father who goes into the house, presumably to get ready to leave for prison, and shoots himself.

Chris is desperate with grief and Kate tries to absolve him with her final injunction, 'Forget now. Live.'

Commentary

Context

Social history

A play about war-profiteering opening in 1947, when the Second World War had so recently ended, must have been pointedly painful to the audience, considering how many had experienced similar losses of a son, a brother, a fiancé. Of course, even for those whose circumstances did not resemble *All My Sons*', the play's lesson is that they are 'all our sons' and thus that the grief and culpability are communal. The play's shocking revelations and Miller's insistence that we must take responsibility for our actions provide a lesson about the destructive self-interest and the greed that drives capitalism, sacrificing human values to material values. This moral force resonates in whatever the current social context is, although it must have been additionally vivid for people who had recently endured the Great Depression as well as the Second World War. In his Introduction to *Plays: One* (1988), Miller writes that *All My Sons* was 'conceived in wartime and begun in wartime . . . at a time when all public voices were announcing the arrival of that great day when industry and labor were one, my personal experience was daily demonstrating that beneath the slogans very little had changed' (22).

In gauging the temper of the times further, it is interesting to note that in 1942, President Franklin Delano Roosevelt ratcheted up industrial mobilisation for the war, requiring, among other equipment, 60,000 new aircraft. In one of his famous 'Fireside Chats' radio broadcasts in 1942, he said, 'In the last war, I had seen great factories; but until I saw some of the new present-day plants, I had not thoroughly visualised our American war effort . . . The United States has been at war for only ten months, and is engaged in the enormous task of multiplying its armed forces many times. We are by no means at full production level yet.' By 1943 the government raised the production goals to 125,000 new aircraft. This is the source of the pressure Joe Keller felt; George explains his father's version of what happened once the defects were discovered and he telephoned Joe to come to the plant: 'No sign of Joe. So Dad called again. By this time he had over a hundred defectives. The Army was screaming for stuff and Dad didn't have anything to ship. So Joe told him [. . .] to cover up the cracks in any way he could, and ship them out.' Joe explains this same desperation near the end of the play: 'I'm in business, a man is in business; a hundred and twenty cracked, you're out of business; [. . .]

your stuff is no good; they close you up, they tear up your contracts, what the hell's it to them?'

In Miller's 1944 *Situation Norma l. . .*, which he called 'a book of reportage', he wrote, 'A man who has known the thrill of giving himself does not soon forget it. It leaves him with a thirst. A thirst for a wider life, a more exciting life, a life that demands all he can give. Civilian life in America is private, it is always striving for exclusiveness. Our lifelong boast is that we got ahead of the next guy, excluded him. We have always believed in the fiction – and often damned our own belief – that if every man privately takes care of his own interests, the community and the nation will prosper and be safe.' In *Tmebends* (1987), his autobiography, Miller's comment on this is significant: 'Though unable to define it in words, they [soldiers] shared a conviction that somehow decency was at stake in this grandest slaughter in history' (277).

In 1947, after *All My Sons* opened on Broadway, Miller's name appeared in an ad in the newspaper the *Daily Worker* (published in New York by the Communist Party) protesting against the treatment of Gerhard Eisler, an anti-fascist German refugee. Miller auctioned off a manuscript of *All My Sons* to support Progressive Citizens of America. During this same year, the Civil Affairs Division of the American Military refused to allow the production of *All My Sons* in occupied Europe, citing its negative criticism of American society. In *Echoes Down the Corridor* (2000), Miller noted that 'I wrote *All My Sons* during the war, expecting much trouble, but the war ended just as I was completing the play, leaving some room for the unsayable, which everyone knew – that the war had made some people illicit, sometimes criminal fortunes' (xi). Similar to this is Miller's recollection of seeing the play in Jerusalem in 1977: 'the audience sat watching it with an intensifying terror that was quite palpable. On our right sat the president of Israel, Ephraim Katzir, on the left the prime minister, Yitzhak Rabin', who explained what Miller felt to be 'an almost religious quality' in the audience's attention: 'Because this is a problem in Israel – boys are out there day and night dying in planes and on the ground, and back here people are making a lot of money. So it might as well be an Israeli play' (*Timebends*, 135).

There are two accounts of the source of the play's plot: one is that Miller read about the Wright Aeronautics Corporation of Ohio (the state where the play takes place); the company affixed 'Passed' tags on defective airplane engines, having bribed Army inspectors; the other source is a story Miller heard in his living room, when 'a pious lady from the Middle West told of a family in her neighbourhood which had been destroyed when the daughter turned the father in to the authorities on discovering that he had been selling faulty machinery to the Army. The war was then in full blast. By the time she had finished the tale I had transformed the daughter into a son and the climax of the second act was full and clear in my mind' (*Plays: One*, 17). It is worth noting Miller's shift from daughter to son: perhaps nothing marks twentieth-century American drama more than the highly charged and very male family battles between sons and fathers, brothers and brothers; note that, like O'Neill's *A Long Day's Journey into Night*, Williams's *Cat on a Hot Tin Roof*, Shepard's *True West*, Parks's *Topdog/Underdog* – an obviously abbreviated list which nevertheless stretches through the entire century – the controversy is almost always between men and always about money. Like all these plays, *All My Sons* is also about two brothers and their father and money, as are two of Miller's own subsequent plays, *Death of a Salesman* and *The Price*.

In *Timebends*, Miller remembers asking his cousin, 'What did your pop want?' His answer: 'He wanted a business for us. So we could all work together [. . .] a business for the boys' (130). Miller realised that his uncle Manny, a 'homely, ridiculous little man had after all never ceased to struggle for a certain victory, the only kind open to him in this society –selling to achieve his lost self as a man with his name and his sons' names on a business of his own'.

In the course of Act One's opening desultory conversation, all three men reveal a reflexive and cheap cynicism about the news: weather reports are automatically discounted as inaccurate, news is automatically assumed to be bad. Note that this is in the ease of post-war America; we can assume that only a few years earlier, during the war, the news was bad in an entirely different way, specifically when it reported the scandal of Joe's factory having shipped the faulty airplane parts that led to the planes crashing and deaths of twenty-one pilots – the newspaper account which caused Larry's suicide. Note that later in Act One, when Chris tells his father that their dishonesty in not discouraging his mother's false hope that Larry is still alive and will return home has been a mistake, Joe's reply is 'The trouble is the goddam newspapers', referring to reports of other missing soldiers who have come home.

The contemporary world has no shortage of bad news. Public endangerment scandals re-inform the play with each re-reading or revival, from the destruction of the spaceship *Challenger* due to faulty O rings, to the twenty-year Canadian Red Cross blood-distribution disgrace which infected people with HIV, to the 2008 outrage in China over milk tainted with melamine causing 300,000 infants to sicken, to the 2009 US epidemic of salmonella caused by peanut butter shipped despite contamination warnings. And, most spectacularly, the global economic crisis begun in

2008 and Bernard Madoff's role in it[1]; his scam wrecked hundreds of thousands of lives, institutions, and corporations, and it is worth noting for our purposes of comparison to *All My Sons* that Madoff's two sons, who ran the company's market-making and proprietary units, said that their father kept them in the dark about the secret business, a 'dark' which may resemble Chris's willed ignorance. Money, as Miller's play warns us, is always likely to triumph over decency until the world learns that they are 'all our sons'. As Miller wrote in *Timebends*, 'I could not imagine a theatre worth my time that did not want to change the world.'

Theatrical history

In the stream of the history of great American dramatists, Miller follows Eugene O'Neill. But where O'Neill's tragic vision suggests that people are doomed – by temperament, by events they cannot control, and by the weight of the past – Miller's is a fighting play, insisting that we can live more moral lives if only we acknowledge our place in the family of man. The tragic lesson is always that that understanding comes too late. Whether this means that *All My Sons* is to be read as a tragedy largely depends on the reader's (and, in production, the director's) optimism: *can* we 'be better'? In the wider, longer stream of the history of great Western dramatists, Miller follows Ibsen, whose plays show that the societal context inevitably influences individual lives and that social context can be altered by social action; thus, although the issues of women's rights and, indeed, all human rights have not been solved in the nearly 150 years since *A Doll's House*, significant changes in both ethics and legislation have achieved some social progress.

In theatrical production, *All My Sons* requires a tricky combination of ensemble work – the cast must seem to be a family, a neighbourhood, creating the comfort of people who are familiar with each other on a daily basis, while also creating a sense of alienation, the very opposite of ensemble. *All My Sons* is about what Miller called 'unrelatedness', the mistake of believing that responsibility stops at the edge of your back yard. And, unlike O'Neill, Miller writes realistic, grounded language, creating speakable dialogue that allows the audience to identify further with the characters in a crucial emotional as well as thematic arc. They sound familiar. They sound like an old-fashioned version of us.

In *Timebends*, Miller recalls his disappointment when Herman Shumlin, Lillian Hellman's producer and director, having read *All My Sons* said he

---

1   The trusted Wall Street broker whose $50 billion Ponzi scheme cheated investors around the world.

'didn't understand it' (268). Miller defines himself, from this early moment, as a 'social playwright', like Hellman, an identity that continues in his pursuit of a production and a director, so he was naturally thrilled when both Elia Kazan and Harold Clurman, 'creators of that thirties mixture of Stanislavsky and social protest which was the real glamour' (*Tmebends*, 270) were bidding for the script. When it opened on 29 January 1947, Brooks Atkinson, the powerful *New York Times* critic, praised Miller as a 'genuine new talent' and added, 'there is something uncommonly exhilarating in the spectacle of a new writer bringing unusual gifts to the theatre under the sponsorship of a director with taste and enthusiasm'; the director was Elia Kazan.

As Miller's first successful play on Broadway, *All My Sons* launched the great career and established Miller as America's social critic, the voice of a collective conscience telling us, as Chris tells his father, 'You can be better!' *All My Sons* also established Miller's style as realistic, thereby launching a commonly held error, since the plays that follow *All My Sons* depart from realism. This becomes especially interesting in the light of subsequent productions of *All My Sons*, influencing set design, lighting, sound, etc. As Miller wrote, 'No, I am not really interested in "realism". I never was. What I'm interested in is reality . . . Realism can conceal reality, perhaps a little easier than any other form, in fact' (Roudané, 362).

Themes

Time

In *Timebends*, Miller writes about 'the hand of the distant past reach[ing] out of its grave', an image which defines the plot of *All My Sons* (as it defines the plot of Ibsen's *Ghosts*, for example), like the iron hand of the past clamped on the present and the future in O'Neill's *Long Day's Journey into Night*. In *All My Sons*, this hand of the 'distant past' substantiates Miller's theme that actions have moral consequences, and essentially builds the structure of the play on a series of surprising revelations. It is worth noting that, like O'Neill's family drama which is also about two grown sons, *All My Sons* is also, temporally, a long day's journey into night, a play which begins with the sunny optimism of morning and ends in grim darkness. Similarly, *Death of a Salesman* is a play about past events which govern the present, but in *Salesman* scenes from the past slice through the scenes in the play's present, refusing the chronological linearity of *All My Sons* and creating a visible psychological landscape.

References to time appear throughout the play: all that happened in the past – not only Joe's decision to save his business instead of lives, but also all that happened to Chris in the past in the Army. We learn about his military experience, his leadership and how his squad's self-sacrificial generosity became central to his ethics and values, and his shock and disgust at returning to a post-war world where it was business-as-usual. There is constant mention of how long Larry has been missing, how long Ann has been single, how long Chris has been waiting, how long Steve has been in prison, how long Jim's time of impassioned medical research lasted, how long the poplars have been growing, how long since Larry's memorial tree was planted.

Significantly, when George arrives, wrecked by the war, enraged by his visit to his father, brimming with accusations as well as self-recrimination, his anger and resolution are quickly defused by Kate's grape drink and her insistence that all is as it was: 'None of us changed, Georgie. We all love you.' Awash in nostalgia (the word means 'homesickness'), George caves in to her affectionate manipulation.

Imprisonment

Much of the history of modern drama could be written in scenes of entrapment; if it is the emblem of modern man's sense of impotence in the face of the enormous forces facing him, trapped as he is by history, psychology, genetics, economics, etc., then the modern stage is, necessarily, a claustrophobic arena. Beckett's *Waiting for Godot* and Sartre's *No Exit* are the paradigmatic examples. An interesting set design will allow the audience to interpret the issues central to the script: it evokes atmosphere and speaks meaning, without ever explicitly telegraphing to the audience what the play is going to be about. Although the setting often echoes the theme by trapping characters in one room (increasingly a thrifty as well as meaningful development in modern set design), in *All My Sons*, the setting is not an indoor room but a back yard. But rather than create a feeling of openness and fresh air, it fences in the family and divides neighbour from neighbour. Even as the barriers between the Kellers' yard and the Bayliss's and the Lubeys' yards are permeable – the neighbours enter and exit constantly – Miller's stage directions nevertheless specify that the 'stage is hedged on right and left by tall, closely planted poplars which lend the yard a secluded atmosphere'. Note that when Ann arrives after three years in New York, she runs to the fence and says, 'Boy, the poplars got thick, didn't they?' How symbolic this setting becomes will be reflected in the many possibilities for design choices.

The scene with Bert in Act One is a microcosm of the entire play: Bert's curiosity about the promised jail in the Keller house prompts Joe to say: 'Bert, on my word of honor, there's a jail in the basement. I showed you my gun, didn't I?' Note how much is packed into this seemingly playful line: the house is, truly, a prison; Joe's gun will be the instrument of his shame-filled and repentant suicide; and Joe's 'word of honor' is, we will learn, worthless. The scene with Bert concludes with Joe telling the boy, 'mum's the word', an unwitting comment on the family's policy of silencing the truth, and thereby denying the guilt that has festered under the surface.

Steve is, literally, in prison. Note, too, that when Sue explains to Ann why she hopes once she and Chris marry they will move away, Sue says, 'it's bad when a man always sees the bars in front of him. Jim thinks he's in jail all the time . . . My husband is unhappy with Chris around' (47). Jim's capitulation to his imprisonment – however pragmatic, however cynical, however sad – is revealed late in Act Two when he reassures Kate about Chris's storming out of the house: 'We all come back, Kate. These private little revolutions always die. The compromise is always made. In a peculiar way, Frank is right – every man does have a star. The star of one's honesty. And you spend your life groping for it, but once it's out it never lights again. I don't think he went very far. He probably just wanted to be alone to watch his star go out.' But Chris's star of honesty does not 'go out' even though he may be imprisoned in other ways, especially by his own need to be good, a need that demands that others 'be better', as he tells his mother at the play's end.

Materialism and the American dream

The first instance of the phrase 'the American dream' occurs in James Truslow Adams's *The Epic of America* (1933); he defines that 'dream of a land in which life should be better and richer and fuller for every man, with opportunity for each according to his ability or his achievement [. . . .] The American dream that lured tens of millions of all nations to our shores [. . .] has not been a dream of merely material plenty. [. . .] It has been a dream of being able to grow to fullest development as man and woman [. . .] unhampered by the barriers which had slowly been erected in older civilizations . . .'. And even in 1933 (the Great Depression had surely challenged the American dream in unprecedented ways), Adams laments the erosion of the values which had constituted the societal understanding of that dream: 'we came to insist on business and money-making and material improvement as good in themselves [. . . to] consider an unthinking optimism essential, [. . .] regard[ing] criticism as obstructive and dangerous [. . . to] think manners undemocratic, and a cultivated mind a hindrance to success, a sign of inefficient effeminacy [. . . and] size and statistics of material development came to be more important in our eyes than quality and spiritual values . . .'. The eerie aptness of Adams's assessment, so many decades after it was written, suggests that the critique may be timeless.

Destructive to society as well as to the individual, materialism is what Miller called 'the petty business of life in the suburbs'. In *All My Sons*, the context is the essentially amoral post-war American prosperity (1947's economic and physical landscape was very different in Europe to what it was in the US). Chris's long speech to Ann tries to explain the shock and dismay he felt when he came back from the war: 'there was no meaning in it here; the whole thing to them was a kind of a – bus accident . . . I felt wrong to be alive, to open the bank-book, to drive the new car, to see the new refrigerator' (38). The sense of corruption related to material success is also eerily apt: Joe Keller, in Act Two, says, 'A little man makes a mistake and they hang him by his thumbs; the big ones become ambassadors.' Compare this cynicism to a nearly identical remark in O'Neill's *Emperor Jones*: 'For de little stealin' dey gits you in jail soon or late. For de big stealin' dey makes you Emperor and puts you in de Hall o' Fame when you croaks.'

Martin Esslin points out that the fundamental premises of the Theatre of the Absurd, as set forth in his landmark book (*The Theatre of the Absurd*, 1962; 3rd edn London: Methuen, 2001), go far towards elucidating the differences between the American and the British societal environment. In brief, they include: 'the sense that the certitudes and unshakable basic assumptions of former ages have been swept away, that they have been tested and found wanting, that they have been discredited as cheap and somewhat childish illusions' (23) and that such Absurdist plays 'express [. . .] the senselessness of the human condition and the inadequacy of the rational approach by the open abandonment of rational devices and discursive thought. [. . .] The Theatre of the Absurd has renounced arguing *about* the absurdity of the human condition; it merely *presents* it in being – that is in terms of concrete stage images' (24–25).

Esslin argues that the 'dearth of examples' of Absurdist drama in the US is due to the fact that the Second World War did not happen there, since Absurdism 'springs from a feeling of deep disillusionment, the draining away of the sense of meaning and purpose in life which has been characteristic of countries like France and Britain in the years after the Second World War. In the United States there has been no corresponding loss of meaning and purpose. The American dream of the good life is still very strong' (311). Instead of despairing, Chris rails against this loss of 'meaning and purpose', refusing to relinquish belief in American progress: 'Everything was being destroyed, see, but it seemed to me that one new thing was made. A kind of . . . responsibility. Man for man.'

Joe senses this in Chris's reluctance to 'use what I made for you . . . I mean, with joy, Chris, without shame [. . .] Because sometimes I think you're . . . ashamed of the money' (41). In their horrific showdown near the play's end, Joe tells his wife, 'you wanted money, so I made money. What must I be forgiven? You wanted money, didn't you?' She replies, underlining her complicity in all this, showing that no one is pure or blameless: 'I didn't want it that way.' And Joe comes back with, 'I didn't want it that way, either! What difference is it what you want? I spoiled both of you.' Jim Bayliss's comment to Kate early in Act Three seems significant, equating materialism with madness: 'Nobody realises how many people are walking around loose, and they're cracked as coconuts. Money. Money-money-money-money. You say it long enough it doesn't mean anything. Oh, how I'd love to be around when that happens.' Kate's realistic response is, 'You're so childish, Jim!' (79).

Like *Death of a Salesman*'s Willy Loman, Joe Keller has subscribed to a set of wrong-headed and self-defeating values: the American dream has been corrupted by materialism, and those who believe in that corrupted version of the dream are, according to Miller, doomed to failure – a failure which both Joe and Willy respond to with suicide. For Willy his suicide is his last sale: his life for the insurance money to launch Biff into his 'magnificent' future; while for Joe the suicide is penance for the material greed he yielded to in the past. One could argue that Joe's death is an easy way out: an escape from repentance, guilt, apologies, years of denial of culpability, in addition to burdening his' son with the guilt of having driven him to death.

Other dominant themes are discussed elsewhere in this commentary; these include:

Moral responsibility: a group of related ideas about responsibility to self and to society.

Family loyalty: this is exclusive and tribal, destructive to the universal family of man, and, as a corollary to this, the maternal is seen as primal, ruthlessly protective of the nuclear family unit.

War: Chris discovers the real nature of loyalty in the brotherhood of self-sacrificial soldiers. It is worth noting that this is not a conventional anti-war play.

Denial: the psychological self-protective device that enables self-interest. As Joe says, 'I ignore what I gotta ignore.' This theme is, obviously, fundamental to the entire play.

Fathers and sons: (Joe and Chris, Joe and Larry, Steve and George)
one of the central relationships of American drama. This is a pattern
particular to American drama (see p. xxvii) as well as to Miller's
plays: consider the similarities to *Death of a Salesman* and *The Price*.
The corollary to this theme is the theme of brothers (also dominating
the aforementioned plays), often struggling – physically and/or
emotionally – with each other.

Characters

Chris Keller

As one of the central and pivotal characters, Chris makes all the plot's
events happen, and thus is, perhaps, the character most representative of
the playwright, whose task it is to make the play happen. On the surface,
Chris is the hero: courageous in war, modest in peace, and entirely decent,
a man deserving of his community's affection and admiration. But despite
having been back home for several years, working in his father's factory
(we never find out what it is he does there – sufficient to say that he is
deeply connected to the Keller business and we presume his is a white-
collar job), he seems to be merely one of the 'sons', somehow still a boy,
despite his history of military bravery. The soldiers in Chris's unit, under
his command, 'didn't die; they killed themselves for each other', as he
tells Ann, and when one of them gave him his last pair of dry socks, he
takes that as an emblem of their self-sacrificial generosity, and thus their
tribute to him as their leader is, for Chris, an emblem of their goodness
rather than his own. He is still troubled by their deaths, but he never
indicates any inner torment about the enemy deaths he must have caused
or the horrors he must have seen. He admires unselfishness, as opposed
to the more aggressive, fiercer forms courage might take. His mildness
extends to his love life, as we see in the scene where he kisses Ann; he is
a sweet rather than a sexually passionate man. Significantly, he achieves
manhood when he stands up to his mother when she tries to drive Ann
away. Miller indicts the American idea of manhood as Joe defines it in his
attempt to explain his past actions to Chris: 'You're a boy, what could I
do! I'm in business, a man is in business' (76). Chris is not 'in business',
and thus is not 'a man'. Although Joe is the designated guilty party, they
are all culpable. Chris's refusal to 'see it human', as Joe pleads, is telling;
his acknowledgment that Joe is 'no worse than most men but I thought you
were better. I never saw you as a man. I saw you as my father (89)' shows
an idealism which seems both laudable and at the same time adolescent:

he is unable to view his parents as people separate from their relationship to him. That confrontation near the end continues significantly: Chris says, 'I can't look at you this way, I can't look at myself!' He then 'turns away, unable to face Keller' (89); and that small stage direction may be Miller's largest clue as to Chris's unacknowledged guilt.

So many grown men in Miller plays – and in American drama generally – seem to be stuck in an arrested adolescence: living in their parents' home, without wives or children of their own. The Kellers' neighbour, Frank Lubey, stands as a foil to Chris; always a year away from being drafted into the army, he now has a wife and three children, with a house of his own. Worth noting, too, is George's lack of a family. As Chris tells his mother, specifically referring to Larry's death but generally speaking of his own condition, 'We're like a railroad station waiting for a train that never comes in' (21). The train, it turns out, will arrive in a few minutes: enter Ann, and with her the incontrovertible evidence of Joe's guilt and the promise of adult life for Chris.

Chris is adored, not just by the soldiers he commanded, but by friends and neighbours – with the significant exception of Sue, the doctor's wife, whose self-interest, financial as well as emotional, is undermined by Chris's idealism: 'Chris makes people want to be better than it's possible to be.' She feels he tempts her husband away from the practicalities of supporting a family with the ideal of medical research, i.e. towards self-sacrifice and away from self-interest, towards altruism. But despite Chris's apparent idealism, he has clearly accepted the materialistic values of his society and the conventional male role of provider; when Ann accepts his proposal of marriage, he is thrilled and expresses his joy by saying, 'Oh Annie, Annie . . . I'm going to make a fortune for you!' (38).

Chris's name is significant, since he seems to be not only the embodiment of Christian virtues but perhaps the embodiment of Christ. Sue tells Ann, 'I resent living next door to the Holy Family. It makes me look like a bum, you understand?' As Joe will plead with him near the end, 'Chris, a man can't be a Jesus in this world!' Miller has Chris, the ultimate son of the ultimate father, reverse the theological roles and demand self-sacrifice from his father as penance for all the deaths; just before he reads Larry's letter aloud, he says 'I know all about the world. I know the whole crap story. Now listen to this, and tell me what a man's got to be!' Larry is an offstage surrogate Jesus, having been, in effect, sent to his death by his father when Larry read the newspaper story. Larry has, in effect, died for the sins of Joe Keller, representing the twenty-one downed pilots. The second son is the one who must bear the burden of moral decision, always the central burden in Miller's world view. It seems unlikely that Chris will be able to follow his mother's advice: 'Don't take it on yourself', since she already knows the theological framework, despite her denial of it: 'God does not let a son be killed by his father.' Here we witness a father killed by both his sons. George, another son, also bears this burden, and Chris chastises him with, 'George, you don't want to be the voice of God, do you?' (58).

Another aspect of Chris's central role in the play is his embodiment of the theme of denial; his is a far more complex psychological portrait than Kate's protective denial or Joe's consciously defensive denial. Chris never admits to himself what he knows; it isn't until his mother confesses for Joe, even before he reads Larry's letter, that he consciously realises what his father has done. But Miller has provided significant clues throughout: why is Chris so uneasy about Joe wanting to change the name on the plant to 'Christopher Keller, Incorporated'? When Joe blusters about Steve, suspecting that he sent Ann to 'find out something', Chris retorts angrily, 'Why? What is there to find out?' When George asks for ten minutes' conversation with Joe, 'and then you'll have the answer', Chris evades the showdown. Perhaps the most damning of all the clues is Kate's saying to Jim, 'I always had the feeling that in the back of his head, Chris . . . almost knew. I didn't think it would be such a shock' (80). As George says to him, 'You know in your heart Joe did it' (60) and then adds, moments later, the heartwrenching line, 'Oh, Chris, you're a liar to yourself!' (61). This element in Chris's character calls for enormous subtlety from the actor: possessing an open face and an open nature, he must remain something of a mystery to his parents ('I'm beginning to think we don't really know him. They say in the war he was such a killer. Here he was always afraid of mice' (83). Worse, he remains a mystery to himself, as most Miller characters do. From Willy Loman in *Death of a Salesman* to Eddie Carbone in *A View from the Bridge,* from Quentin in *After the Fall* and Victor in *The Price,* to Lyman Felt in *The Ride Down Mount Morgan* – they all appear to be self-searchers but are also self-deluders. John Proctor in *The Crucible,* Miller's most powerful moral hero, may be the exception, although there are those who find his moral clarity oppressive, and sanctimonious, just as there are those who find Miller's moral clarity oppressive, and sanctimonious, as some of his protagonists even resort to suicide, and therefore self-condemnation.

Joe Keller

Miller's Everyman is both an individual and an archetype, 'a man among men' as the stage directions introduce him to us. The play demonstrates that this Everyman needs to be replaced: he is 'nearing sixty' (although in explaining his desperation to Chris he says he's sixty-one). Joe's values

All My Sons 41

belong to a pre-war world, where strength was defined by physical power and making money and where loyalty was defined by caring for one's family. Note that he has no sense of loyalty to Steve, his business partner, neighbour and longtime friend, although Chris feels deep loyalty to the men he fought in the war with – loyalty that will ultimately supersede his loyalty to family. Joe's is a world where a man supports his wife and children, where he builds a legacy for his sons, and where material prosperity and conspicuous consumption are the gauge of success. Uneducated, he is not inclined to think about the world (note his wonder at the newspaper's want-ads as well as his refusal to read any news) or to introspection, and has swallowed society's values whole. Joe is a man who has not heard the Socratic dictum that the unexamined life is not worth living, and it is his tragedy to examine the moral principles by which he has lived only to discover, too late, that he has followed the wrong path.

Nevertheless, Joe's style as 'a man among men' is bluff, good-natured, and confident enough to have faced down the neighbours – his long walk down the street after he was exonerated is both hubristic and impressive – and to have won them over, so that despite their knowing he is guilty, they enjoy his company enough to play cards, to chat about what's in the newspaper, to talk and joke about families. Joe is crass and despite his white-collar success, he remains distinctly blue-collar and working-class in his manner.

His shrewd ability to handle people is clearly demonstrated when he suggests to Ann that her father could come back to work at the factory once his prison term is over; Joe is clearly trying to subvert any of their family's impulse towards revenge, and what seems like generosity is self-protection: 'I like you and George to go to your father in prison and tell him . . . "Dad, Joe wants to bring you into the business when you get out,"' Ann, 'Surprised, even shocked' replies, 'You'd have him as a partner?' Joe qualifies his offer, explaining, 'nervously', 'I want him to know that when he gets out he's got a place waitin' for him. It'll take his bitterness away. To know you got a place . . . it sweetens you' (53). Although Ann is amazed, we should recall that only a page earlier she has said, 'You're not so dumb, Joe.' Chris's rejection of Joe's notion is angry and forcible, eventually provoking Joe's outburst, 'A father is a father!' (53), a remark which seems so fraught with meaning that Joe himself is appalled.

Joe tries to explain his guilt – both to Chris and to himself – by asking that he 'see it human'. He replies to Chris's insistence that he should be in jail with the pragmatism of capitalism: 'Who worked for nothin' in the war? When they work for nothin' I'll work for nothin'. Did they ship a gun or a truck outa Detroit before they got their price?' (89).

Kate Keller

Although she seems to have the smallest role of the family, she is the paradigm of the play's deepest psychological anguish, revealing the cost of her values as well as the cost of her repression of the truth. She is unable to grieve straightforwardly over the death of her son and fabricates an elaborate self-consolatory fiction by which she lives for three years. Harold Clurman noted that 'If there is a "villain" in the piece, it is the mother – the kindly, loving mother who wants her brood to be safe and her home undisturbed' ('Thesis and Drama', *Lies Like Truth: Theatre Reviews and Essays*, New York: Macmillan, 1958). Frank Rich's *New York Times* review of the Broadway revival in 1987 calls Kate 'an unwitting monster who destructively manipulates everyones' guilts, enforces the most conformist social values, and attempts, with intermittent success, to disguise psychotic impulses as physical ailments and familiar self-martyrdom'.

We don't meet Kate until the middle of Act One when she steps on to the porch. Miller describes her as being 'in her early fifties, a woman of uncontrolled inspirations, and an overwhelming capacity for love'. It is worth noting that her dialogue in the script is ascribed to 'Mother' and, although she is referred to by her name by the characters, Miller clearly sees her as a maternal archetype more than as an individual. She occupies the conventional role of mid-twentieth-century suburban housewife, having devoted herself to husband and children and house; one aspect of her relationship to her husband is sarcasm; after Joe mistakenly throws away a bag of potatoes, believing it to be garbage, he says, 'I don't like garbage in the house.' She replies, with tart wisdom, 'Then don't eat' (18). Chris comments on this exchange: 'That settles you for the day', to which Joe remarks, 'Yeah, I'm in last place again.' This mild bickering is clearly a marital habit, and represents a passive-aggression understandable in women whose lives are completely defined by husbands who may strain their loyalty and the expected wifely admiration. The garbage exchange is also telling in that Kate is metaphorically reminding Joe of cause and effect: there are consequences to everything.

Miller's subtle portrayal of Kate's manipulative nature, shows her bending the men around her – Joe, Chris, George, Larry, Jim, Frank – to her will by making them worry and protect her; she brings out their gallantry and eagerness to please. The younger generation, especially the unmarried Chris and George, she infantilises, reducing them to the boys they were by making them nostalgic for the innocent pleasures these battle-scarred men used to enjoy. When George appears in the middle of the play, she speaks for the America Miller indicts: 'You had big principles, Eagle

Scouts the three of you; [. . .] Stop being a philosopher and look after yourself' (67). It is worth noting that the women in the play – Ann and Sue and Lydia – are not susceptible to her charm or manipulation and resist her for their own survival. These gender lines are drawn early in the play and offer a compelling picture of sexual politics at mid-century, as well as the particular pathology of a woman trapped by truths so intolerable that the only way she can deny them is by distorting her personality. How much this denial rises to the conscious surface – and how to reveal that – is the problem every actress playing Kate must solve.

Kate cannot sleep – we hear of her late nights in the back yard and the kitchen – and is, as well, tormented by disturbing dreams when she does sleep; she has headaches, which we, unlike the family, understand to be symptoms of her repressed knowledge, both of Larry's death and Joe's guilt. If she admits to herself that Larry is not coming home, that he is dead, she must also admit to herself that her husband bears some responsibility for that death. Further, if she admits her husband's guilt, she must admit her own complicity – both in keeping silent when Steve went to prison and in enjoying the material benefits of her husband's ill-gotten prosperity. Neither Chris nor Joe do anything more than merely worry about her symptoms which seems to be further indication of their own repressed knowledge and guilt. Despite looking like a 'normal' family, the Kellers are deeply troubled, a family who only seems to be 'functional'. By the end of the play, Kate's wifely loyalty shifts to maternal loyalty: no longer able to protect her husband, she must now protect her son by forgiving him: 'Don't dear. Don't take this on yourself. Forget now. Live' (91). Her sobbing is the play's final sound.

Ann Deever

Ann is introduced to us by Miller in a puzzling way: 'Ann is twenty-six, gentle but despite herself capable of holding fast to what she knows.' The implication seems to be that this wholesome, lovely woman – it is clear from everyone's reactions to seeing her again that she has grown into a beauty – is also self-assured and determined. She understands Kate's power over Chris and, with startling clarity, attempts to strike a quid pro quo deal: 'You made Chris feel guilty with me. Whether you wanted to or not, you've crippled him in front of me. I'd like you to tell him that Larry is dead and that you know it. You understand me? I'm not going out of here alone. There's no life for me that way. I want you to set him free. And then I promise you, everything will end, and we'll go away, and that's all' (84). Kate refuses Ann's terms, forcing Ann to produce Larry's suicide letter. Ann's insistence on their all knowing the truth is more for her own benefit than for any higher morality: she wants Chris for her husband and she wants him free of his mother's psychological oppression. Sue Bayliss says that Ann is 'the female version of [Chris]' (49), though her motivation is purely self-interest; it could, however, be argued that everyone in the play is similarly motivated.

When Kate reads the letter, saying, over and over, 'Oh, my God . . .', Ann's reply ('Kate, please, please . . .') is said, Miller's directions tell us, 'with pity and fear'. These emotions suggest the classic Aristotelian definition of tragedy. If Joe is the tragic figure whose death comes as a result of wisdom gained too late, then Ann's tragic emotions mirror ours; the girl next door, who is both insider and outsider, is our surrogate. Once she insists that Chris read the letter – she 'thrusts' it into his hand – she has fulfilled her dramatic role and is silent for the last intense moments of the play which belong exclusively to the family.

George Deever

George Deever is an interesting character, although the role seems minor. George is Chris's Laertes: the foil to the complex hero, the son whose relation to his father throws the play's central father/son relationship into high relief. (Note, too, that Laertes' father, Polonius, is pivotal in *Hamlet's* plot just as Steve is pivotal to *All My Sons* in that Polonius is seen to be weak and easily misled.) George's arrival is anxiously discussed before he finally appears; we have been keenly aware of his presence 'in the car', i.e. Offstage, as the struggle about his surprising visit continues on stage. When he ultimately enters, Miller provides this information: 'George is Chris's age, but a paler man, now on the edge of his self-restraint. He speaks quietly, as though afraid to find himself screaming' (55). Like Chris, George is a veteran; unlike Chris, he was seriously wounded – enough to spend a long time in hospital, and long enough to have been studying law while recuperating. 'When I was studying in the hospital it seemed sensible, but outside there didn't seem to be much of a law. The trees got thick, didn't they?' (59). Although that last sentence seems to be merely a quick and nervous shift in subject, it is, in fact, causal: the trees have indeed grown, enclosing the backyard, shielding the family from the outside world. When Kate first sees him she greets him with 'Georgie, Georgie' and with sad sympathy takes his face in her hands and says, 'They made an old man out of you [. . .] He looks like a ghost' (63). Significantly, she reminds him that when he was drafted into the military she told him, 'don't try for medals'. She insists that 'You're all alike', implying that, like Chris (and by extension Larry), George was too self-sacrificial. 'Relishing her solicitude', he succumbs to her pity and maternal concern, demonstrating once again the way the Kellers' charm has always worked.

Although we understand that brother and sister shared a view about their father's guilt, we learn, as Ann does, that something has radically changed George's attitude; their joint rejection of him – not a word, not a visit, not a Christmas card – George now sees as a 'terrible thing. We can never be forgiven' (59). That 'terrible thing' was not only to have abandoned him to prison, but also to have abandoned him as family, accepting, without question, the public view of the crime. When Chris wonders, 'The court record was good enough for you all these years, why isn't it good now? Why did you believe it all these years?', George's powerful reply, often oddly buried in the scene's commotion, is, 'Because you believed it . . . That's the truth, Chris. I believed everything, because I thought you did' (61). Thus, Chris's denial of the buried truth has caused even larger collateral damage. This also indicates the truth of what Sue Bayliss points out to Ann: Chris's charismatic idealism is dangerously persuasive.

We learn how determined Ann has been to marry Chris; not only had she told George she was going to marry Chris before Chris's proposal, even before the visit, before their first kiss, but George then felt obliged to break the years' silence and visit his father for the first time to tell him the news. Trying to imagine the motivation, there seem to have been equal parts of love and spite in his decision, just as there are in his decision to come and prevent Ann marrying Chris: he arrives demanding she collect her things and leave with him, that 'she's one item he's not going to grab. [. . .] Everything they have is covered with blood' (61).

The grim and desperate mood is broken by the arrival of Lydia with a hat she has made for Kate, whose lack of tact and sensitivity in the ensuing scene is a gauge of her crassness and her self-protectiveness: nowhere else in the play does she show how much like Joe she is. Lydia was 'Laughy' in the old days and she is repeatedly embarrassed by Kate's insistence that George should have married her; her three babies and her husband Frank having escaped the war, as well as her new womanly beauty, all make George understandably envious. Kate relentlessly pursues this theme, harping on George's seriousness with remarks like: 'Don't be so intelligent', and 'While you were getting mad about Fascism Frank was getting into her bed' (67). Despite what may well seem like Kate's cruel mockery, George succumbs to Kate's charm again, '(*laughing*). She's wonderful' (67). Part of what is so painful in this scene is the way it reveals George's nostalgia, his need for both maternal solicitude (we never learn what his relationship is with his own mother) and the ease of the past when he lived next door. Nostalgia, the longing to go back to an unrecoverable past, is an inevitable theme in a post-war play, and George embodies that theme. While Chris and Ann look forwards to a future, George, stuck in an intolerable present, looks back to a happier, more innocent past. His heartbreaking remark 'I never felt at home anywhere but here' (71) is emblematic of the hopelessness of nostalgia and the sense of alienation and anomie that marks post-war America.

Joe's approach to containing the danger George represents is to browbeat him with the past, pointing up example after example of his father's weakness. His most revealing accusation 'There are certain men in the world who rather see everybody hung before they'll take the blame' is, ironically, a self-accusation. When he accidentally reveals the lie of his 'flu' on the day of the fateful decision at the plant, George, Miller's stage directions tell us, '*stands perfectly still*' (72). The ensuing suspicion is apparently lost in Frank's arrival with Larry's horoscope, then in the cab's honking, waiting to take George to the train station. Chris and Ann seem on the verge of a showdown; George says to his sister, 'He simply told your father to kill pilots, and covered himself in bed!' Chris threateningly says, 'You'd better answer him, Annie. Answer him' (74), but this climax, too, is undermined by Kate's declaration that she has packed Ann's bag, trying to evict her from their lives. But Chris rises to Ann's defence, indignant at his mother's highhanded interference, and the moment is subsumed: 'Now get out of here, George!' George tries to pursue Ann's confrontation of the truth, and we hear their voices arguing offstage as George leaves. Unlike the main characters, George is the only one whose life is unresolved; he is, perhaps, the most modern of the play's characters: damaged, guilt-ridden, rendered aimless by his existential crisis, and exiled to a life bereft of family, friends, and meaning.

The neighbours

The Baylisses and the Lubeys serve to create a sense of neighbourhood, living as they do on either side of the Kellers' house; they also provide a spectrum of personality types, serving as foils both to each other and to the central characters. Early in Act One Frank tells Jim, 'The trouble with you is, you don't *believe* in anything', and Jim replies, 'And your trouble is that you believe in *anything*' (6). Not only do they represent distant ends of the philosophic spectrum, from optimism and credulity to pessimism and cynicism, but Frank Lubey's interest in astrology is set against Jim's medical science, which has in itself deteriorated to, as he sees it, the hand-holding of hypochondriacs.

The two couples, along with the Kellers, provide a portrait of the institution of suburban, mid-twentieth-century marriage: while Frank seems to be cheerfully married to a good-natured woman, Jim is grimly married to a sniping, unhappy woman. It's worth noting that Jim and Sue Bayliss are older than Frank and Lydia, perhaps implying that their disillusionment is yet to come. Although Kate had once thought Lydia would be George's wife, he replies, 'sadly' and with obvious regret, 'she used to laugh too much' (67) – and clearly she still does. The Lubeys' little tiff about repairing a toaster is entirely pleasant, while the Kellers' little tiff about Joe's throwing out the potatoes elicits a more biting response from Kate; and the Baylisses' about the patient on the telephone is distinctly mean-spirited.

Frank is seen as an affable, puppy-ish man, likable, but not respected or admired. His happy life may be due to his innocence as well as to good luck: he beat the draft (as a result of the year in which he was born: no wonder he is addicted to astrology), escaped the war, and got the girl. That girl, Lydia, now the mother of three children, is a 'robust, laughing girl of twenty-seven' who knew George and Ann when they were all young together. Lydia, like Ann, is literally 'the girl next door', wholesome and easily amused.

Jim's wife Sue, is a former nurse; as Joe tells her, 'You were a nurse too long, Susie. You're too . . . too . . . realistic' (8). Sue seems both disappointed and resentful, not only of her husband's attitudes but at having lost her youth and looks; when Joe tells her that Ann has arrived and that 'she's a knockout', Sue replies sardonically, 'I should've been a man. People are always introducing me to beautiful women' (9).

Jim is the one of the four neighbours Miller is most interested in: he has the largest role and, not insignificantly, the bleakest outlook on life. No longer willing to participate in his family (maintaining it is too hot to drive to the beach, despite his having just driven to the station to pick up George), he resents the compromise marriage requires; no longer the idealistic researcher, he is now embittered and resigned to supporting them by doing medicine of the most pedestrian kind. His resignation gives his character the most depth and intensity; as he tells Kate, 'I live in the usual darkness; I can't find myself; it's even hard sometimes to remember the kind of man I wanted to be' (80), which gives him a profound and tragic modernity. Jim's cynicism would be summed up years later by the American comedian George Carlin who said, 'It's called the American dream 'cause you have to be asleep to believe it.' He also said, 'Inside every cynical person, there is a disappointed idealist', a perfect description of Jim.

Structure

As the legendary director and critic Harold Clurman shouted out after sitting through a rehearsal of *All My Sons'* first production, 'Goddamit, this play is *built*!' The architecture of a play, its structure, is what shapes the plot, links scene to scene, works towards (or refuses to, as is the case with some modern/contemporary plays) a decisive, climactic event. *All My Sons* is Miller's most conventional play structurally, and, like his early plays which immediately followed it, *Death of a Salesman*, *The Crucible* and *A View from the Bridge*, it raises the controversial question of the possibility of a modern tragedy. In his 1949 essay 'Tragedy and the Common Man' (*Theatre Essays*), he argues against the Aristotelian assumption that tragedy befalls only the great; Miller wrote: 'I believe that the common man is as apt a subject for tragedy in its highest sense as kings were . . . I think the tragic feeling is evoked in us when we are in the presence of a character who is ready to lay down his life, if need be, to secure one thing – his sense of personal dignity . . . Tragedy, then, is the consequence of a man's total compulsion to evaluate himself justly.'

As regards *All My Sons*, these remarks raise the question: is Joe a tragic hero? This can, perhaps, be answered in Miller's own terms since the essay goes on to argue that, 'Tragedy enlightens – and it must, in that it points the heroic finger at the enemy of man's freedom. The thrust for freedom is the quality in tragedy which exalts. The revolutionary questioning of the stable environment is what terrifies.' That last sentence could function as a summary of *All My Sons*. Tragic dramatic structure always begins in order and disintegrates into chaos, while the comic dramatic structure begins in chaos and moves towards order, an order which acknowledges the possibility of a stable future (thus comedies often end in weddings). 'Too late' is the classic tragic lesson, and like classical tragedy, Miller's protagonist discovers what he needs to discover too late to rectify his moral error. The analysis becomes more complex if we consider that Chris – hiding from the truth of what he has known all along – is the tragic figure, rather than Joe whose error is an act of will, an incorrect moral choice. Modern thought is steeped in both psychology and sociology, and both tend to diminish the stature of the individual who, for reasons of nature or nurture, could not help doing what he did. Because Miller optimistically believes that human beings can be better than they are, he believes that life can be remediated; this is fighting drama, like Ibsen's, lacking the bleak finality of Lear's definitive 'Never, never, never, never, never.'

To trace the structure of the play, we watch the peace of Act One dented by intimations of trouble: the fallen tree, Kate 'getting just like after [Larry] died', the arrival of Ann, 'Larry's girl' as Kate sees her, *must* see her. Each family scene threatens to – or actually does – turn ugly until a neighbour arrives to lighten the mood; this is a pattern established throughout the play. There are expository speeches built naturally into the dialogue – Ann explains why she isn't married, Chris describes his experience in the war and its effect on him, and, just when Chris and Ann declare their love and kiss, George telephones to say, mysteriously, that he will be arriving shortly, creating suspense to carry us through the first intermission.

Act Two postpones George's arrival while Joe attempts to assert his authority, his seeming generosity to Steve, and thus enlist Ann as an ally; Chris's anger at Joe's willingness to forgive Steve (entirely self-serving, but in ways we do not know about yet), demolishes the conciliatory atmosphere. Enter George, with 'blood in his eye', and once again the action alternates between anger and affection, as it does over and over again. When the showdown between Chris and George nearly reaches its climax, Lydia arrives from next door with the hat she has made for Kate, defusing the tension again. The pivot of the plot appears so inconspicuously that we barely register it as the staggering revelation it is; George is yielding to the nostalgic tug of the place when he says, 'I never felt at home anywhere but here [. . .] Kate, you look so young [. . .] You too, Joe, you're amazingly the same. The whole atmosphere is.' Joe fatefully replies, 'Say, I ain't got time to get sick', and Kate makes a' dreadful misstep: 'He hasn't been laid up in fifteen years . . .', to which Joe quickly replies 'Except my flu during the war' (71). This is the inadvertent disclosure that will bring the whole false structure of their lives crashing down. This time Frank's bumptious entrance with Larry's horoscope only fuels the flame, and the passionate, heartbreaking confrontation between Joe and Chris ends Act Two as Chris storms off. Act Three brings its own startling revelations: Chris returns, Ann reveals Larry's suicide letter, and Joe accepts his guilt. The structure of the conclusion of the play is based entirely on exits.

In his Introduction to the Methuen Drama volume *Plays: One*, Miller notes that in his first produced play, *The Man Who Had All the Luck*, he had tried to write a sense of the 'amazing': 'I had tried to grasp wonder, I had tried to make it on the stage, by writing wonder' (15). After the failure of this first venture, Miller returned to that master of wonder, Dostoevsky, discovering the effectiveness of the Russian novelist's structure: 'the precise collision of inner themes during, not before or after, the high dramatic scenes'. Miller turns then to Beethoven and discovers another crucial lesson in structure: 'the holding back of climax until it was ready, the grasp of the rising line and the unwillingness to divert to an easy climax until the true one was ready. If there is one word to name the mood I felt it was *Forego*. Let nothing interfere with the shape, the direction, the intention' (16).

Acknowledging 'the shadow of Ibsen', Miller points out that 'as in Ibsen's best-known work, a great amount of time is taken up with bringing the past into the present' (20). Although he acknowledges that this kind of structuring may be out of fashion, he writes that '*All My Sons* takes its time with the past, not in deference to Ibsen's method as I saw it then, but because its theme is a question of actions and consequences, and a way had to be found to throw a long line into the past in order to make that kind of connection viable' (20). When Kate tells Ann why she's certain Larry is still alive, she says – finding the only way she can to deny a truth that is too terrible to admit – 'Because certain things have to be, and certain things can never be. Like the sun has to rise, it has to be. That's why there's God. Otherwise anything could happen. But there's God, so certain things can never happen' (29). The point, of course, is that here randomness would be a comfort: Larry's death is not meaningless but meaningful, the iron-clad logic of cause and effect; here the cause – Joe's immoral act – has created this terrible effect – Larry's suicide and the deaths of twenty-one other young men.

Finally, the structure of the play rests on Miller's vision as he expressed in *Timebends*: 'Whenever the hand of the distant past reaches out of its grave, it is always somehow absurd as well as amazing, and we tend to resist belief in it, for it seems rather magically to reveal some unreadable hidden order behind the amoral chaos of events as we rationally perceive them. But that emergence, of course, is the point of *All My Sons* – that there are times when things do indeed cohere' (135). Thus, the hints and clues about who knows what need to be fully available to us without revealing too much too soon; it is not simply a matter of our suspense, but of the characters' suspense: the connections are not merely between the present and the past, between events and moral consequences, [but also] between the manifest and the hidden' (*Timebends* 24).

Productions

A few key productions

1947   *All My Sons* opens on Broadway, directed by Elia Kazan

1976   Production in Jerusalem directed by Hy Kalus, starring two of Israel's leading actors, Hanna Marron as Kate and Yossi Yadin as Joe. Miller attends (in 1977) with both the President and Prime Minister of Israel, where the play has a record-breaking run.

1981   West End production in London, directed by Michael Blakemore.

2000   Production at the National Theatre, London, directed by Howard Davies (four Olivier Awards).

2002   Production at the Guthrie Theatre, Minneapolis, directed by Joe Dowling.

2008   Revival on Broadway, directed by Simon McBurney.

Screen adaptations

1948 Universal Studios, directed by Irving Reis.
1986 American Playhouse (television), directed by Jack O'Brien.

Productions are, necessarily, interpretations of a script. The director makes choices and decisions, the actors make choices and decisions, as do the designers of the lighting, sound, and costumes. When reading a play, the reader makes all those choices, consciously or not, as we see the play happen in our mind's eye. It is crucial to read all the stage and set directions, and not to skip the italicized portions of the script eager to get on with the story.

Actors, directors, and other playwrights have much to say about Miller: for example, Patrick Stewart, the powerful British actor (who will, to some degree, always be Captain Jean-Luc Picard of *StarTrek*) said during an interview while starring in Miller's late play *The Ride Down Mount Morgan*:

He [Miller] likes actors. Not all playwrights do, which may be surprising. But Arthur does and when I began to realize that, it's very relaxing. On numerous occasions, he said to me [sudden shift to American accent], 'I don't know how you do it! I sit there and I watch and I don't know how you do it!' [Switch back to own voice and accent] Well, that's so *charming*. [Switch back to American accent] 'I couldn't do it, it would kill me!' He likes actors, he knows that a play is not complete until it's been given flesh and blood and sometimes that flesh and blood requires that there's input from the actors and the director. (*Arthur Miller's America*, 178)

Rosemary Harris played Kate in *All My Sons*, in the 1981 production in London; it ran for a remarkable nine months at Wyndham's Theatre. She recalls:

One of the fascinating aspects of playing Kate is the question of how much she really knows or suspects. It is a very thin line. The hope of Larry's return has to be kept alive at all costs and some of the profoundest feelings I've felt on a stage I felt during Ann's reading of Larry's suicide letter. It's hard to describe: a complete and utter emptiness engulfed by grief. I was always awfully jolly after the curtain came down but I used to wake up in the morning with a curious sense of heaviness and sorrow. After all, 'my husband' and 'my son' had killed themselves the night before. Playing Kate has been one of the joys of my theatrical life . . . I am grateful to Arthur for that character and all the people of his imagination. And I retain more than memories. All these years later I still have the costumes from that play. (*Arthur Miller and Company*, 50–1)

Making this admiration mutual, Miller told the critic Mel Gussow:

Nobody like Rosemary Harris had ever played that part, except once, in, of all places, Jerusalem . . . She was fantastically *there*. Rosemary and Blakemore [Michael Blakemore, the production's director] didn't assume at all that the basic thing was a father and son play [. . .] with Rosemary Harris, it wasn't simply narrowed down to the conflict. She created an ambience there that you could cut with a knife. It was quite wonderful. (*Conversations with Arthur Miller*, 100–1)

The original Broadway production in 1947 won two Tony Awards: Arthur Miller for Author of Best Play and Elia Kazan for Best Direction, as well as the New York Drama Critics' Circle Award (winning over Eugene O'Neill's *The Iceman Cometh*). Brooks Atkinson, the powerful *New York Times* critic, wrote that Miller

brings something fresh and exciting . . . Told against a single setting of an American backyard, it is a pitiless analysis of character that gathers momentum all evening and concludes with both logic and dramatic impact. Beth Merrill as the neurotic and tired mother gives us the impression of an inner strength that dominates at least one corner of the crisis. As Joe Keller, Ed Begley dramatizes the whole course of the father's poignant ordeal without losing the basic coarseness of the character. As the son, Arthur Kennedy is giving a superb performance with great power . . . [Miller is] a playwright who knows his craft and has unusual understanding of the tangled loyalties of human beings. (30 January 1947)

Miller felt that it was Atkinson's 'campaign for *All My Sons* that was responsible for its long run and my recognition as a playwright' (*Timebends*, 138).

The British production in 2000 won four Olivier Awards: Howard Davies for Best Director, William Dudley for Best Set Design, Ben Daniels for Best Supporting Actor and Julie Walters for Best Actress. In the *Independent* David Benedict wrote:

The overwhelming passions of Julie Walters, James Hazeldine and Ben Daniels are shockingly convincing . . . At root this is a 'what

did you do in the war daddy?' drama in which retribution comes to
call. . . All the five main characters fill the theatre with tension as if
holding five sticks of lit dynamite. (8 July 2000)

In the *Evening Standard* Patrick Marmion wrote:

It is an intense, immaculately conceived production packed with
compelling performances . . . Miller's writing is packed with
wit and wisdom and follows an Ibsenite dramatic procedure of
stripping away layers to reveal previously dormant, now deepening
conflicts. Not only does Howard Davies create a vivid sense of this
particular family's life, he also creates a subliminal sense of the
whole community, illustrating the warring themes of responsibility
and self-interest. William Dudley's design, meanwhile, creates an
environment best described as wrap-around theatre. He lays a real
grass lawn, canopied with a curtain of weeping willow. To this he
adds naturalistic sounds and smells emanating from all around the
theatre. But with the stage perfectly set it is the acting that blows
you away. (7 July 2000)

In production, the design decisions most obvious and influential to the
audience are those affecting the set. The audience can 'read a set', which
is to say that the set tells you what the play is about. The great American
playwright Edward Albee, talking about sets, observed 'It is impossible
NOT to have a set – even the total absence of a set is a set. The only
requirement is that the set be right for the production – there are many
possibilities for a play, as long as the designer understands the play. I'm
very leery of a set that wants to tell you what the play is about – a set
is a container' (Toby Zinman, *Edward Abee*, University of Michigan
Press, 2008, 3–4). Miller's set directions, on the other hand, describe the
Kellers' back yard in minute detail, even down to the presumed real-estate
value. Miller specifies an apple tree, although a cherry tree must have
been tempting. (American apocrypha: George Washington, America's first
president, chopped down a cherry tree when he was a boy. When confronted
by his father, he said, 'I cannot tell a lie. I did it.') The apple tree also has
its source in Miller's life: after the stock market crash of 1929 in which
his father lost a great deal of money, the family moved to Brooklyn, New
York, and in the new back yard, Miller, then a teenager, planted an apple
tree and a pear tree; the apple tree was later knocked down in a storm. But
an apple tree has unavoidable biblical associations, suggesting that the
Kellers' suburban back yard is Eden, and the choice of an apple tree thus
tells us what the play will be about: the loss of innocence, the acceptance
of the knowledge of good and evil and thus of moral responsibility; and,

further, that this pre-lapsarian world is doomed. But this is a faux Edenic world: the Kellers' fall into error happened years before the play begins, and it only remains for the denials, ignorings, and self-protective delusions to be stripped away.

Everyone *in* the play reads the apple tree as a symbol, too: for Kate the storm's wreckage signifies that it was too early to memorialise Larry's death, that it's a sign he's still alive. When she says at the start of Act Two, 'You notice there's more light with that thing gone?', we feel that she means one literal thing, while Miller means another, metaphoric, thing. When George asks about the apple-tree stump and Chris tells him, 'We had it there for Larry', George replies, 'Why, afraid you'll forget him?' It's worth noting at this point that *Timebends* ends with Miller's evocative declaration: 'the truth, the first truth, probably, is that we are all connected, watching one another. Even the trees.' Miller's 'secluded atmosphere' is created by 'closely planted poplars', trees that, we will learn, have grown taller and denser over the years, and thus symbolically as well literally seclude the back yard even more. Seclusion, of course, keeps in, imprisoning, as well as keeping out, protecting and isolating.

Historically, Miller's directions for this play invited the most realistic of sets, but almost always the realism is laced with symbolism. The original set was designed by Mordecai Gorelik for the 1947 Broadway premiere; Gorelik organised his sets, as Miller explains in *Timebends*, 'around a metaphoric statement condensing the central image of the play'. He had designed a back yard with a bump, and Miller worried the actors would fall over it. 'What's the point of it, Max – a rise like that in the middle of the stage?' The reply was, 'You have written a graveyard play and not some factual report. The play is taking place in a cemetery where their son is buried, and he is also their buried conscience reaching up to them out of the earth. Even if it inconveniences them [the actors] it will keep reminding them what the hell all this acting is really *about*. The bump stays!' (275).

Looking at photographs of a dozen productions reveals that they are all remarkably and interestingly similar: the same back yard, the same wooden lawn furniture, the same fretworked gazebo. There have been productions where the back yard was picket-fenced, as though to signify the bars of a prison, picking up Joe's ongoing game with the neighbourhood boys who believe there's a jail in the house, as well as implying the real prison Steve is in and Joe should be in. The possibilities for easy symbolism are all remarkably similar.

John Lee Beatty, the pre-eminent set designer, acknowledged that his inspiration for the 2002 Guthrie production in Minneapolis was the Grant

Wood painting *American Gothic*; what he hoped to achieve was an 'ironic twist', wanting it to seem 'attractive and yet, oddly, a little bit off, not quite realistic'. Beatty noted that 'underlying that painting and through his other work, [Wood] explores solid philosophical and aesthetic backgrounds having to do with American identity. His idyllic images of America are rendered through a potently ironic perspective.' In his comments to his actors and staff early in the rehearsal process, Beatty quoted Miller saying that 'nothing should interfere with its artifice'. His interpretation aimed to avoid the 'nostalgically naturalistic'.

The American playwright John Guare recalls an uproarious lunch with Miller:

> I told Arthur how my feelings about him as a writer had changed.
> I had at one time thought him the enemy, consigned to the poetry-
> free pits of naturalism Hell. Not until I saw *The American Clock*
> did I realise how shot through to its very bones the play was with
> surrealistic imagery and that this surrealism was indeed responsible
> for that which was most powerful about the play. I subsequently
> saw a conventional revival of *All My Sons.* I closed my eyes and
> simply listened to the play's madness and realized one day some
> visionary director will find a way to liberate Arthur's plays from
> their cage of traditional psychological realism. (*Arthur Miller and
> Company*, 223)

Simon McBurney would be that director. His production opened on Broadway in 2008. He was the least likely director for this American classic, being both British and wildly experimental (he is the artistic director of the antirealist company Complicite). McBurney was asked by Rebecca Miller, Arthur Miller's daughter, to direct *All My Sons*, and he remembers Arthur Miller telling him in 2001, 'In America I've always felt that people have either tried to honor it [the play] too much to the letter or there has been this heavy hand of naturalism on it, and nothing has been taken to the hilt.' As a *New York Times* interview noted, there is no better guide to the hilt than McBurney who said that rather than adding to the play, he wanted to strip it down, which turned out to mean removing the written set directions. In Tom Pye's set design there were no wings where actors could hide in order to preserve the realistic illusion on stage, no poplar trees, and not even a house: the upstage wall was an immense weathered wood construction, dwarfing the actors, with one small window set eerily far above the normal height of an upstairs room.

The production made other intrusions on the naturalistic perspective: Keller (played by John Lithgow) enters the stage carrying the playbook from which he reads the opening stage directions; a free-standing screen door signified entering and leaving the house; a pay-phone was stuck on to the proscenium arch; and huge cinematic projections punctuated the action with memories and highlighted historical context. The result was not a back yard, but a stage.

McBurney began the play earlier than Miller does: the tree is still standing, the storm occurs, Kate comes out in her robe, reaching up to the heavens, and the tree is knocked over. At the National Theatre in London in 2000, Howard Davies's directorial choice began the play with Kate watching the lightning strike the apple tree. McBurney, like Miller, but unlike Davies, does not seem to want to shift the burden of responsibility to the cosmos; his inclination is, like Miller's, far more on the human, the psychological, and the ethical.

Dismantling the furniture of realism yielded surprising meaning, making this play both more interesting – which is to say less moralistic – and more clearly and persuasively connected to the vision and the style of Miller's late plays: *The Ride Down Mount Morgan*, *Resurrection Blues*, and *Mr Peters' Connections*. This is a valuable kind of rereading, starting from the end and looking backwards. *All My Sons* battles through the human tug-of-war between destiny and free will – the human question inherent in the myth of Eden, and thus fundamental to Western culture – and this production emphasised that battle. And as the Edenic drama in Genesis shows us, the hardest thing for human beings is to take responsibility for our actions. The Judeo-Christian implications of *All My Sons* are immense, but if we read this production set, we feel what McBurney, interpreting Miller, wanted us to feel. McBurney said that: 'Miller is creating a modern American tragedy here . . . it's attempting to find the explosive animal questions of humanity in the play, which of course are the questions at the heart of Greek drama' (*American Theatre*, December 2008, pp. 88–9). A case made, in this instance, partly by the set design.

Rebecca Miller said of the McBurney production: 'the raw power of the play has never been unleashed in this way . . . It is the purest manifestation of the play I can imagine. I hope this will open the door to more extraordinary, unexpected productions of Miller plays' (*American Theatre*, December 2008).

The films

The first film version makes every Hollywood mistake in adapting a successful play to the screen. Directed by Irving Reis in 1948 and rewritten by the producer, Chester Erskine, the film 'opens up' the play to many settings; we go inside the house, out to dinner at the shore restaurant, to the Keller factory, to the prison to hear Steve's actual version of the fateful day (his name is changed to Herb), and on a romantic, moonlit drive. This undermines the effect of imprisonment of the play's single set and the significance of the hedged-in back yard. Further, almost all the ambiguities of character stemming from denial have been erased, and the motivations, by being flattened out, make much less sense, all, apparently, in the interests of making the moral lesson overly explicit. For example: Chris tells Joe, 'If it turned out you weren't telling the truth, I'd kill you', which is a far different and less persuasive foreshadowing of the conclusion than Joe's line in the play, 'I'm his father and he's my son, and if there's something bigger than that I'll put a bullet in my head.'

Edward G. Robinson's Joe is grim and self-important; he is particularly unlikable at the poker game, where he treats people like lackeys, wins everyone's money and gloats, although this behaviour seems to win everyone's admiration, including Chris's. The film's old-fashioned mores startle, especially Joe kissing Ann on the lips. Burt Lancaster as Chris is earnest throughout, never suspicious, always eager to please his parents; his face registers little emotion. All the war stories and the resentment he feels about post-war America have been erased from the screenplay. Like Chris, Ann seems to lack a vivid personality, providing only for the requirements of the plot.

Kate was Mady Christians' last film performance, and her Austrian accent and Germanic hairdo lend the role an unsettling old-time movie-villain quality. We see her eavesdrop (accompanied by spooky music) on Ann's phone conversation with George (Howard Duff), and her affection seems too blatantly predatory and cloying. The Baylisses have been transformed into a high-spirited, sexy couple.

The 1986 made-for-television film is, on the other hand, faithful to Miller's script. Under Jack O'Brien's strong direction, the actors find every nuance within a vivid naturalistic style. Filmed in unobtrusive colour, acknowledging the breaks between acts, this production is passionate and deeply moving. Aiden Quinn (as Chris), James Whitmore (as Joe), Michael Learned (as Kate), Joan Allen (as Ann), and Zeljko Ivanek (as George) all turn in impressive performances.

Notes

The notes below explain words and phrases from the play, with page numbers referencing the Student Editions published by Bloomsbury Methuen Drama.

page

3   *back yard*: garden.

3   *porch*: veranda.

9   *Thomas Edison*: an American inventor (1847–1931), whose numerous inventions included the phonograph, the motion-picture camera, and the light bulb.

10   *oilstone*: a whetstone used for sharpening blades; it is generally lubricated with oil.

22   *dast*: should dare.

31   *Post Toasties*: a breakfast cereal.

32   *cylinder heads*: in an internal combustion engine, the valves and spark plugs are encased in the cylinder. The cylinder is a pressure vessel that contains the forces of combustion. A crack that grows around the circumference of the vessel will increase until the head is weakened enough to blow off.

32   *P-40s*: when the Second World War began, the P-40 was America's principal foremost fighter plane.

39   *Well, nobody told me it was Labor Day?*: Joe's remark when he sees Ann and Chris kissing refers to an annual American holiday, traditionally the first Monday in September, giving workers a long weekend. It marks the official end of the summer season. Joe's reference is an old-fashioned one: at small-town carnivals on Labor Day there would be a kissing booth, where a person – usually a pretty girl – would allow people to kiss her for a fee.

42   *He's in Columbus*: this is the name of the capital city in the state of Ohio, where Steve is in prison. This indicates that although it's still a long-distance phone call, Columbus is fairly close to the 'outskirts of an American town' where the play is set.

49   *I resent living next door to the Holy Family*: the Holy Family is, in the Roman Catholic Church, Jesus, his mother the Virgin Mary, and his human father figure, Joseph.

49   *But if Chris wants to put on the hair shirt let him take off his broadcloth*: a hair shirt is traditionally a means of religious mortification by wearing undergarments made of rough and

scratchy animal hair. Broadcloth is a densely woven, smooth fabric, no longer much used in contemporary clothing.

51 *Every time I come out here it looks like Playland*!: an amusement park.

51 *roué*: French for what used to be called a 'rake', a playboy.

56 *Zeppelin*: a Zeppelin was a dirigible, an airship used in the 1930s. In America they can still be seen flying as novelties (not as transportation) and are sometimes called 'blimps'.

64 *Mahatma Gandhi*: (1869–1948) the pre-eminent political and spiritual leader of India during the struggle for Indian independence. He employed tactics of non-violent resistance and civil disobedience. He led a simple, abstemious life and was very thin, hence Chris's joke.

66 *No, he was always one year ahead of the draft*: in 1940 (still peacetime in the US) the government instituted a system of compulsory, one-year military service for men between the ages of twenty-one and thirty-five. After Pearl Harbor, when the US entered the war, the draft law was amended, eliminating the exemptions (married men, etc.). All men between twenty and forty-five became eligible for the draft. Ultimately more than ten million men were drafted in the Second World War.

67 *Eagle Scouts the three of you*: Eagle Scout is the top rank in the Boy Scouts of America, a nationwide club subscribing to high moral principles.

67 *Andy Gump*: Andy Gump was a popular cartoon-strip character in several national and local newspapers.

Questions for Further Study

1 Consider the significance of the play's title.
2 Compare and contrast Joe Keller to Miller's most famous character, Willy Loman in *Death of a Salesman*: Do they share values? How are each man's values tested? Are their suicides similarly motivated?
3 What symbolic elements illuminate the meaning of the play?
4 Some readers/spectators have found Larry's letter, whipped out at the last minute, too contrived as a plot device. Argue for or against its timing and its dramatic necessity.
5 What is the effect of the play taking place in the Kellers' back yard? Consider the importance of neighbourhood.
6 What can be deduced about mid-twentieth-century American society from this play? What evidence supports your ideas? Consider the spectrum of attitudes articulated by the characters, ranging from optimism to cynicism.
7 *All My Sons* is, like O'Neill's most famous play, also a 'long day's journey into night'; how does the morning-to-night time-scheme function as a way of understanding the play's vision?
8 We see four couples in the play: what does Miller seem to be saying about the institution of marriage?
9 'Denial', a self-protective psychological device for hiding an unpleasant truth from oneself, is prevalent among these characters. Why do they need to persist in denial?
10 What is the symbolic significance of Chris's name as it affects the dynamica of the plays?
11 To what extent is *All My Sons* an anti-war play?
12 Bert's role is small, although significant. What does Miller reveal by Bert's appearance in Act One?
13 *All My Sons*, it could be argued, is Miller's only completely realistic play. Miller seems to adhere to the conventions of realism, especially that of the 'fourth wall'; discuss the necessity of naturalism for the impact of this play in performance.
14 The elaborate set directions indicate how important it was to Miller to create a very specific world: which elements of the set directions seem crucial and why?
15 What do you understand 'ensemble' to mean? Should the cast create the sense of an ensemble to indicate family or neighbourhood?
16 Do you think the confrontation between Joe and Chris should be a physical fight? Different choices are made by different directors.

17 The lighting design needs to create visual clues for the audience to indicate that time has passed, but it can also create an emotional atmosphere. How do you imagine this evocation?

18 Imagine you are the casting director: describe the central qualities you are looking for in the four major roles. Although accomplished actors can transcend physical attributes, nevertheless audiences tend to 'read' a character through the actor. How might this affect the play?

19 How crucial is it that the play be located by costuming, etc. in mid-twentieth-century America? Can you imagine this play successfully relocated to another time and place to make a similar sociopolitical statement?

20 George's entrance is postponed as he waits in the car offstage; what is the effect of this delay? What does it tell the audience about the approaching climax? Like many plays, *All My Sons* is built on entrances and exits. Consider the timing of the comings and goings. How does this work, for example, in the conclusion?

21 Sophoclean irony depends on the audience knowing more than the character does, so that it is not the revelation of the secret but the character's reaction to the secret that we wait for. Analyse the way Miller has built his play on this classical device.

Death of a Salesman

commentary and notes by
ENOCH BRATER

Commentary

When Willy Loman, suitcase in hand, walks slowly on to the set *of Death of a Salesman* in one of the most famous stage entrances in twentieth-century drama, he begins the long requiem that finally announces itself as such in the play's closing moments. The work, Arthur Miller said, 'is written from the sidewalk instead of from the skyscraper'. Unlike Willy's two sons, the audience hardly needs to wait for his wife's pronouncement to understand that 'the man is exhausted. A small man can be just as tired as a great man'. The playwright's proletarian spirit permeates the entire drama. Willy Loman, the salesman working on commissions that no longer come, is down on his luck, not that he really ever had any. Happy, who talks big, is the perpetual assistant to his company's assistant; Biff, who (unlike his father) knows that he's 'a dime a dozen', is the ageing, fair-haired boy gone to seed; and their mother, Linda, the homebody, ignored by time and the men around her, is unable to stem the tide that soon engulfs them all, try as she might. The whole question of 'Tragedy and the Common Man', the subject of one of the playwright's seminal essays of the same period, is neatly captured in the play's evocative subtitle, '*Certain Private Conversations in Two Acts and a Requiem*'.

Salesman's immediacy, accessibility and inter-generational appeal is a final tribute to Linda's great moment of lucidity, which occurs early in the play: 'Attention, attention must finally be paid to such a man.' Miller's challenge was formidable: how to construct a play that was on the one hand anecdotal and particular, and on the other widely and richly representative, symbolic, at times even mythic. From early on, the work originally called *The Inside of His Head* seemed to cry out for a practical stage solution as difficult and innovative as it was elusive: how to render the past, the present and the protagonist's increasingly desperate imaginings as one continuous whole, without resorting to mechanical 'flashbacks' (a term the playwright disliked). *Salesman's* tone here is realistic, but it presupposes a realism with a marked difference. The naturalistic set Miller relied upon for his previous success, *All My Sons*, would no longer serve his purpose. To make this play work, stage space would have to be explored imaginatively, recalibrated and in fact reinvented. His much-celebrated collaboration with the director Elia Kazan and the brilliant designer Jo Mielziner resulted in the construction of a highly atmospheric platform set that gave *Salesman* the look and flexibility its narrative drive demanded. On a multi-level set time past and time present could be in constant dialogue with one another as a rhythmic pattern of renegotiation instantly emerged. All that was needed to signal temporal transition was stage lighting, accompanied by the sound of a flute playing somewhere in the distance. Given such a highly unusual design concept, Miller's '*dream rising out of reality*' could be rendered concrete, material and dead-centre – on stage.

No one involved in the original production of *Death of a Salesman* in 1949, least of all the author, was sure that the gamble would work. The producer Kermit Bloomgarden, one of the play's principal backers, recommended a different title for the play. Convinced that no one would buy a ticket to a show with 'death' advertised on the marquee, he suggested *Free and Clear* as an alternative, highlighting Linda's speech in the Requiem, which brings closure to the play. The playwright refused: 'The work I wrote is called *Death of a Salesman*.' When the curtain came down on the first night of the out-of-town tryout in Philadelphia, followed by an awkward silence, the tension, as Miller relates in his autobiography *Timebends*, was palpable and real. A lot was at stake, not only for Miller, but 'for the future of the American theatre'. There was, finally, thunderous applause, followed by the oddest thing of all: 'men and women wept openly' and, after the applause died down, 'members of the audience refused to leave and started talking to complete strangers about how deeply they had been affected by the play'. Miller, who thought he had written a tough, hard-hitting exposé of the dangerous and deceptive myth of 'making it in America', was entirely unprepared for the emotional punch *Salesman* delivered in performance. His play had at once found a life of its own.

The strong effect *Death of a Salesman* continues to have on Miller's audiences can be so daunting, the emotions it excites so raw, that the drama quickly becomes, despite its author's stated intentions, something quite different from a thesis play. And this may have little to do with the protagonist's socio-economic status as the quintessential 'low man'. The playwright took the name from Fritz Lang's *The Testament of Dr Mabuse*, the 1933 film in which a detective hopes to redeem himself by exposing a gang of forgers. Duped by them instead, he shouts into a telephone to his former boss, 'Lohmann! Help me for God's sake! Lohmann!' Later in the same film, we meet the crazed detective in the asylum as he shouts into an invisible phone, 'Lohmann? Lohmann? Lohmann?' 'What the name really meant to me,' Miller said, 'was a terrified man calling into the void for help that will never come.' And thinking about his own Loman in the notebook he kept while working on the first draft for the play, he wrote this: 'Remember [the character's] size', his 'ugliness'. 'Remember his attitude.' 'Remember', above all, '*pity*'.

Although we generally think of Miller as a playwright with a narrative rather than a visual imagination, *Death of a Salesman* relies on a profound sense of stage imagery: the set is Miller's play. Dwarfed by looming apartment blocks that rob the sunlight from Willy's garden (as well as his soul), the Loman house belongs to some other moment in time and a very different sense of place. What threatens both is impermanence and the flux of change. America is on the move, but the Loman sanctuary stands still. This is still Brooklyn, but a reimagined borough in which windows, like so many threatening eyes, stare down on a diminished world that seems ever more diminished and inconsequential. 'There's more people now!' Willy cries out in an anger that is really a sign of his despair. 'Bricks and windows, windows and bricks' frame his claustrophobia, which the set renders as agonisingly real. Music, too, tells the story. Each of Willy's journeys into the past, including one double journey, is signalled by the sound of a single, plaintive flute. His father, significantly, made his own flutes by hand, then sold them from a wagon by himself, always on the move. Willy's suitcase carries unspecified 'samples' of factory-made goods. Other sounds will be similarly evocative and similarly advance the plot. The recorded sound of a child on tape reciting the capital of every state in alphabetical order drowns out Willy's cry for help, and Biff is cautioned against whistling in elevators (he does so anyway; the Lomans are great whistlers and they all say 'Gee', a boy's word, not a man's). Finally, when Willy's life come crashing down all around him, we hear the '*frenzy of sound*' as his car starts up and races away, ominously, at full speed. What follows his 'accident' is '*the soft pulsation of a single cello string*'.

In *Salesman*, as elsewhere in the Miller repertory, the play's atmospheric dimension is there to enhance the work's narrative authority and appeal. This is first and foremost the theatre's most compelling representation of the dark underside of the so-called American Dream. Here it is rendered as half-fantasy, half-phantasmagoria, configured as it is as some triumphalist and everywhere disturbing guy-culture. Willy, as we are told in the Requiem, 'never knew who he was'. But he was also, as Miller said elsewhere, a man who 'chased everything that rusts'. He had 'all the wrong dreams'. Caught up, like most of post-war America, in the vain and unobtainable lure of success, which he equates with material wealth, popularity and the making of a good impression ('be well liked and you shall never want'), he realises all too late that what he has been searching for all his life he has had all along, and this is something that is not negotiable: Biffs unqualified love. What makes the play a tragedy – and it is certainly that – is that the father's unfulfilled ambitions, rather than any insurance premiums, are the only inheritance he can offer his sons. His legacy is their peril. 'I'm not bringing home any more prizes.' What Biff is saying is that you will have to love me anyway. But by that time it is too late. Willy drives off and kills himself. In *Death of a Salesman* Miller transforms Greek tragedy and brings it down, crashing, to earth.

Plot Summary, Structure and Dramatic Style

It is all but impossible in *Death of a Salesman* to separate the plot line from the highly stylised structure through which it has been carefully designed for maximum theatrical effect. Much is told through Willy's point of view, and the scenes sited in the past are nearly always, though not exclusively, his. In the frequently staged moments of his selective memory that seem to merge spontaneously and seamlessly into the present, we are literally, not figuratively, 'inside his head'. In such instances anything resembling an objective point of view is hard to pin down. The play builds its momentum symphonically, through the rich intersection of what Willy chooses to remember, how he remembers it, and other memories that he struggles to suppress but that intrude nonetheless. The other characters in the play, who also appear as figures in his past, bear witness in the present, as we do, to his increasing inability to locate the logical boundaries imposed by time, place and the contingencies of resolving a single dramatic action. The taut line of tension is sustained by observing them observe him. Willy's memories move swiftly to the rhythm of their own ebb and flow, but they follow very closely the expository demands of each dramatic encounter; their staging, however, requires a far more concrete system of synchronisation. Miller relies on a surprising new framework for narrative continuity, employing a deft transformation of apparent discontinuity: the plot develops through an atmospheric rather than a strictly linear arc. Plot summary, therefore, rarely does justice to the movement and meaning of this landmark play, though it is worth considering how economical the author has been in building so many resonances into the events that dramatically unfold.

Act One

Miller's stage directions for the opening of the play are a marvel of invention and display his dramatic imagination at full stretch. Everything is geared to tone, mood, atmosphere and gesture, and it is impossible to understand all that follows without an appreciation of the strategy outlined here. The emphasis is on lighting and lyricism, for this stage space has an '*air of dream*' that '*clings to the place, a dream rising out of reality*'. The play begins in silence, as all plays do, but that silence is soon interrupted when a melody is heard, '*played upon a flute*'. Significantly, '*It is small and fine, telling of grass and trees and the horizon*' as the curtain slowly rises on a set that seems to come from another world entirely: the salesman's house, surrounded by '*towering*', '*angular*', even '*angry*' shapes on all sides. In the ominous shadows cast by encroaching apartment blocks – the stage direction calls' them, tellingly, '*vaults*' – the Loman house makes its last stand, out-of-date and out of time, as a '*small, fragile-seeming home*'. Oddly enough, the lines that follow detail the nuts-and-bolts multidimensionality of the platform set, as Miller turns his attention to the logistics of the *mise-en-scène*. Place and placement are designed for flexibility and impermeability. Abandoning the narrow constraints of fourth-wall realism, Miller prepares the stage for scenes that blend swiftly and unobtrusively one into the other, then another. Such spaces must be everywhere configured to accommodate themselves not only to the specific locations for the actions that follow (kitchen, boys' bedrooms, parents' bedroom, garden, backyard, office, restaurant, hotel room), but equally so – and perhaps even more crucially so – to time past, time present and time remembered. It is into this deliberately staged world that Willy Loman enters, tired and exhausted. And as he does so, carrying two large sample suitcases, he is first and foremost an image before he is a personality.

Willy crosses the stage to the doorway of the house, unlocks the door and, muttering to himself, enters the kitchen. He occupies these spaces with authority; each of his movements defines them for the audience before he moves into the offstage living-room, where he will deposit his bags. As he does so, the focus turns to Linda, who has stirred in her bed in another stage space on the right. She has heard her husband come in unexpectedly, and '*with some trepidation*' cries out the play's first real line of dialogue, 'Willy!' Their encounter relays pivotal information: she's worried that he may have 'smash [ed]' the car; he tells her that he was on his way but just 'couldn't make it', couldn't drive any more; and she tries to mollify him by suggesting any number of excuses for his sudden return ('the steering again', 'you never went for your new glasses', and most revealing of all in terms of dramatic foreshadowing, 'Well, you'll just have to take a rest, Willy, you can't continue this way'). Willy hardly hears her as he recites his first of many monologues, this one detailing what happened to him on the road when he 'opened the windshield' and 'let the warm air bathe over me'. 'I have such thoughts, I have such strange thoughts.' Willy is confused; later in the same scene he will rebuke Linda for even mentioning the removable windshield, for that clumsy apparatus belonged to the model he owned years before, not the one he drives off the road now. It is through a reliance on seemingly minor details like this that Miller begins to establish key elements of his plot (later in the play silk stockings play a similar role, those darned by Linda and the new ones given to his mistress in a Boston hotel room). Their discussion turns to the practical, at least on Linda's part, as the couple begins to speculate on his chances for shifting his sales 'territory' from New England to more local markets in New York. Willy isn't really interested: 'They don't need me in New York. I'm the New England man. I'm vital in New England.' What Willy fears is change.

But this isn't any ordinary evening, and not just because Willy has been unable to make a sales trip. Biff, the one-time golden boy whose sports trophies are getting dusty, has come home. His lack of completion is just as troubling: thirty-four years old, he is still not able to '[find] himself'. Father and son have already had one of their brutal encounters before the play began: an argument which took place just after Biff got off the train from nowhere in particular. Their antagonism – and the history behind it – forms the basis of the play's rising action, though at this early point in the drama it serves as a device to establish conflict and expose psychological texture.

Both of these elements are considerably amplified as stage lighting illuminates yet another space, this one the raised platform outlining the dimensions of Biff and Happy's childhood bedroom. This is an unusual place in which to find two physically grown men, and yet it is the perfect setting in which to localise their emotional paralysis and perennial adolescence. Each son is stunted in his own way: Happy, who usually sleeps in his own bachelor apartment, is more 'bum' than playboy, and Biff, more 'guy' than 'man', still uses words like 'gee' and 'naa' and 'pal'. The vocabulary they use as they listen across their twin beds to their parents' give-and-take – Willy gives and Linda takes – is laced with wished-for macho wonders that turn out to be more like blunders. Even they can barely disguise the changes that have come over them: 'I don't know' – and Biff is probably speaking for both of them at this point – 'what I'm supposed to want.' Happy shies away from self-reflection like this, and tries hard to avoid it throughout the play; though his brother, the former high-school football hero – he peaked much too soon – can be cauterised by his awareness of the waste he is making of his own life. Yet once together, they spur one another on to create another childlike fantasy, this one quintessentially American: moving together 'out West', raising cattle, using their 'muscles', and ripping off their shirts in the middle of a hot afternoon in Montana or Nevada or Arizona or some other place that ends in an 'a' where people couldn't locate Brooklyn on a map, even if they wanted to.

Their reverie is cut short when they hear from below that their father is talking to himself, memorialising and sentimentalising a past he tries so desperately to recapture. This is nostalgia writ large. The scene not only shifts back to the kitchen, then to the garden, but more significantly to the past; this is the first of the play's many temporal leaps. Biff and Happy must now play down, performing the younger versions of themselves their father so much longs for them to be again. Their shared past is a world of football passes, hammocks, punching bags, sneakers, college logos, Simonised cars, youthful vigour, firm male bodies, inevitable sunshine – the way it was or should have, could have been. It never rains in the past (though the skies will turn dark for Willy's funeral).

And yet there is a serpent in every garden, including Willy Loman's. The site of his elaborate myth-making is quickly and fatally compromised even in this first journey into the rosy past, and it is accomplished by the smallest of gestures – a 'borrowed' football from the high-school locker room ('The coach told me to practice my passing'); Biffs plan to up-end his team's passing game by taking off his helmet and 'breakin' out' for an unauthorised touchdown; Biffs driving without a licence; above all the threat of failing maths. To his son's questionable behaviour Willy offers no repudiation; in fact, he encourages it, filling Biff with an unearned sense of self-esteem and its corollary, success-at-any-price, even if it means bending the rules or worse: lie, cheat, steal and deceive. 'Be liked and you shall never want' is Willy's false mantra, and he has stuffed his sons, as they say in Brooklyn, 'full of it'. Make 'an appearance', create' 'personal interest' and the world will be their oyster because they are – what? – 'both built like Adonises'. Biff, the captain of the team, will always be in first place, or so his father makes him believe.

What the Lomans are full of is talk: Willy exaggerates the number of his commissions, misrepresents the amount he earns, puffs up his position in the firm and fantasises about his popularity with the buyers. Yet he knows he is 'fat' and 'foolish to look at', and behind his back he heard another salesman liken him to a 'walrus'. However, Linda still thinks him 'the handsomest man in the world'. No matter, in either case. Biff will be his redemption. Suddenly, strange laughter is heard '*to the left of the house*': 'The Woman' comes into full view from behind a scrim, exposing herself and the charade of domestic tranquility. In his imagination and in the stage blocking Willy moves into this new scene before Linda's laughter merges with the Woman's and returns him to the kitchen. We're still in the past, but we have just made a double journey into it.

As Linda exits, the scene returns to the present. Happy comes down the stairs in his pyjamas and discovers his father still talking to himself. Willy, returning to everyday reality, gradually becomes aware of his son's presence and rehearses with him the 'awful scare' he had today that brought him back home: 'Nearly hit a kid in Yonkers.' What he yearns for is release, some alternative existence, the one he might have had with the myth-like figure of his brother Ben.

The scene becomes more complicated with the arrival of Willy's neighbour, Charley, who is also the only friend he has ever had. The kind-hearted Charley invites himself into the house because he is worried about Willy, having just heard disturbing noises in the night. They play a game of cards to while away the time, but the tricks go awry when Willy 'sees' Ben walk, umbrella in hand, straight into the set. Willy must now carry on a double conversation, one with his uneasy casino partner, the other with an apparition from his past. Charley, growing impatient with the lack of connection, gives up on him, picks up the cards and departs. Willy is now free to move directly into his dream-world, and as he does so he brings his whole family, as well as a younger version of Charley, with him. In this key scene, re-drawing the lines of the past on the space before us, a number of important details quickly accumulates: Linda meets Willy's brother for the first time and is unsure about him, as well as critical of his underhand sportsmanship in boxing with a teenage Biff, whom he humiliates. Ben, another great talker ('William, when I walked into the jungle, I was seventeen. When I walked out I was twenty-one. And, by God, I was rich!'), also relates the flamboyant history of the boys' grandfather, 'a wild-hearted' flute-maker and inventor of gadgets, and a travelling man who rarely stayed in one place for very long. Willy longs to spend more time with his elder brother and find out something more, anything more, about a father he has never really known: 'Dad left when I was such a baby and I never had a chance to talk to him and I still feel – kind of temporary about myself.' Details like this add a great deal of poignancy to the dramatic moment, just as they serve to open up and expand the psychological range of the drama as a whole.

Linda re-enters, signalling our return to the present. Willy, still reeling from the mental encounter with his brother, asks about the diamond watch fob he gave him when he visited the family from Africa, and she reminds him that they pawned it long ago. Willy's departure for a late-night walk, shuffling away in his slippers, clears the stage for the famous confrontation scene she has been waiting to have with her two negligent and (in different ways) troubled sons.

The scene brings us to the very heart of Miller's drama. What it reveals so clearly is that Linda's allegiance is to her husband before it is to her sons. As the opening stage directions have already told us, '*she more than loves him, she admires him, as though his mercurial nature, his temper, his massive dreams and little cruelties, served her only as sharp reminders of the turbulent longings within him, longings which she shares but lacks the temperament to utter and follow to their end.*' As her sons descend the stairs to enter her space, the well-kept kitchen, Biff attempts to establish her as a potential ally and partial confidante (he will, of course, not tell her everything – what happened in Boston remains strictly off-limits), while Happy plays the choral part, backing up his brother. Linda steadfastly resists their manoeuvres, and displays her metal even further by repudiating them, most especially Biff, the son Willy adores, for their 'hateful' treatment of their father, a man crying out for help: 'Biff, dear' – and her line is loaded – 'if you don't have any feeling for him, then you can't have any feeling for me.' One of Miller's great strengths as a writer of stage dialogue is on display here: his ability to find eloquence even in the rhythms of everyday speech. Linda's lines that follow, for example, say more about the entire issue of 'tragedy and the common man' than anything the playwright or his critics have had to say about it elsewhere:

> I don't say he's a great man. Willy Loman never made a lot of
> money. His name was never in the paper. He's not the finest
> character that ever lived. But he's a human being, and a terrible
> thing is happening to him. So attention must be paid. He's not to be
> allowed to fall into his grave like an old dog. Attention, attention
> must be finally paid to such a person. You called him crazy . . . a
> lot of people think he's lost his balance. But you don't have to be
> very smart to know what his trouble is. The man is exhausted . . . A
> small man can be just as exhausted as a great man. (pp. 44–5)

So convincing is Linda's moving speech that she even succeeds in turning Biff around, at least temporarily: he'll find a job and stay at home now, a declaration that seems even more heartfelt once he learns that his father has been trying to kill himself. There is, nonetheless, an important caveat: Biff insists that his mother should not blame everything on him. 'What happened to the love you had for him? You were such pals!' a distraught Linda cries out in an emotional outburst that reveals as much about her momentary insecurity as it does about her anger. The answer to that question will be the furtive through-line that keeps the rest of the play going.

Linda's big scene also reveals something else that is fundamental to the dynamics of this family drama: her unacknowledged complicity in its steady unravelling. As powerful as her speech is – it more than adequately conveys her anxiety about Willy, her real fear of the emptiness that awaits her if he is no longer there, as well as the play's central thesis – it nevertheless encapsulates the extent to which she has been the enabler of Willy's self-delusions. She has not only put up with the disgraceful way he treats her (no wonder Happy talks about women with such disrespect), but she has made excuses for her husband all her life long. Worse still, she has never intervened when Willy filled their sons with so many illusions of grandeur, not to mention the imbalance with which he has meted out his affection for them. Happy has been, at best, an afterthought. Much of this remains deeply buried in the play's subtext, even in this critical scene. These disturbing tensions are in any case quickly overwhelmed by others when Willy, who has overheard Biff in the last part of the scene, delivers his Parthian shot: 'Even your grandfather was better than a carpenter. You never grew up.'

As the act draws to a close, it is important for Miller to demonstrate the *modus operandi* of this family's customary but still lethal dysfunctionality: Biff takes the bait and once again assumes his assigned role as his father's main antagonist; Linda engages in her vain attempt to calm the waters, and is promptly put down for it; Happy interjects with the bright promise of a new day dawning, a business opportunity for the Loman brothers – 'sporting goods'; and Willy turns around and betters Happy's feisty game plan. Then, as always, and almost without noticing that they are doing so, the characters turn on one another. Willy stalks off, followed by the transference of guilt and the inevitable, vain apologies. The pattern is bound to reinscribe itself: 'you got a greatness in you,' Willy serenades Biff, 'remember that. You got all kinds a greatness . . .' He's still 'like a young god', a 'Hercules – something like that', he confides to Linda. 'And the sun, the sun all around him . . . God Almighty, he'll be great yet. A star like that, magnificent, can never really fade away!' Earlier in the act it was Happy who said that his brother was 'a poet'. But it is really their' father, '*staring through the window into the moonlight*', who lyricises his feelings as the curtain slowly falls: 'Gee, look at the moon moving between the buildings!' This luminous nightscape, however, comes with a cautionary note: Biff takes the tubing with which his father has tried to kill himself and walks quickly up the stairs.

Act Two

The scene opens with the dual promise that both father and son, now reconciled (for the moment, at least) will move forward with their plans for the future: Biff will meet Bill Oliver and Willy will meet Howard, the young man who has inherited the family business. As the curtain rises, the music is '*gay and bright*', a sharp contrast to the lone sound of a flute that frames our entry into the opening of the play. The action is set in the kitchen, the site of so much of the turmoil and confrontation that has taken place in the first act, but here the mood is positive, generative, even comforting. Willy sits at the table sipping coffee, he dreams of planting his garden again, and the whole house smells of shaving lotion: the Loman boys are already out and away. Yet such textures can be deceptive. Linda notes that Biff looked 'so handsome' in his blue suit when he left the house early that morning, before her husband was even awake. Later in the act we will learn that Biff was recently in jail for three months for stealing a suit very much like the one he is wearing today.

Miller builds this act on the foundations he has carefully laid in everything that occurs in the preceding scenes. And it's the attention to the small details in the ominous undertones of the previous dramatic action that will soon overtake this one as well. Money's short: the Studebaker's recent 'motor job' still hasn't been paid for, the refrigerator needs a new fan belt and, most significantly of all, the premium on Willy's life insurance is overdue (Linda reminds him that they're in 'the grace period now').

Everything they own has been purchased on 'time'; and by the time everything's paid off, everything's broken. Linda reminds Willy of one more item, the one that will come to haunt her at the play's conclusion: the final installment on their mortgage. 'After this payment, Willy, the house belongs to us.'

Willy departs, but not before several homely reminders: Linda cautions him to be careful on the subway stairs, to take his saccharine and his glasses, to be sure to meet Biff and Happy for dinner at Frank's Chop House. The telephone rings as Linda is left alone on stage; her one-sided conversation with Biff is filled with both disappointment and the frailest of hope. She discovers that it was Biff, not Willy, who removed the fateful attachment to the gas heater, but his high spirits as he just left the house have nonetheless buoyed her. 'Be sweet to him tonight, dear,' she implores her son, '*trembling with sorrow and joy* ', 'Be loving to him. Because he's only a little boat looking for a harbor.' In the middle of her speech the light fades on her as the scene shifts to Howard's office. Willy has appeared, but Howard barely notices him, intent as he is on threading a new tape into his latest acquisition, a voice-recording machine. We already know this is all going to end badly for Willy Loman.

And it does. Each of his appeals for what Linda has just called a safe 'harbor' is summarily dismissed. Howard is cruel, with the cruelty and insensitivity of a young man who has always had it good and has never had to grub for a living – or for anything else for that matter. Yet he reminds us, too, that Willy has never been that much of an earner; he never made the sales or commissions he brags about and, after all, 'business is business'; 'everybody's gotta pull his own weight'. Willy romanticises a time when there was 'friendship' and 'personality' in this very same office; but it is in this same space, instead, that he is now fired. The scene's framing device is the sound of a child's voice reciting the names of the capital of every state in alphabetical order, and the irony cuts to the quick, adding insult to injury. But not before Miller provides Willy with a stunning monologue, the one that gives him the title for his play:

> . . . my father lived many years in Alaska. He was an adventurous
> man. We've got quite a little streak of self-reliance in our family.
> I thought I'd go out with my older brother and try to locate him,

and maybe settle in the North with the old man. And I was almost decided to go, when I met a salesman in the Parker House. His name was Dave Singleman. And he was eighty-four years old, and he'd drummed merchandise in thirty-one states. And old Dave, he'd go up to his room, y'understand, put on his green velvet slippers – I'll never forget – and pick up his phone and call the buyers, and without ever leaving his room, at the age of eighty-four, he made his living. And when I saw that, I realised that selling was the greatest career a man could want. 'Cause what could be more satisfying than to be able to go, at the age of eighty-four, into twenty or thirty different cities, and pick up the phone, and be remembered and loved and helped by so many different people? Do you know? when he died – and by the way he died the death of a salesman, in his green velvet slippers in the smoker of the New York, New Haven and Hartford, going into Boston – when he died, hundreds of salesman and buyers were at his funeral. Things were sad on a lotta trains for months after that . . . In those days there was personality in it, Howard. There was respect, and comradeship, and gratitude in it. Today, it's all cut and dried, and there's no chance for bringing friendship to bear – or personality. You see what I mean? They don't know me any more. (p. 66)

This resonant monologue serves as a stirring counterweight to Linda's in the previous act; but as Willy brings an all but mythic dimension to the art of selling, embodied as he still sees it in a heroic figure from the past, Howard hardly looks up at him: 'Now pay attention!' he suddenly cries out, and his anger is justified. His language can be just as pointed, and as eloquent in an entirely different way, when Miller provides him with lines heavily inflected by the rhythms of New York speech: 'I put thirty-four years into this firm, Howard, and now I can't pay my insurance! You can't eat the orange and throw the peel away – a man is not a piece of fruit!' Using a metaphor without ever realising that he is doing so, he, too, like Linda, demands that 'attention' – and the word has been carefully chosen – must be paid. His voice falls on deaf ears. 'Whenever you can this week,' Howard intones, disenfranchising him completely, 'stop by and drop off the samples.'

As Willy stares blankly into space, Ben's music, '*first distinctly*, *then closer, closer*', all at once intrudes, signalling yet another retreat into the past. The scene rehearses the fateful visit when Ben made his final appeal for Willy to join him. 'He's got a beautiful job here,' Linda interjects, revealing her own complicity in holding him back. 'Don't say those things to him!' she states firmly, even adamantly. 'Enough to be happy right here, right now.' The moment is inopportune all around; Biff, the golden boy, is about to have his tryouts at Ebbets Field. Happy as well as Charley's son Bernard are beside themselves with excitement, though Charley himself introduces a note of caution, if not downright ridicule. Willy counters this by characterising his neighbour's remarks as entirely out of bounds, and declares that for his son 'This is the greatest day of his life.' It is; but no one on stage yet realises just how potent the line is in dramatic irony.

The scene that follows is a sombre one. We are now in the present, in the reception room of Charley's office. A great deal of the play's back story is revealed: Charley has been handing out money to Willy so that he can pretend to Linda that he is still an adequate, albeit marginal, provider. Bernard, the worrier and the studier, now grown up and working as an accomplished attorney on his way to Washington, DC, to argue a case before the United States Supreme Court, is present, too. And it is this figure from Biff's boyhood past who asks the crucial questions: why was Biff so changed when he came back from Boston? What happened there? Why didn't Biff take the summer make-up course when he 'flunked' high-school maths? The audience already knows that before the curtain comes down on this drama the answers to all of Bernard's questions will be made painfully clear, though Miller keeps the suspense going by not giving away more than he has to at this point. There's another kind of drama going on in this scene anyway; Willy refuses the job Charley offers him because he sees this as his final humiliation.

Little does he see that there's more to come. 'Raucous music' and 'a red glow' bring us to the restaurant where Willy is to meet his sons for a celebratory dinner. Happy is discovered on stage with a waiter, and the setup provides him with the opportunity to display his credentials as small-time operator and pathetic 'philanderer', the word his mother has already used to characterise his refusal to accept any responsibility for his actions. Before Willy and Biff arrive on the scene, he tells the waiter that his brother is an important 'cattle man' from the Far West, and plays the role of big-time spender when he propositions a young woman and tells her a different tale about his brother's status, now configured as a professional football player. Biff appears, and 'the Girl' soon exits to 'make a phone call' to complete what she assumes will be a wild night out. She is not on stage to hear about his diminished state: he waited six hours to see Bill Oliver, then finally saw him for 'one minute' as he left his office. 'I realised what a ridiculous lie my whole life has been!' he confesses. 'We've been talking in a dream for fifteen years.' All he can do now is repeat the self-destructive pattern that has never been broken: this time he finds his way into Oliver's office, steals a pen and runs down 'all eleven flights' of stairs. Yet he knows instinctively that something must now change: 'Hap, I'm gonna tell Pop.'

What Biff has in mind is nothing less than full exposure of the kind of 'life lie' that has haunted the Loman family forever. Happy says he's 'crazy'; they must protect their father at all costs. When Willy comes into the restaurant a few moments later, Biff seems more determined than ever. But his determination is slowly undermined as Willy reveals that he has been fired and the cycle of deception and denial asserts itself once again. Happy is only too willing to aid and abet, editing his brother's commentary and finally distorting it completely, Willy only too willing to fall back into their mutual fantasy. Biff is undone. But not more so than his father as a '*single trumpet jars the ear*'. Young Bernard enters crying 'Mrs Loman, Mrs Loman!', forcing Willy to remember the painful day when they got the news that Biff 'had to go and flunk math'. But only Willy relives the scene. Biff and Happy are still in the present. 'What math?' Biff demurs. 'What're you talking about?' Willy is both in and out of the present, more out than in, as the past replays itself kaleidoscopically. Young Bernard announces to Linda that Biff has run off to Boston to see his father. 'Oh, maybe Willy can talk to the teacher,' Linda suggests, participating as she has always done in the family game of illusion and reality. In the meantime, Willy hasn't really heard a word of what Biff has been trying to say, as the scene from the past he has so much wanted to repress begins to insinuate its ugly presence. 'Standish Arms, good evening!' the voice of a hotel telephone operator declares from the vast nowhere. 'I'm not in my room!' Willy shouts on stage. Biff is suddenly frightened: 'Dad, what's the matter?' And as the stage directions tell us, Biff is not only frightened, but horrified. He falls down on one knee before his father and utters the very words he had promised himself never to say again: 'Dad, I'll make good. I'll make good.' The lethal trap in which they find themselves has no exit.

At least not yet. The new presence on stage of Letta and Miss Forsythe, who may or may not 'sell' (the former has answered the latter's telephone summons to join the young men), forces Willy to reactivate the sad moment when Biff discovered him alone in a hotel room with 'The Woman'. Biff took the train from Grand Central Station in New York all the way up to Boston in order to seek his father's help – surely Mr Birnbaum, the recalcitrant maths teacher with a lisp, will succumb to Willy's charm when he speaks so smoothly and persuasively on his son's behalf. Willy is his son's hero after all; he will now become his saviour, too – or so Biff imagines. The impressionable boy is forced to witness a scene of adultery instead. Vain attempts at concealment make matters even worse, as does the handing-over of a pair of shiny silk stockings: 'You,' Biff cries out accusingly, 'you gave her Mama's stockings!' You fake!', 'you – liar!', You phony little fake!' soon follow. In this powerful scene, father/son behaviour with women is, from a dramatic point of view, very efficiently turned on its head. Biff, crestfallen, returns to New York; and we can now piece together all of the information we have been given leading up to this fateful encounter. There's worse to come for Willy. Though earlier Biff has told Miss Forsythe that she's 'just seen a prince walk by. A fine troubled prince. A hardworking, unappreciated prince. A pal, you understand? A good companion' (p. 97), both sons have now carelessly abandoned their father and taken off with their own 'chippies' instead. Stanley, the sympathetic waiter who lies on their behalf, stuffs Willy's money back into his pocket even though his sons have walked out without paying the bill. Willy needs the cash; he wants to buy seeds to plant in his garden one last time.

The sound of the flute is heard as light gradually rises on the kitchen. The sons appear at the door; Linda is unseen, but she has been waiting up for them all night. As she enters from the living-room, her fury is evident even before she speaks. Disgusted by their behaviour and their gift of appeasement, flowers, she knocks them to the floor at Biff's feet. To Happy she is even more unmerciful: 'Did you have to go to women tonight? You and your lousy rotten whores!' Miller handles this final scene of confrontation skilfully. Biff wants 'an abrupt conversation' with 'the boss', but Linda is determined to protect her husband from what she knows in advance will be his final undoing. All the while Willy, flashlight in hand, is planting seeds and talking about a 'proposition' to a Ben no longer remembered, but a Ben now fully imagined. 'Twenty thousand,' his brother considers, 'that *is* something one can feel with the hand, it is there.' That the 'twenty thousand' involves his insurance policy prepares us for how this play is going to end:

> Oh, Ben, how do we get back to all the great times? Used to be
> so full of light, and comradeship, the sleigh-riding in winter, and
> the ruddiness on his cheeks. And always some kind of good news
> coming up ahead. And never even let me carry the valises in the
> house, and simonizing, simonizing that little red car! Why, why
> can't I give him something and not have him hate me? (p. 109)

A monologue for Willy, but a soliloquy for us, what this moving speech reveals is that it is Biff, Biff, it has always been Biff.

What happens next is inevitable, only because Miller has made it so. Biff moves to the central position, finds his voice, and tells his father, simply, and in a great moment of self-revelation, 'I'm a dime a dozen.' But in what the text calls '*an uncontrolled outburst*', his father tries for one last time to counter such defeatism, shouting out – in despair? in agony? in frustration? all three? – 'I am not a dime a dozen. I am Willy Loman and you are Biff Loman!' Truth will out, nevertheless, even at this late date: Biff says his father was nothing 'but a hard-working drummer who landed in the ash can like all the rest of them.' As for Biff, 'I'm not bringing home any prizes any more, and you're going to stop waiting for me to bring them home!' Their world of illusions comes crashing down: 'Pop, I'm nothing! I'm nothing, Pop . . . I'm just what I am, that's all . . . Will you let me go?', and that final appeal is indeed 'remarkable'. What Willy has been looking for he has always had all along: his son's unqualified love.

The imaginary Ben summons Willy to his final action in the play as his car speeds off.

Requiem

It should come as no real surprise that Miller, who has built his play so deliberately to the accompaniment of a variety of musical motifs, should choose to close *Salesman* with a scene richly dependent on the kind of atmosphere we associate with such master composers as Mozart, Verdi, and Fauré. For a requiem, as in the one Beethoven wrote 'for a Fallen Hero', is both a prayer and a homage to the dead. Here it comes in the shape of a spare funeral scene, and one that emerges virtually spontaneously from the sounds that signal Willy's demise. Unlike the massive attendance for the legendary Dave Singleman's memorial ceremony, Willy's has had few attendants, only those whose emotional attachment to him has always been fixed: his wife, his two sons, and a single friend. 'He had the wrong dreams,' Biff intones at his father's grave. 'He never knew who he was.' Happy disagrees, but it is the faithful Charley who is the one to speak in his friend's defence: 'Nobody dast blame this man. A salesman is got to dream . . . It comes with the territory.' Linda, carrying flowers like the ones she refused to accept from her sons in the previous scene, somehow cannot cry. But release will come, for Miller gives her the curtain speech. Alone on stage, and finally occupying it with authority, it is her words that echo in our ears as the curtain slowly falls: 'Willy, I made the last payment on the house today. Today, dear. And there'll be nobody home . . . We're free and clear . . . We're free . . . We're free.'

Yet in the final movement of this haunting requiem, even Linda's words are no longer necessary, for '*Only the music of the flute on the darkening stage as over the house the hard towers of the apartment buildings rise into sharp focus.*'

Themes

One of the signature virtues of *Death of a Salesman*, and of Miller's work in general, is its ability to speak to audiences around the world with astonishing immediacy and clarity. The accessibility of the playwright's themes, and the multiple resonances his drama gives rise to, is especially notable in *Salesman*, the play which is, among many other things, about a man who lives in a dream and mistakes it for reality. The author's characterisation of his central figure has a way of monopolising many discussions about the play, and yet its position as one of the most significant works written for the American theatre should lead us to a number of other considerations as well, all of them interrelated. Some of these issues might be understood as follows:

'Tragedy and the Common Man'

The subject of a major essay by the playwright, which he wrote in response to the critical reception of *Salesman* when it first reached Broadway in 1949, tragedy as it might be experienced by the workaday, working man displays Miller's huge proletarian ambition for one of the major themes in his play. Willy Loman is designed to be a protagonist capable of sustaining the scope, depth and sheer dramatic tension traditionally associated with legendary figures from the grand theatrical past, a repertory that ranges widely and even includes figures of the heroic dimension of Oedipus and Lear. In *Death of a Salesman* Miller's indebtedness to the shape of tragedy in the theatrical past is everywhere apparent, as is his effectiveness in adapting its conventions to the scaled-down economies of the modern world. In the story that unfolds Miller emblematises the inescapability of tragedy by concentrating on elements that are little and local, then discovers in them a symbolic dimension far beyond the anecdotal. Willy's story is in the first instance personal, as tragedy always is; yet its resonances stretch far beyond a given time and a given place. The scene is Brooklyn, 'Willy Loman territory', but it is a Brooklyn of the imagination, dramatically transformed.

The American Dream: Materialism, consumerism and happiness

It is probably something of a truism to say that *Death of a Salesman* represents the dark underside of the so-called American Dream, a phrase that originated in the early 1930s. As the play demonstrates time and time again, that dream is likely to become a nightmare for individuals caught in-between the dualities of an encroaching materialism and the rampant consumerism it implies. Happiness is equated with material success; anything less than being 'rich' signifies failure. Willy fully buys into this myth, as well as its deceptive corollaries: be liked and you shall never want, look good and make an impression, be athletic, nice and 'manly'. This is the legacy he wills on his sons, handicapping any chance they might have had to find out who they really are or what they might have become under the influence of a different father. Willy never realises until it is far too late that 'business is business', a far more lethal game than anything he has ever had in mind as the ticket to the misbegotten 'success' that continues to elude him. Neither does he have any sense that the growing corporate culture –an unsentimental conglomerate of take-and-take, not give-and-take – has stacked all the cards against him.

(Dysfunctional) family values

Because the Lomans have built their life together on denial and deception – and, above all, on self-deception – it is only a matter of time before fate, which they experience as exposure – undoes them all. And because they have never broken the cycle of denial and its deceptions, they are fated, too, to rehearse their dysfunctional family dynamics over and over again. Biff tries to break through the false values that have corrupted him; he tries, then tries again. When he finally succeeds in doing so – *if* he does so at the play's conclusion – the price he pays is a heavy one indeed.

The great generational conflict of father and son

As in the play that precedes it, *All My Sons*, the mighty antagonism in *Salesman* is embodied in another father and son, Willy and Biff Loman. Their battle, too, is a fight to the finish, for each represents a different version of what it means to be truly alive in this world. That battle is all the more heartrending in that each is emotionally bonded to the other: while Willy's love manifests itself in the form of an unhealthy obsession, Biffs has progressed from adolescent hero-worship to something far more profound, something intangible based on his own growing self-awareness. To say that their relationship is intense is an understatement. Built into it, too, is a wider generational conflict; the world that Willy has lived in is no longer possible; times have changed. How is Biff to find a place for himself in this new world that no one, certainly not his father, has prepared him for? Willy, too, is perilously involved in a conflict with *his* father, a man he has never known: witness his need to romanticise substitute father-figures like his much older brother Ben and the mythic salesman Dave Singleman.

Illusion, delusion and the madness of reality

Many of the key scenes in *Death of a Salesman* take place inside Willy Loman's head. These are illusions, of course, and as members of Miller's audience we experience them as such. Yet they may be delusions, too, for some of them, especially the scene when his sons plan to hang a hammock in the backyard, may represent the past as Willy wants to remember it, not as it actually was. His delusions in the real world are of much greater concern; they have to do with his exaggerations about himself and his overvaluation of his sons. Yet for Willy the greatest madness of all is reality, the world that has changed all round him. 'They don't know me any more,' he sighs in what may be his only instance of self-awareness in the entire play.

Growing old and growing up

Salesman is an unusual play in that it follows a double trajectory. On the one hand, and most significantly so, it shows the difficulty Biff faces, and the psychological obstacles he must overcome, as he tries to assert himself in reaching for his much-delayed maturity. But the play also demonstrates what it means to grow old in a culture that seems quite willing to pass you by, as Charley says in the Requiem, when 'you get yourself a couple of spots on your hat'. That's 'when they start not smiling back' and you know 'you're finished'.

The marginalised role of women

That *Salesman* represents a male-centred universe should be readily apparent. The women play predictable secondary parts, and that may be putting things mildly: there's an office secretary and worse to come, two call girls and The Woman caught in adultery. Not a very promising start. Linda, of course, is a far more complicated personality; as one of the four major protagonists, she is in fact the only fully developed female character on board. Initially assigned the satellite parts of wife and mother, she negotiates a great deal of dramatic space for herself when she confronts her sons, and it is she – and she alone – who commands the empty stage in the final moments of the play.

Masculinity in American culture

Props and properties in *Salesman* define a stereotypical masculine culture of athleticism, machines, muscles and brawn: football, basketball, baseball, carpentry, cars and 'women'. Willy disparages Charley because he doesn't know how to handle tools, and dismisses Charley's son Bernard because he's a lot better at books than at sports. Biff deplores the confinement of holding a steady office job, which he interprets as more than a mild form of emasculation. He'd much rather be out herding cattle, doing man's work. Happy, who does work in an office (but only as one of two assistants to the assistant), plays out his masculinist fantasies by having meaningless sexual encounters with the wives of his superiors; as he says, he can't help himself. Surely the male figures in this play feel that their masculinity is threatened, as they define it in such a circumscribed way. Willy can't take the job offered by his only friend because he would feel humiliated by it; but his greatest humiliation as a 'man' is that he can no longer earn a living.

The myth of the Far West and other dreams of leaving

Escape from the picayune existence of everyday life seems to be much on everyone's mind in *Death of a Salesman*. Biffs wandering has taken him to the prototypical American landscape, the Far West, to which he longs to return. Happy says he'd like to join Biff there – someday, but perhaps not right now. Uncle Ben thought he was going off to Alaska a long time ago, but ended up in Africa instead. He wanted his brother to join him, and for a moment Willy was tempted until Linda drew him back. And of course their father, the flute-maker, was always on the move. Escape routes seem to be a Loman family trait. Willy, in fact, has two of them: one to his garden, the other to his past. Oddly enough, it is Linda, the play's only significant female figure, who seems firmly planted in the here and now.

Advertising and adversity

Miller's play is loaded with consumerist goods that are always in need of repair. Things fall apart – refrigerators, vacuum cleaners, cars, the roof – just when they're about to be paid off. The world imagined here is perennially on the installment plan. The Lomans bought a Hastings refrigerator, clearly a lemon, because 'they got,' as Linda said in the past, 'the biggest ads of any of them!' Years later Willy seems to have forgotten this prophetic exchange when he says, 'I told you we should've bought a well-advertised machine. Charley bought a General Electric and it's twenty years old and it's still good, that son-of-a bitch.' Miller presents an America on the verge of a consumerist rampage – tape recorders and other electronic gadgets loom large in the not-too-distant future – where buyers are at the mercy of ad-men, and where products are timed to break down so that new and not necessarily improved ones can be purchased. The Lomans' biggest consumer asset, bought on time of course, is their out-of-date house. At the end of the play the mortgage is finally paid off, but there's nobody at home to live in it.

Characters

Willy Loman

Miller once described his lead character in *Salesman* as 'a man trying to write his name on ice on a hot July day'. The statement goes to the heart of the matter, for it reveals the way in which this figure is meant to be both mundane and metaphorical, localised and lyrical, eccentric and yet at the same time hugely emblematic. A working man in his sixties – Linda gives his age as sixty-three – he has been a salesman all his life, but as he tells his brother Ben, 'I still feel – kind of temporary about myself. The large sample cases he carries seem to be almost an extension of himself, though oddly enough we never find out what is inside them. While his father sold flutes and other items he made with his own hands, Willy has no real connection to the inventory he hawks – dry goods? We never know for sure. What motivates Willy, instead, is the sales and the sales pitch. And yet he has never been much of a success at either; he has merely eked out a modest living and a marginal existence, all the time exaggerating his take. Everything he owns has been purchased on time. What he loves to do most of all is work in his garden, though this pastime conflicts with the image of himself he tries to project as a social animal, cracking jokes, giving people a few laughs, shaking hands with small-town dignitaries, above all being popular and 'well liked' as he drives his car up and down the New England 'territory'. He takes it for granted that his wife loves him, that she is totally devoted to his well-being, and that she will stand by him and up for him no matter what happens during their married life. He addresses his real attention and affection to his sons, most especially and almost obsessively so to Biff. It is this golden boy who will fulfil the unrealised dreams he has always had for himself, or so he believes. He never understands the psychological burden he places on his son until it is far too late.

In the play we meet Willy at the most perilous moment in his career: things are falling apart. The trajectory moves relentlessly downwards as he loses his job, the confidence he once had in himself and, most perilously of all, his ability to distinguish illusion from reality. Haunted by visions sited in the past, Willy experiences them as part escape-mechanism, part phantasmagoria, part painful reminder of the road not taken. At the end of the play he will move into this illusory world completely.

Linda

Linda is configured and sometimes even marginalised as Willy's long-suffering wife, but the play doesn't quite work unless we consider that she must be more than that, too. Her status in the drama depends in part on our understanding of the historical period in which she is placed, a moment in post-war America when the complementary roles of wife, mother and homemaker are featured in popular magazines and in the popular imagination as every woman's *sine qua non*. In his stage directions Miller tells us that 'she more than loves' Willy, 'she admires him'. Nothing she does on stage challenges her fixity and her loyalty, implying that she accepts the roles assigned to her and even embraces them – though to contemporary eyes this may seem like some sort of pre-feminist nightmare.

Does she suspect her husband of infidelity? If so, she lets her guard down only once, when, confused, she asks 'What woman?' in the midst of a conversation that seems to be heading elsewhere. Linda, however, outsizes her role at those moments when she speaks up – and decisively so – as if she perceives that the safety and frail security of her sheltered world is being threatened. She is, for example, the only character on stage who effectively counters her brother-in-law's arguments for taking Willy off with him to Africa, empowering Willy to offer his own defence for establishing himself 'here', and she will let Ben know exactly what she thinks of him when he spars unfairly with her son (one can only imagine what his business scruples must be like). More to the point, she is fierce and fearless in seeking to protect her mate, even against Biff, knowing full well that any self-awareness forced upon him at this late date would be lethal. In this sense it could be argued that, like Kate Keller in *All My Sons*, she knows everything, though she may not yet be ready to accept the part she has played in enabling Willy to construct the elaborate fantasies about himself and the boys who still call him 'pal'. In the context in which we discover her, boxed-in as she is as much by the looming apartment houses as by the limitations of her assignment to the secondary part, one wonders if she would really have been any better off had she pierced through the shell of mutual denial. As if to complicate matters, Miller surrenders the stage to her in the final moments of the play, providing her with an eloquent curtain speech. But just what is going through her mind when she utters words like 'free' and 'clear' and must now confront the bleak future awaiting her?

Biff

The much-favoured elder son in the Loman family, Biff has been brought up to play the featured role in an elaborate game of charades fated to end badly. That he peaked too soon is only a part of the problem. A terrible thing has been done to him by the father he loves only too well. For that same father's love, in return, has always been conditional: bring home prizes, throw the strongest athletic pass, 'borrow' whatever you need – construction supplies, a football, a carton of basketballs, a suit that lands him in jail for three months, a pen – and don't worry about taking answers on a high-school maths exam from someone else, even from the 'puny' Bernard, for you are a leader of men because 'I say so'. Disillusion and demystification were always waiting for him around the corner, but when he meets them the encounter comes in the ugliest of ways: discovering that the father he has been trying to please all his young life, and whose authority he never even dreamed of questioning, is nothing more than a common adulterer. Everything he had been taught to depend on is suddenly swept away. In a certain sense Biff makes the same mistake Chris Keller does in *All My Sons*, never thinking of the man who stands before him as a person in his own right, but only as the larger-than-life figure who is his father. In the case of *Salesman*, Willy has gone a long way to foster such unsustainable hero-worship. Biffs rebellion after the shock of his discovery – he is, after all, still an adolescent – takes the form of anger, fear and above all, retribution: ruining his life is the best way to get back at his father.

As the play begins Biff, now in his early thirties, has returned to Brooklyn on one of his periodic visits, this time determined to assert his freedom from the tyranny of his dysfunctional family's false expectations and the weighty burden of guilt that have kept him in check. His maturity and self-awareness are long overdue. But this homecoming is fraught with more pain than even he might have imagined: his father has been trying to kill himself. His freedom requires a heavy purchase, one that Biff is at first reluctant to make: forcing his father to confront reality and see his son for who he is and what he was always fated to become.

Happy

All his life Happy has been in the shadow of his elder brother, reluctant or simply incapable of asserting himself in the strange chemistry of family dynamics. He carves out a workable space for himself by dodging any formidable challenge that comes his way. He doesn't resent his brother, nor does he blame his father for putting him (at best) in second place; he merely tries to stay out of their way, though he will offer the occasional comment from the sideline when their antagonism reaches a fever-pitch. Linda seems to have given up on him completely, though it should be noted that he is the child, however negligent, who has chosen to stay behind, not run off to find himself in 'the Far West'. In the scenes from the past, Happy sometimes tried to gain Willy's attention – 'I'm losing weight, you notice, Pop?'; but when he realised that this was never forthcoming, he simply gave up on it. He seems to have bought into the family myth that if Biff turns out well, he will too. Happy talks big, and in this respect, as in several others, he may be the true inheritor of Willy's public posture – minus, of course, the sinking anxiety that goes along with it in his father's case.

The Woman

Though the fact that she is unnamed might suggest that she plays a minor role in the play's trajectory, she is in fact the principal device Miller uses to pierce through Biffs illusions and extend his father's guilt, despair and disappointment (in himself as well as in his son). She lives on in Willy's memory, and she haunts him; but for Biff, who discovers her in his father's hotel room in Boston, she will always be brutally present in the guise of infidelity, a betrayal as much of his mother as of himself.

Uncle Ben

Willy's brother always remains 'inside his head' even in those scenes when his presence doesn't materialise on stage. A figure who, on a narrative level, represents the road not taken, he is on another level the mechanism for elevating the play above the here-and-now, bringing its full symbolic and psychological dimensions to light. Ben is the link to the father Willy has never known; but he also provides access to the material success that has always eluded him. Willy needs to romanticise both, just as he does in his monologue about Dave Singleman.

Charley

In contrast to the mysterious presence of Ben, Willy's neighbour Charley plays the choral role, attempting to bring him back to earth when dangerous reveries intrude. Some of them involve the hagiography surrounding Biff – he says that 'the jails are full of fearless characters' who steal items like six-by-tens from construction sites, and jests when everyone goes off to cheer the home boy on in a city-wide tournament. But the more threatening reveries are of a different sort; they have to do with Willy's misconception that he can succeed in business merely by being 'well-liked'. 'Who liked J.P. Morgan?' Charley interjects, piercing Willy's balloon. Throughout, he remains a loyal friend. And he bankrolls Willy when the chips are down.

Bernard

Charley's hardworking and conscientious son is the foil for the high-school football-hero who is Biff. Willy disparages him for studying, but nonetheless encourages his son to make use of him, for he can be helpful in passing answers on to him during exams. Like the other boys in the neighbourhood, Bernard is susceptible to the Lomans' charms, but in the end it is his deliberateness and commitment to the straight-and-narrow that wins the day. As the young lawyer he becomes, he is described in the text as '*a quiet, earnest, but self-assured young man* '.

Howard Wagner

Another son, this time the boss's, he has inherited and now runs the family business for which Willy has worked for many years. Unlike Bernard, he has obviously done nothing to gain this privileged position other than have the good luck to be born in the right place at the right time, something he does not seem to take into account. He likes the toys that come along with his status, most particularly his new tape-recorder. Howard is more contemptuous of Willy than sympathetic, for he seems to see him as a throw-back to past inefficiencies, which he dismisses as no longer practical in an economy where 'business is business'. He may feel a little sorry for Willy, but not enough to prevent him from firing him.

Jenny

Charley's secretary, she has worked in his office for some time, and tries to elicit the adult Bernard's help when she sees that Willy is distressed in the outer hall.

Stanley, Miss Forsythe and Letta

Three figures who appear in the restaurant scene, where Willy is supposed to meet Biff and Happy, they play functional roles in the unravelling of what was supposed to be a celebratory dinner. Miss Forsythe is a quick pick-up for Happy, and Letta is the friend she calls to make up a foursome with Biff. Stanley's role as the waiter is more nuanced; he may or may not see through Happy's pose as big-time big-spender – the bill doesn't get paid in the end – and his tenderness to Willy, the father they leave behind, is in marked contrast to the behaviour of Willy's two grown sons.

Major Productions

An iconic work like *Death of a Salesman* is naturally to be found in the repertory of theatre companies around the world. The play is appealing because it is at once concrete and full of mysterious suggestion – not to mention the fact that it contains in abundance one of the things the playwright said he wanted to be remembered for: 'Some good parts for actors'. Each time *Salesman* is staged, the drama reaches out to find new audiences, renewing itself in the process. Miller said he was at first surprised by the huge emotional pull of the story; but as he approached his eightieth year, he observed that he now realised that you had to make an audience 'feel before it can be made to think'.

That combination of reactions has been characteristic of the effect the play has had in its most successful interpretations. The world premiere on 10 February 1949 at the Morosco Theatre in New York is by this time the subject of legend. Directed by Elia Kazan on a famous multi-platform set designed by Jo Mielziner – a set that has left an indelible mark on the history of stage scenography – the production starred Lee J. Cobb in the pivotal role of Willy Loman. The actor was such a sensation in this part that for years afterwards it was impossible to imagine any other Willy Loman. A big, burly man who could look as crumpled on stage as off, Cobb was nonetheless a player with huge and unexpected resources of dignity and understated eloquence, all of which he brought to the play. Mildred Dunnock was cast as Linda; she wanted the part so badly that she kept coming back to the casting calls, even after she was told her demeanour was far too dignified for the role. It was perhaps her greatest professional success. Featuring Arthur Kennedy as Biff and Cameron Mitchell as Happy, the production itself was also a huge critical and box-office success. The play won a Pulitzer Prize, a Tony Award and, coming just two years after *All My Sons*, Miller's second award from the New York Drama Critics' Circle. Later that same year Kazan directed *Death of a Salesman* in London, with Paul Muni as Willy Loman.

Thirty years later Michael Rudman, then a young director at the National Theatre in London, mounted a forceful revival in the Lyttelton Theatre, casting the veteran actor Warren Mitchell in the lead. The director wanted to bring the work back to Miller's Jewish roots. The playwright had been clear about not giving the Lomans a specific ethnic identity; his aim was to tell a story not about *some* Americans, but about *all* Americans. Besides, the drama of working-class Jewish America had already been portrayed with clarity and vigour by Clifford Odets, whose Depression-era *Awake and Sing! was* the single most important play presented in New York by the Group Theatre in the 1930s. Rudman's set included minor details – a Hebrew/English calendar, for example – in an attempt to make a point, and Mitchell used East End inflections to give his character the authenticity his director required. This was certainly an imposition on the play, but it worked. Though Miller was Jewish, his family was by no means working-class. Rudman, however, was a close reader, and he was perceptive in picking up on the rhythms of New York speech, heavily inflected as it is with a syntax based on the rich metaphorical flavour of Yiddish, the language the large number of Eastern European Jews brought with them to America: 'You can't eat an orange and throw the peel away,' Willy tells Howard Wagner, ' – a man is not a piece of fruit!' Willy also uses the ultimate New York Jewish phrase paying homage to the departed: 'may he rest in peace.'

Among those who saw the 1979 National Theatre production was the American film actor Dustin Hoffman. He remembered how much he had been impressed with the taped version of *Salesman* prepared for American television in the early 1950s (see below). Hoffman brought the production to New York, then back to London, casting himself in the role of Willy Loman. Hoffman said he had been waiting all his life to play a part like this; when he began his career as a young actor, ads for 'leading man' never meant 'short' and 'ethnic'. His Willy Loman, like Warren Mitchell's, could be both; but in order to accommodate the part to Hoffman's physical stature, in this interpretation Willy became a 'short' man instead of a 'fat' one.

The play became susceptible to even more dynamic changes in 1983. As part of the cultural exchange accompanying the normalisation of diplomatic relations between the Chinese People's Republic and the United States during the Nixon administration, the playwright was invited to supervise a major production in Beijing. The play was to be presented at the People's Art Theatre in the translation by Ying Ruocheng, who played Willy Loman under his own direction. Miller wasn't convinced that a highly personal story about the cost of a defeated life in capitalist America would make any sense in a collectivist, communist society. But as *'Salesman' in Beijing*, the book he did with his wife Inge Morath clearly illustrates, Willy Loman's story was experienced in China as a family tragedy created in its own national image.

The Chicago-based director Robert Falls prepared a fiftieth anniversary production of *Death of a Salesman* as early as 1997, substituting a double stage-revolve for the original's platform set, thereby making us rethink the play's sense of stage geography and stylised spatialisation. Two years later Falls's ambitious production for the Goodman Theatre settled in for a sold-out run at the Eugene O'Neill Theatre on Broadway. Brian Dennehy, a powerful Willy Loman for a new generation of theatregoers, earned one of this show's several Tony Awards.

Recreating the aural and visual landscape of the original 1949 Broadway production with set design by Jo Mielziner and music by Alex North, Mike Nichols' staging of *Death of a Salesman* opened at the Barrymore Theater in New York on 15 March 2012. The stage and screen actor Philip Seymour Hoffman headed the cast in the lead role of Willy Loman, with Andrew Garfield as Biff, Finn Wittrock as Happy, Linda Edmond as Linda and John Glover as Willy's fortune-seeking brother, Uncle Ben.

Film and television

1952   Laszlo Benedict directs a film version of the play starring Frederic March as Willy; Mildred Dunnock as Linda; Kevin McCarthy as Biff; and Cameron Mitchell as Happy. March had been Lee J. Cobb's replacement in the original New York production, and later took the show on tour in the US. The film incorporate many of the acing choices made in the original Kazan stagings in London and New York.

1966   Lee J. Cobb stars as Willy Loman with Mildred Dunnock as Linda in Alex Segal's production for American television. The adaptation wins three Emmy Awards, and features the young actors George Segal as Biff and Gene Wilder as Bernard. This production offers documentary evidence of Cobb's and Dunnock's legendary performances in the roles of Willy and Linda Loman.

1966   Alan Cooke directs Rod Steiger as Willy Loman for the 'BBC Play of the Month'. Steiger was oddly cast in the role – the wrong physical and vocal type for Willy Loman – but the rest of the cast shed new light on the other main characters.

1984   The director Volker Schlondoff directs a new adaptation of *Death of a Salesman* for television. Dustin Hoffman reprises his stage role as Willy Loman and also serves as co-producer. With John Malkovich as Biff, Stephen Lang as Happy, Charles Durning as the Lomans' neighbour Charley, and the Canadian actress Kate Reid in an exceptionally fine and nuanced portrayal of Linda, the CBS broadcast is seen on one night by 25 million viewers. In Spain and other venues around the world, the film is also screened in movie houses. Despite the exceptional cast for this production, film editing never fully succeeded in capturing the spontaneity of the stage play's temporal fluidity.

Notes

The notes below explain words and phrases from the play, with page numbers referencing the Student Editions published by Bloomsbury Methuen Drama.

page

1   *Requiem*: a mass for the dead; it has inspired a number of musical compositions, often characterised by a solemn, dirge-like setting.

2   *today*: The 'today' of Miller's note refers to the late 1940s, the time in which the action of the play takes place.

3   Miller's stage directions call for the use of a platform set, i.e. a stage space constructed on multiple levels in order to allow for swift transitions from one time and one place to another.

4   *Yonkers*: a city in Westchester County just beyond the northernmost border of New York City

4   *Studebaker*: a car manufactured in the US until 1963.

5   *arch supports*: these are inserted into shoes for greater comfort and to prevent fallen arches, something from which people who spend a good deal of time on their feet can suffer – as a salesman might, waiting to show his wares.

5   *windshield*: windscreen; in the earliest automobiles, they were removable.

5   *New England*: the north-east section of the US that includes Connecticut, Rhode Island, Massachusetts, New Hampshire, Vermont and Maine.

6   *Portland*: the largest city in Maine.

8   *high school*: in the US, high school means grades 9 to 12.

9   *Thomas Edison*: an American inventor (1847–1931), whose numerous inventions included the phonograph, the motion-picture camera and the light bulb.

9   *B.F. Goodrich*: an American industrialist (1841–88) whose company produced tyres.

10   *Chevvy*: the popular abbreviation for Chevrolet, an automobile still manufactured by General Motors today.

10   *simonize*: simoniz is a trademark brand for a car wax that originated in 1935.

11   *Bushwick Avenue*: a main thoroughfare in the Flatbush section of Brooklyn, New York.

13   *subway*: the New York City counterpart of the London Underground.

13   *Nebraska . . . Arizona*: the states Biff mentions here are all in the western part of the US. 'The Dakotas' is a usual way of linking two of them, North Dakota and South Dakota.

14   *counties*: each state in the US is divided into smaller geographical units known as counties.

15   *bowling*: the American version, an indoor game in which players attempt to score points by rolling a ball on a flat surface into objects called pins.

18   *chamois*: (pronounce 'shammy') leather, made from the skin of the chamois (pronounced 'shamwa') goat. It absorbs water and cleans shiny surfaces to a high gloss.

19   *Albany*: the capital of the State of New York.

19   *football*: this ball will be used for the rough-contact American game.

19   *a punching bag*: this is used for practice by professional boxers. Gene Tunney (1897–1978) was the world heavyweight champion from 1926 to 1928. He defeated the legendary Jack Dempsey twice.

20   *regulation ball*: only regulation balls, of a specific dimension and weight, could be used in a tournament game of American football.

21   *Providence*: the capital of Rhode Island; Waterbury Connecticut, was a prosperous mill and manufacturing town at the time in which the play is set; and Bangor is a city in northern Maine. 'Mass.' is the abbreviated form for Massachusetts, with Boston as its major city. Boston is frequently referred to as 'the cradle of the Revolution' because of the Boston Tea Party (1773), one of the signal events precipitating the rebellion of the thirteen American Colonies against Britain. It was also the place where the phrase 'taxation without representation is tyranny', summarising the colonists' primary grievance, took hold.

22   *captain*: leader of a football team; a goal in this game, called a touchdown, is worth six points; players 'pass' the ball from one to another in order to avoid a 'tackle' from the opposing team as they attempt a run to the end of the field to score.

22   *Regents*: the Regents Exams are standardised tests given in a variety of subjects to high-school students in the state of New York. Each test is in a different discipline, and a student must have a satisfactory grade in order to achieve credit from the New York State Department of Education.

22   *sneakers*: trainers.

23   *Adonises*: Adonis was a complex cult figure from Greek
     mythology. He had multiple roles, most of them as an annually-
     renewed, ever-youthful vegetation god. His name is applied to
     handsome young men.

26   *Hartford*: the capital of Connecticut; it is part of Willy's New
     England 'territory'.

27   *scrim*: a translucent theatre curtain usually made of a thin textile
     such as gauze. It can be used to create interesting visual effects:
     when light is thrown on the front of a scrim it becomes opaque,
     but if objects are brightly lit behind it they will become visible.

32   *shoot*: in the game of cards Charley and Willy play, they 'shoot'
     several rounds or hands. On the next page Willy says he's
     'clean', meaning he has no cards that match (this also refers
     to the statement he has just made, that he has nothing to leave
     behind for Biff).

33   *nickel*: a five-cent coin.

34   *Brooklyn*: one of the five boroughs that make up New York City.
     The others are Manhattan, the Bronx, Queens and Staten Island.

35   *a pot . . . my build . . . an ace*: all terms in a game of cards.
     The first refers to the money that is at stake; the second to the
     placement of one card on an opponent's for a better chance to
     win; and the third is the strongest card in the pack. The game
     Willy and Charley like to play is called casino (see p. 40).

36   *a deck of cards with five aces*: this would be "loaded", as it
     should only have four.

37   *Ketchikan*: a city in south-eastern Alaska.

38   *Ohio, and Indiana, Michigan, Illinois*: northern Midwestern states.

39   *hunt*: when Willy talks to Ben about the opportunities to 'hunt' in
     Brooklyn, he is remembering the time long ago, before its huge
     population growth and eventual urbanization.

39   *knickers*: knickerbockers, men's short trousers, also known as
     knickerbockers, plus-twos or plus-fours in Britain.

39   *stock exchange*: the New York Stock Exchange on Wall Street is
     the US centre for stockbrokers and traders.

41   *yard*: garden.

49   *to take a fade*: an old-fashioned way of saying 'take unauthorised
     time away from work'. To do so, you need someone to 'cover'
     for you.

50   *Filene's . . . the Hub . . . Slattery's*: Filene's was the most
     famous department store in Boston in its time. Slattery's and the
     Hub were well-known restaurants in the same city

50   *Spalding*: a major manufacturing company of sporting goods and related items.

51   *the Royal Palms*: a resort hotel in Florida. Its original site was in Miami.

55   *Ebbets Field*: the home of the Brooklyn Dodgers before the Major League baseball team moved to Los Angeles after the 1957 season. The stadium was demolished in 1960.

56   *Hercules*: the Roman name for Heracles who in Greek mythology was celebrated for his great strength and courage. He was the son of Zeus and the mortal Alcmena, but he later became a god in his own right as a result of his extraordinary deeds and bravery.

59   *General Electric*: most often known as G.E., a well-established home appliance conglomerate. Hastings Home Appliances is a much smaller company.

59   *Sixth Avenue*: in Manhattan, now officially called Avenue of the Americas, but inveterate New Yorkers still refer to it by its old name.

61   *wire-recording machine*: an early version of a tape recorder.

62   *The capital of Alabama . . .*: naming the capitals of every state in alphabetical order (without making any mistakes) was a popular game American children sometimes played.

63   *Bulova watch time*: a reliable brand well-known throughout America; on radio the company advertised itself by giving the exact time of day in order to remind potential customers how accurate its instruments were designed to be.

63   *bandsaw*: a tool used in carpentry; it uses a blade consisting of a continuous band of metal with teeth along one edge.

64   *Jack Benny*: (1894–1974) one of the most accomplished radio (and later television) comedians of all time.

66   *the Parker House*: one of Boston's most elegant hotels. It is America's longest continuously operating luxury hotel and is located along the historic freedom trail on Beacon Hill.

66   *the New York, New Haven and Hartford*: the name of a train and train route stopping in several New England cities between Grand Central Station in New York and Boston's South Station.

67   *Al Smith*: Alfred Emanuel Smith, Jr. (1873–1944) was elected Governor of New York State four times. In 1928 he was the Democratic Party candidate for President, the first Roman Catholic and the first Irish-American from a major political party to seek this office. He was defeated by Herbert Hoover.

71   *shoulder guards*: part of the protective gear worn by the players of American football.

71   *the Commodore Hotel*: built as part of the terminal complex surrounding Grand Central Station on 42nd Street in New York City. It is now the Grand Hyatt.

73   *homer*: a home run in baseball that allows the player at bat to run all the bases to score a point, and also bring 'home' players on other bases to score additional points.

74   *Red Grange*: Harold Edward "Red" Grange (1903–91) was a professional American football player for the Chicago Bears.

74   *Touchdown*: a touchdown in American football, when a player catches or carries the ball across the opposing team's end-of-field line, scores six points. There are goal posts at each end of the field; a team scores three points when a player kicks the ball between the posts of an opposing team.

77   *flunked*: failed an exam.

79   *vest*: a waistcoat.

79   *the Supreme Court*: one of the three branches of government in the United States, the highest judicial authority in the country.

81   *J. P. Morgan*: John Pierpont Morgan (1837–1913) was the most powerful American banker of his time.

83   *Hackensack*: a city in New Jersey across the Hudson River, frequently disparaged by self-satisfied New Yorkers as a reference point for all things provincial, naive and out-of-town.

83   *buck*: a colloquialism for one US dollar.

83   *hit a number*: to win a big return on an illegal gambling scheme.

84   *Sotto voce*: to speak quietly.

84   *Strudel*: Happy uses 'strudel', a kind of sweet pastry usually made with apples, honey and raisins, as a circumlocution (and a not altogether polite term) for an enticing young woman.

86   *the New York Giants*: a professional football team. The 'quarterback' is the key player in the game.

86   *West Point*: located fifty miles north of New York City the prestigious United States Military Academy.

86   *She's on call*: she is a call girl, i.e. a prostitute.

87   *no soap*: an idiomatic way of saying 'this won't work'.

89   *scout*: like 'pal', another of those colloquial terms the Lomans use with one another to express intimacy. Its use in this context may derive from 'boy scout'.

90   *bullin' around*: used here in the same sense as the blunt expression 'bull shit'.

93   *Grand Central*: how New Yorkers refer to Grand Central Train
      Station, one of the two major railway terminals in Manhattan
      (the other is Penn Station).

94   *Standish Arms*: a hotel in Boston.

100   *a malted*: a milkshake drink, very popular with New Yorkers.

100   *a sixty-one*: Biff needs a passing grade of sixty-five points; he
      received only sixty-one.

102   *J.H. Simmons*: a Boston retailer.

103   *the chippies*: slang for prostitutes.

108   *gilt-edged*: a safe investment.

108   *coolie*: a highly derogatory term for a worker of Chinese or other
      Asian origin.

114   *a dime*: in the US a dime is a ten-cent coin.

114   *drummer*: a travelling salesman who sold goods wholesale in
      large lots to retailers. The term is slightly derogatory as it implies
      someone who is always trying to sell you something, whether
      you want it or not.

114   *one dollar an hour*: a very low wage, even for the time in which
      the play is set.

119   *free and clear*: in a literal sense, the Lomans have paid off
      the thirty-five-year mortgage on their house, and now own it
      outright.

120   *dast*: should dare.

Questions for Further Study

1 To what extent is *Death of a Salesman* fundamentally a play about America, and to what extent is it a play whose issues reach far beyond the American experience?

2 Several important plays, ranging from Eugene O'Neill's *The Iceman Cometh* to David Mamet's *Glengarry Glen Ross*, use the character of a salesman to make a statement about America. How does Miller's play emblematise this figure as the prototypical American personality?

3 How might the scope and focus of the play have changed had Miller used one of the alternative titles under consideration, *The Inside of His Head* and *Free and Clear*?

4 How aware is Willy Loman that his situation in the play is determined by the rules of a new, post-Second World War economy?

5 To what extent is *Death of a Salesman* a play of its time and how is it relevant today?

6 How might you wish to present the play to bring out any particular aspect or refresh it for new audiences?

7 Do you think Linda Loman is partly responsible for holding her husband back from the risk-taking that might have made Willy more successful financially?

8 What might Willy have done had he had daughters instead of sons?

9 Discuss the roles Miller assigns to women as satellite figures in the play Can Linda be considered as a character who plays a secondary part?

10 Many of the scenes in the play take place in the kitchen, yet the family never sits down to have a meal together in this domestic space. What might this say about the Loman family dynamics?

11 Why does Biff seem to be addicted to stealing? What do you think he is attempting to accomplish through this repeated transgression?

12 In the play Willy continually equates masculinity with athleticism, success in sports competitions, handling tools with authority and making an impression as a 'manly' man. What might this say about his anxiety regarding his own masculinity?

13 What is it that Willy fears about the new apartment buildings that have been constructed all around his Brooklyn neighbourhood?

14 How does Miller show the ways in which Biff's point of view impinges on his father's?

15 In the play Happy, the second son, rarely if ever speaks up for himself. Do you think his psychological situation is better or worse than Biff's?

16 What part does *Death of a Salesman* play in representing America as an automobile culture?

17 Miller dresses his stage with a number of consumer products: a vacuum cleaner, a tape recorder, a refrigerator, etc. What role do these props play as the drama unfolds?

18 Is *Death of a Salesman* tied to the multi-platform set? How would you like to present it?

19 Is *Death of a Salesman* a marriage play? What does Willy's infidelity and adultery say about the relationship Willy has with his wife?

20 Why does Charley's son succeed while Willy's sons do not? How does Charley's role as a father differ from Willy's? Consider the roles that other father figures play in the drama, including the offstage father Willy has never really known.

21 Is it significant that Uncle Ben made his fortune in Africa? What does the play imply about his ethics as a fortune hunter there?

22 What is it that Willy finds so consoling about planting seeds and working in his garden?

23 In what particular ways does *Death of a Salesman* expand our sense of how fourth-wall realism can be made to work in the theatre?

24 Music is often used as a framing device in the theatre, to establish atmosphere as the curtain rises and to extend its effect as the curtain falls. But in *Salesman* music plays a far more integral role. Discuss the role of music in advancing the form and meaning of Miller's play.

25 Linda is the only mother figure who appears in the play. Along the way we learn that Willy and Ben's mother died long ago, and Bernard's mother, like Howard's, is not even mentioned in the play. Is this significant, or merely the result of the playwright not wanting to crowd his stage with extra characters?

26 What is the effect of the Requiem? What would the play be like without it?

The Crucible

commentary and notes by
SUSAN C. W. ABBOTSON

Plot

Act One

Set in the Puritan town of Salem, Massachusetts, in 1692, *The Crucible* begins in the sparsely furnished bedroom of Reverend Samuel Parris's daughter, Betty, who is in a coma. His West Indian slave, Tituba, asks after Betty but is sent away. Parris, who spied Betty and her friends in the woods the night before, worries about how his parishioners will react to rumours that witchcraft is afoot. He questions his niece, Abigail Williams, who insists they were only dancing. Abigail has been dismissed from the Proctors' service under suspicious circumstances, but she asserts her innocence, saying that Elizabeth Proctor is spreading lies about her. Ann and Thomas Putnam's daughter, Ruth, is also acting strangely and they arrive to raise additional suspicions. Insisting that witchcraft is at fault, they encourage Parris to lead the townspeople outside in prayer. He agrees as the Putnams are important in the community, and he wants to stay in their favour.

Meanwhile, we learn more about what happened in the woods from a discussion between Abigail and two other servant girls who arrive, Mercy Lewis and Mary Warren. Mercy was dancing naked and Abigail was involved in a spell to harm Elizabeth Proctor, while Mary had watched from behind the trees. When they forcefully wake Betty she tries to fly. She is threatened by Abigail not to reveal the truth. John Proctor arrives to find out what is going on and send his servant, Mary, home. Proctor is left alone with Abigail. She admits the girls were playing games in the woods but were not involved in witchcraft. She also complains of his neglect, and it is clear that she believes he still has feelings for her. He insists they will never be together again. Betty screams and the others return, along with two elders, Rebecca Nurse and Giles Corey. Rebecca calms Betty, while Proctor antagonises Parris by accusing him of stirring up unfounded suspicions. Proctor states his dislike of Parris's authority and Putnam gets drawn into an argument over property. Reverend Hale, who has been sent for by Parris, arrives to interrogate the people of Salem.

Hale, rather pompously, takes charge. Proctor leaves, unhappy with the idea of a witchhunt, warning Hale to be circumspect. Ann confesses she sent her daughter to Tituba to ask her to conjure up the dead to find out why Ann has lost seven children in childbirth. Rebecca dislikes this superstitious conversation and leaves. Giles asks Hale about his own wife's tendency to read books, explaining that it disturbs his praying. Hale and Parris question Betty, who does not respond. They question Abigail further about events in the woods. She blames Tituba, saying that Tituba made her drink blood and tempted her to ally herself with the Devil. Tituba denies she has any contact with the Devil, but when Parris declares, 'You will confess yourself or I will take you out and whip you to your death', she becomes fearful for her life. Tituba confesses and is led by her questioners to name Sarah Good and Goody Osburn as conspirators. Abigail and Betty add more names and the adults scurry to arrest the accused.

Act Two

Eight days later at the Proctors' house, we see evident tension between Elizabeth and Proctor as she is hurt over his affair with Abigail, and he feels guilty. He has tried to make amends and is annoyed by her lack of forgiveness, but she suspects that he still harbours feelings for the girl. Mary has become an official of a court organised to try the witches, and fourteen people are in jail. Elizabeth urges Proctor to proclaim what Abigail said about the girls only playing games. He is fearful that he will not be believed and grows angry at Elizabeth's continued suspicion. Mary returns and gives Elizabeth a poppet, a homemade doll, which she has sewn while sitting in court. She informs them of the escalation of arrests and threatened hangings, saying that even Elizabeth has been suspect. She insists she spoke in Elizabeth's defence, but recognising her newly acquired power, stands up to Proctor when he threatens her, before going to bed. Realising his wife's danger, Proctor agrees to go to town. At this point, Hale arrives.

   Hale is uncertain about the girls' latest accusations, but sure that evil is at work. He has just come from Rebecca Nurse, whose name has also been mentioned. He questions the couple about their religious adherence, asking why they do not regularly attend church, and why their youngest son is not baptised. Proctor admits he dislikes Parris, but has done many things for the church. When asked to name the Ten Commandments, he significantly forgets adultery, until his wife reminds him. At Elizabeth's prompting Proctor shares his doubts about Abigail's veracity, but Hale is unsure. Francis Nurse and Giles arrive to announce their wives have been arrested. Hale is shaken, but insists the court will be fair, a belief he reasserts as the Marshal arrives to arrest Elizabeth, who has been denounced by Abigail. They take the poppet as proof that Elizabeth has been involved in questionable practices. It has a needle in its stomach, and Abigail has behaved in court as if someone were stabbing her. Although Mary insists she made the poppet and gave it to Elizabeth, Elizabeth's violent response to Abigail's accusations, insisting that, 'She must be ripped out of the world', convinces them that she needs to be cross-examined. Although Proctor angrily tears the warrant, his wife agrees to go. The husbands urge Hale to act, but as he insists that the town must be guilty of something for this to have happened, Proctor falls silent, evidently thinking about his own sin. Left alone with Mary, Proctor insists she help him clear his wife, but she is fearful of Abigail. He asserts a preparedness to confess his own adultery to destroy the court's faith in Abigail.

Act Three

In an anteroom outside the courtroom, we overhear Judge Hathorne cross-examine Martha Corey. Giles disrupts the proceedings to defend her and is brought before the court by Governor Danforth, who is now in charge. Francis, whose wife, Rebecca, has been condemned, also comes forth to insist the girls are lying. Though threatened with contempt, he and Giles stand firm. Proctor arrives with Mary as their witness, for he has convinced her that she must testify against Abigail. Danforth fears that Proctor is trying to undermine his court, rather than just save his wife. Elizabeth has declared herself pregnant, and Proctor insists it must be true as his wife is incapable of lying. Pointing out they will not hang a pregnant woman, Danforth suggests Proctor drop his protest, but Proctor refuses, as other innocents are involved. Danforth is shown a list of people who feel the wives are wrongly accused, but to the horror of the husbands, he orders everyone on the list to be arrested for questioning. Giles accuses Putnam of prompting his daughter to cry witchery on people to get their property, but when he refuses to name his source, he is arrested. Hale is becoming concerned about these high-handed responses, his doubts evidently on the rise, and he suggests a lawyer be engaged to deal with Mary, but Danforth insists on continuing the investigation himself. Danforth harshly questions Mary, but with encouragement from Proctor she stands firm.

Danforth has Abigail and the girls brought in to defend themselves. Abigail tries to deflect the charges, but Proctor's insistence on her bad character begins to make Danforth unsure. Proctor gets Parris to confess to seeing Abigail dance in the woods to help build his case. To reassert control, Hathorne asks Mary to illustrate how she pretends to faint in court. When she cannot, they decide she must be lying. Abigail leads the girls to act as if Mary were sending a spirit against them, and Mary panics. Proctor pronounces Abigail to be a whore and confesses his adultery. Since Abigail denies it, Elizabeth is brought to confirm the charge, as Proctor says she knew. Not knowing her husband has confessed, she lies to save his reputation and declares no adultery took place. Despite Hale's claims that it was 'a natural lie to tell', Danforth refuses to believe adultery has taken place. As the girls reassert that Mary's spirit is attacking them, Mary breaks down and accuses Proctor of being in league with the Devil. All the judges, except Hale (who now denounces the proceedings), are convinced by this performance, and have Proctor arrested. When asked to confess, Proctor declares that 'God is dead', and accuses them of being damned for their part in such events.

Act Four

Three months have passed and Sarah Good and Tituba, who confessed themselves witches, languish in jail. A drunken Marshal Herrick moves them to a different cell as they call to the Devil for release. Danforth and Hathorne, having had twelve people hanged, are about to hang seven more, including Proctor, Rebecca and Martha. Hale is advising prisoners to confess to avoid death, and they feel that Parris is becoming unhinged by the pressure. They hope to get someone to confess to make their case valid, and Parris suggests delaying the executions. Abigail and Mercy have absconded with his savings, and he is fearful that the rumoured rebellion in nearby Andover will spread to Salem. Hale enters to admit his failure in getting Rebecca to confess and demands that those awaiting execution be pardoned. Danforth insists they must continue, to justify the case against those already hanged.

They decide to ask Elizabeth to encourage her husband to confess, and although she suspects a trick, she agrees to speak with Proctor. Left alone with her husband, we see by their physical descriptions that both have suffered in jail. Elizabeth relates how Giles died under torture and Proctor confides his decision to confess, not feeling worthy enough to die beside Rebecca and Martha. Elizabeth insists on his worthiness and shoulders blame over his adultery because of her former coldness. She leaves him to make his own decision, but wanting to live for her sake, he announces he will give them the confession they want.

The judges return, excited about Proctor's confession, to which they bring a horrified Rebecca as witness. To Proctor's growing discomfort, they have Cheever write it down for Proctor to sign. However, Proctor refuses to name anyone else as an accomplice, and although he signs the confession, he refuses to hand it over for public display, knowing it will be used against the others. Admitting his confession is a lie, he tears it apart. Proctor recognises the dignity of his moral stance and chooses to die beside the others. Danforth orders the hangings to proceed, and Proctor and Rebecca are taken outside. First Parris, then Hale plead with Elizabeth to intervene, but honouring her husband's decision, she refuses. The curtain falls to the sound of the drums heralding the executions.

Appendix

Miller wrote a short additional scene for Act Two, not always included in performance, which takes place five weeks after Elizabeth has been arrested, on the day before her trial. Proctor secretly meets Abigail to warn her to tell the truth or be exposed, but Abigail does not believe him. She seems close to madness: still passionate about Proctor, and paranoid about the township. Her body is covered in scars she believes caused by spirits. She refuses to help and Proctor is left with few options.

Afterword

'Echoes Down the Corridor' is a brief note which follows the play, in which Miller relates subsequent events. Parris is voted from office, Abigail is alleged to have become a Boston prostitute, and Elizabeth eventually remarries. Twenty years on from these proceedings, the government awarded compensation to the victims still living, and to the families of the dead.

Commentary

Context – Historical, Social and Theatrical

The Crucible takes for its point of departure the Salem witch trials of 1692, but it also reflects Miller's reaction to how the House Un-American Activities Committee (HUAC) operated at the time when the play was written, and the dangers of the McCarthyist fervour that gripped America in the 1950s. It is typical of his work in its sense of purpose, humanity and the desire to bring society to a better understanding of itself.

Salem witch trials

Miller's interest in the Salem witch trials was prompted by reading Marion Starkey's *The Devil in Massachusetts* (1949), which suggested that attitudes towards race and nationality during the Second World War made the Salem witch trials an allegory for that period. While Miller saw additional parallels in the climate of the 1950s, he decided to research the original trials by visiting the Historical Society in Salem, Massachusetts. Miller found the core of his plot in Charles W. Upham's 1867 *Salem Witchcraft*, in which all of the play's characters are referred to and many of its events related. He also read the original court transcripts.

Salem was settled in 1629, but by the 1690s had become divided between the agricultural farms of Salem Village and the adjacent, more mercantile port of Salem Town. There was much rivalry between the two, and jealousy of those like the Nurses and Proctors who owned property on the lucrative roadway between them. In January 1692, the Reverend Parris's daughter, Betty, aged nine, and her cousin, Abigail, aged eleven, apparently became afflicted with contortions and fits, making complaints about being pinched and pricked with pins. After the local doctor found no physical evidence for their condition, and other girls experienced the same symptoms, witchcraft was suspected. Parris's slave, Tituba, was asked to bake a 'witch cake' to discover who was responsible for this. Soon after, Thomas Putnam and other men of the town accused Tituba and two disreputable women of the neighbourhood, Sarah Good and Sarah Osborne, of causing the afflictions. Examined in March by the local magistrates John Hathorne and Jonathan Corwin, Tituba confessed, and all three were sent to jail in Boston. More accusations followed from the girls, including ones against Martha Corey, who had voiced scepticism over their credibility, as well as Rebecca Nurse and Elizabeth Proctor. The local innkeeper John Proctor, who had written to Boston complaining about the proceedings, was imprisoned in April after objecting to his wife's arrest during Deputy-Governor Danforth's examination. Even a former minister of the town, George Burroughs, was accused, and three of Proctor's children. After Osborne had died in jail, magistrates were assigned to trials beginning in May, by which month's end there were sixty-two people in custody and more to follow.

Most of the accused were found guilty on controversial and questionable evidence. The afflicted would claim an apparition of the accused had attacked them, and since the courts decided that the Devil needed a person's permission to take their bodily form, the accusations were considered believable. Some confessed, usually after being unpleasantly cross-examined, or condemning testimony was given against them from other self-confessed witches. Discoveries of poppets, ointments, horoscopes or books on palmistry were also considered as evidence against them. Though several men were accused, the majority were women, as they were considered the weaker gender and therefore more susceptible to the Devil. After being interrogated, the accused would later stand trial, at which most were condemned to death. The first to be hanged on 10 June was Bridget Bishop, an outspoken woman close to sixty years old; she claimed innocence to the moment of her death. Rebecca Nurse, Sarah Good and three more women were hanged in July. Elizabeth was given a stay of execution because she was pregnant, but Proctor was hanged alongside Burroughs and three others on 19 August. Burroughs unsettled onlookers by reciting the Lord's Prayer on the scaffold, a feat supposedly impossible for an agent of the Devil. Martha was hanged in September along with seven others. All were excommunicated and none were allowed proper burial.

The courts were dismissed in October after several complaints, and when they reconvened the following year, with Danforth serving for the first time, evidence based on apparitions was no longer admissible. Although three additional women were found guilty, many charges were dismissed. There were no more hangings, and by March the trials had been much discredited. By May, Elizabeth and the rest of the prisoners were released. One judge, Samuel Sewall, repudiated the trials and formerly apologised; he would go on to write the first attack on slavery in America. Hale, who was the great-grandfather of the American Revolutionary War hero Nathan Hale, had changed his mind late in the court proceedings after his wife was accused of witchcraft. She was acquitted and he would go on to speak out against the trials, publishing a highly critical text of the proceedings in 1697, *A Modest Enquiry into the Nature of Witchcraft*. In 1702 the General Court declared the 1692 trials unlawful, and by 1711 restitutions were made to victims. In 1752 Salem Village was renamed

Danvers, but it would not be until 1957 that Massachusetts made a formal apology for the debacle. In 1992, on the three-hundredth anniversary of the trials, a park in Salem was opened with a stone bench in memory of those executed; Miller spoke at the dedication ceremony.

In a note at the beginning of the play Miller declares that his account is predominantly truthful, and while he has made some changes for 'dramatic purposes', the nature of the events themselves is historically accurate. The major alterations are the fusing of various original characters into a single representative, reducing both the number of judges and the girls 'crying out', slight alterations to the time-line and locations, decreasing Proctor's age (originally in his sixties, with Elizabeth, his third wife, twenty years his junior) and increasing Abigail's age to allow the possibility of an affair, as well as making her the girl who denounces Elizabeth. While he based characters on what he learned through letters, records and reports, Miller asks for them to be properly considered as 'creations of my own, drawn to the best of my ability in conformity with their known behavior'. Despite this disclaimer, critics have noticed a number of the play's historical inaccuracies. Since the 1958 edition, however, the play contains additional notes detailing the situation of Salem society in the 1690s. These supply facts regarding the lives of the main characters involved that go beyond the events of the play itself, and stand as a tribute to the extent of Miller's research.

Many details in the play are firmly supported by trial transcripts and other records of the time, such as Sarah Good's condemnation on being unable to recite the Ten Commandments, the Putnams' rivalry and desire for more land, Rebecca's steadfast claim of innocence, Giles Corey's complaint against his wife preventing him from saying his prayers and his death by being crushed under stones. There is also proof of Mary Warren's poppet being given to Elizabeth, Mary's repudiation of the girls' accusations and subsequent change of heart. Notable details from Miller's dramatic imagination include the presentation of Abigail and her lust for Proctor; the character development of both the Proctors, with John especially depicted as a liberated thinker; and Proctor's subsequent confession, recantation, and death alongside Rebecca and Martha (all three were hanged on different dates). Miller also makes Governor Danforth and Reverend Hale the central and direct antagonists to Proctor. Hathorne (the great-great-grandfather of the writer Nathaniel Hawthorne) was probably the most despicable of the real judges, being the only one who never publicly repented the key part he played in the trials. It was the uncompromising moral absolutism of that era's Puritans that Miller wished to capture and expose. The original prosecution was as blind to facts and relentless as they appear to be in the play; and there were many, like the Putnams, who took full mercenary advantage of the situation or stood by and allowed the atrocities to happen.

House Committee on Un-American Activities (HUAC)

The concept of HUAC had begun in 1938 with the Dies Committee, charged with investigating German-American involvement in Nazi and Ku Klux Klan activity, but the committee soon became more interested in the communist threat. This committee had been behind the closing of the Federal Theater Project that Miller had briefly joined after his graduation from the University of Michigan. They concluded, erroneously, that it was being overly influenced by the Communist Party. HUAC became a permanent committee in 1946 charged to investigate suspected threats of subversion or propaganda that attacked 'the form of government guaranteed by our Constitution', but their real target was anyone who exhibited left-of-centre sympathies. People were subpoenaed to prove that they were not or had never been active in the Communist Party. If they confessed to any such activity, they were expected to name names of anyone else who might have been involved. It was not illegal to belong to the Communist Party, but HUAC could convict anyone of contempt if they refused to cooperate, and send them to jail. This conveyed an implication that to be a communist sympathiser was a criminal act, despite the laws of the United States. People were often called before HUAC on inconclusive or even questionable evidence; and even if the committee's investigation came up empty, many lives were subsequently ruined. Suspicion and ostracism led to loss of employment and the end of many professional careers.

Few noticed while the committee investigated government employees, but when it began to go after more prominent public figures in the entertainment industry, beginning with an investigation into alleged communist propaganda in the Hollywood film industry, HUAC caught people's attention. After nine days of hearings in 1947, a group of writers and actors was convicted on charges of contempt of Congress for refusal to answer questions. Each of 'The Hollywood Ten', as they became known, took the Fifth Amendment, refusing to testify on the grounds that they might incriminate themselves. Even though none had confessed to any communist sympathies, they were sent to jail for sentences ranging from six to twelve months and subsequently 'blacklisted', which meant they would not be offered work. The example of such harsh treatment scared many into going along with whatever the committee asked, rather than face punishment themselves. The hearings escalated in the 1950s and the anti-communist fervour they provoked became known as McCarthyism, named after its instigator, Senator Joseph McCarthy. His involvement began in 1950 with a speech to a Republican Women's Club. A flood of press attention followed when he produced a piece of paper that he claimed contained a list of known communists working for the State Department.

Although McCarthy would serve on committees covering both government and military investigations into communist infiltration, as a United States senator he did not serve on HUAC, although his scaremongering helped create the atmosphere that gave the House Committee its credibility. In Miller's 1999 essay 'The Crucible in History', he discusses what he saw as the mood of the 1950s, and admits that it was partly his horror of what he saw that led him to write The Crucible as a means of both conveying his anger at such proceedings and exposing the collateral damage they caused. Connecting McCarthyism to the way people acted in Salem, Miller felt that the 1950s American vision of communism was a moral issue, which viewed communists as in league with the Devil. This he linked to the Puritan sense of rectitude, that seemed to suggest that anyone with whom they disagreed must be allied to Satan.

Miller initially resisted the idea of depicting the HUAC hearings in the form of an old-fashioned witch trial as too obvious. However, as the HUAC hearings grew more ritualistic and cruelly pointless, he could no longer resist, despite the obvious risks, for the parallels were far too apt to ignore. He saw how both sets of hearings had a definite structure behind them, designed to make people publicly confess. In both cases the 'judges' knew in advance all of the information for which they asked. The main difference was that Salem's hearings had a greater legality as it was against the law to be a witch, but it was not illegal to be a communist in 1950s America. Miller does not attempt a one-to-one analogy between his characters and those involved in HUAC, because this would have made the play too immediately paradigmatic and temporal. Miller himself appeared before HUAC three years after he wrote The Crucible. Summoned before a group of hostile and opportunistic politicians he presented a speech that virtually echoed that of John Proctor, in which he, too, refused to name names or bring trouble on anyone else. Miller was convicted of contempt, but his lawyer was able to get his one-year sentence reduced to the suspension of a single month and a $500 fine. Rather than accept a conviction that represented wrongdoing, Miller appealed. By August the following year the conviction was overturned by the United States Court of Appeals on the grounds that the questions that he had been asked served no legislative purpose.

Miller insisted that while McCarthyism may have informed The Crucible, it is not its major theme. We never go inside the courtroom, because Miller is not interested in the proceedings as much as the motivations behind them, and the fears and reactions of those involved. The play's continued success depends on the realisation that it offers more than a straightforward history lesson of either HUAC or the witch trials. Rather, *The Crucible* explores the prevailing conditions that precipitate such events. This allows Miller's play a continuing resonance as historical conditions of persecution, intolerance and sanctimonious denunciation continue to repeat themselves in a variety of political and historical circumstances. *The Crucible* speaks to every conflict between an individual conscience and tyranny, whether it is the tyranny of religion, government, race, economics or simply that of public opinion. Connections to past and present injustices and periods of overly zealous patriotism or fundamentalist fervour find their resonance in this work. Miller viewed the right-wing attacks on President Clinton over the Lewinsky Affair as redolent of the Salem magistrates attacking the accused while revelling in the potent sexual details of a supposed allegiance to the Devil; and directing the play in 2006, Dominic Cooke saw parallels to 'Bush and Blair generating hysteria over terrorism and the frightening rise of Christian Fundamentalism in the US'.

The play's theatrical context and place in Miller's oeuvre

While the extensive notes that Miller added to his script may recall the social earnestness of George Bernard Shaw, *The Crucible* follows an American theatrical tradition, advanced by the agitprop plays of the 1930s, of drama that seriously addresses key social and political issues. Miller's outspokenness against such dangerous manifestations as McCarthyism, encoded within the play, was the kind of moral stance that made Miller so admired by both contemporary and subsequent playwrights. His theatrical goal was to appeal to the best instincts of the society for which he wrote.

Not as formally innovative or experimental as *Death of a Salesman* or *After the Fall*, *The Crucible* can be viewed as one of Miller's more realistic pieces. Like his earlier *All My Sons*, it has strong connections to the social realism of Henrik Ibsen, in which earlier indiscretions return to haunt the protagonist as 'the chickens come home to roost'. Just prior to *The Crucible*, Miller adapted Ibsen's *An Enemy of the People*, and that play's central character, Dr Thomas Stockmann, shares something of the moral authority of John Proctor.

Miller viewed *The Crucible* as a companion piece to *Death of a Salesman* in the way both plays explore the role of the individual in conflict with the dictates of society. Having argued in 1949 that tragedy could be written about the common man, in *The Crucible* Miller presents us with another working-class tragic protagonist whose actions are partly determined by forces outside himself. However, unlike Willy Loman, Proctor exhibits a greater degree of conscience, and ends with a better understanding of himself and the events around him. For Miller art has only been useful when it tries to change society for the better, and *The Crucible* is the play he wrote which is most clearly informed by that sense of purpose. The play's ability to span the distance from 1692 Salem to contemporary times allows for a study of the nature of America herself, with some striking lessons. Miller raises disturbing questions about the function of authority and the rights of the individual that speak to people who have never even heard of Salem or McCarthyism. It is this wide-ranging aspect that gives the play its theatrical appeal.

Although the work's initial reception was lukewarm, partly due to its controversial political analogy, *The Crucible* cemented Miller's reputation as one of America's foremost playwrights, and it has grown to become Miller's most resilient play. Its popularity is due both to its craft, which makes it a solid choice for stage production, and the widely applicable aspects of its subject and theme, which continue to fascinate audiences throughout the world. The large cast, including a number of parts for young female players, has made it a staple of school, college and community theatre, along with its frequent presence on academic syllabuses both on the secondary school and university level. *The Crucible* has become the most produced drama in the Miller repertory, and, after Thornton Wilder's *Our Town*, the most performed of any American drama.

The Principal Themes

Individualism vs. community

In the spring of 1692, Salem was a recently founded, religiously devout township, a communal society, it was supported by an autocratic theocracy to help it attain the discipline necessary for survival. Its inhabitants were suspicious of individuality because they saw it as a threat to the imposed sense of order. Authority, and obedience to that authority, had long defined their lives. Constantly threatened by the surrounding wilderness, Salemites worked hard to survive. Their way of life was strict and sombre, with dancing and frivolity frowned upon as wasteful. Concentrating on survival left them little opportunity to misbehave. Ironically, although their families had come to America to avoid persecution, they became intolerant, constantly judging each other's behaviour. The witch trials offered them a release of pent-up frustration and emotion. Under the guise of morality they were given the opportunity to take vengeance on neighbours towards whom they felt envy or hostility. Growing family sizes had led to disputes over property rights, and the fact that anyone accused of witchcraft would have had their lands forfeited either to a claimant or the Church gave many the opportunity, like the Putnams, increase their holdings by making accusations.

The Crucible explores how societies define themselves, the dangers inherent in this process, especially to the individual, and the nature of power itself. Given Miller's democratic views, he is fearful of the consequences of allowing too few too much power, largely because, given natural human weakness, it is all too easy for those few to put their private interest before the common good. The play depicts a conflict between individualism and community, with a single conscience pitted against the weight of a social authority that has been corrupted by selfishness and hypocrisy. We see in the actions of the prosecutors, the blindness that results from paranoia and inflexible belief. The drama illustrates how an entrenched system leads to a desire to negate the opinions of others. What results is a totalitarian social structure where those with a voice, given to them by a financial or political standing, effectively silence dissent. Such societies become intolerant of individual thinkers who question or refuse to accept all they are told to believe. The Proctors are already partly damned by their scepticism over the presence of witches and their refusal to kowtow to a venal minister, both of which make them easy targets.

Miller demonstrates how social forces operate on people, in part to show the falsity of our belief in individual human autonomy. Total freedom, he suggests, is largely a myth in any working society. The actions of Proctor and others in the play are partially dictated by forces beyond themselves, which demand of them sacrifices they have little choice but to make. While Proctor, Rebecca, Martha and Elizabeth stand trial individually, the refusal to confess or name others is as much dictated by a social conscience as a personal one. The ideal would be a balance between the desires of the individual and the needs of the community, but this is a hard balance to attain, especially in a hierarchical society such as the one developed in Salem, where the few are given power over the many.

From the Putnams, to Parris, to the trial judges, *The Crucible* depicts how the unscrupulous can declare the presence of evil to cripple whoever disagrees with them, not just religiously, but politically and socially. They assume a moral high ground, so anyone who disagrees is deemed immoral and damned, without recourse to defence. Tituba and the children were trying to commune with dark forces, but if left alone their exploits would have bothered no one – their actions an indication of how young people react against social and sexual repression. A community stays strong by allowing its individual members some measure of autonomy; when any society becomes too restrictive, trouble is bound to ensue.

Guilt and responsibility

The Greek playwrights and Henrik Ibsen were strong influences on Miller from the beginning of his career. Both wrote plays in which past mistakes inevitably impinge on the present. Miller was interested in the role guilt might play in such circumstances, and how characters deal with guilt is a common theme in much of his work. Earlier plays, such as *All My Sons* or *Death of a Salesman*, have narrative arcs that lead to the uncovering of a literal or moral crime, at which point they end. In the character of Proctor, Miller wanted to move beyond the discovery of guilt to a more circumstantial study of its effects. What follows in this case is an exploration of how guilt can be transformed into responsibility.

In *The Crucible* Miller explores what happens when people allow others to be the judge of their conscience. Through Proctor, Miller examines the conflict between a person's deeds and that person's conception of himself. Proctor is presented as a man caught between the way in which others see him and the way he sees himself. He has betrayed his wife, ruined a young girl, and feels he must pay for his indiscretion. His private sense of guilt leads him to make a false confession for a crime of which he is patently innocent, although he later recants. What allows him to recant is the release of guilt given to him by his wife's admission of her coldness and her refusal to blame him for his adultery. Elizabeth insists that he is a good man, which finally convinces him that he is. This allows him to accept his death rather than 'confess' and damage the reputation of others, which would return him to a guilt he can no longer accept. His death is less atonement for any earlier sin than a martyrdom to help the people of Salem regain their sanity. Thus he transforms his personal guilt into a wider responsibility for others.

Marriage

The Crucible dramatises a debate on the theme of marriage, and what a marriage requires to make it work. At the time of writing the play Miller, a father of two and married to Mary Slattery, was considering an affair with Marilyn Monroe. It is unsurprising, then, to find the issue of marriage explored. The director Elia Kazan introduced him to Monroe in 1951 while the two were in Hollywood to find a film producer for *The Hook*, but Miller resisted her temptations, returning to New York to try and patch up his already failing marriage. His confession to Slattery put a further strain on their relationship. While he dedicated the play 'To Mary', and hopefully depicted a couple who were able to transcend a past indiscretion, his own marriage did not last. Unlike Elizabeth Proctor, Mary took no blame upon herself and their relationship remained strained. In 1955 Monroe came to

New York and began her relationship with Miller, which led to his divorce from Slattery and subsequent marriage to Monroe.

The Proctors' marriage lies at the play's centre, and the love triangle Miller creates between Abigail and the Proctors echoes his own. But just as the play transcends its historical basis, it also goes beyond the autobiographical. Issues of trust, love and what a partner owes the other are discussed in a number of scenes. It is Giles Corey's idle tongue and distrust of his wife that contribute to getting her hanged, while Francis Nurse staunchly defends his wife even at risk of being found in contempt.

Proctor and Elizabeth profoundly love each other, but seven months before the play begins, while his wife was sick, he had an affair with their serving girl, Abigail. We do not know how long this might have continued had not Elizabeth discovered her husband's adultery, but Proctor insists it was nothing more than animal passion. Abigail is sent away, but the trust between the married couple has shattered, and all ease between them is gone. Insecure about her own attractiveness, Elizabeth looks for signs that her husband continues to stray. Tortured by guilt over what he sees as a moment of weakness, Proctor vacillates between apologetic attempts to make his wife happy and anger at her continued distrust. It is not until both suffer at the hands of the court that they come to an understanding of each other and their mutual love. Each is willing to sacrifice everything for the sake of the other. Proctor tries to free Elizabeth by ruining his own name with a public confession of adultery, while she lies for the first and only time in her life to save him. Their final scene together is deeply touching, as we see Elizabeth declare her love, and willingness to sacrifice that love, by allowing Proctor to die rather than relinquish his integrity. The re-establishment of trust between them is made evident when Proctor regains a sense of his own worth by accepting his wife's vision of him as a good man.

Sex and religion

The dangers of orthodoxy and desire are part of a discussion through which Miller represents the puritanical fear of sex. The girls go to the dark woods to indulge in their sexual fantasies, as they are given no room to do so in a fiercely restricted society. Sexual repression within this puritanical community is revealed to be a major factor in the troubles that ensue. It is also a determining factor in the behaviour of many of the play's characters.

Puritanism coloured every aspect of how the people of Salem lived. This meant giving full obedience to the Church – each man, woman and child was expected to attend services each week. Sermons were measured by hours, often full of references to hellfire, and inattention was scorned. Puritans felt chosen by God for a special purpose; He would be watching every moment, so discipline was imperative. Discipline of others and of the self, and anything that threatened that discipline, would be scrupulously observed. Salem believed in both the Devil and the existence of witches, and felt under constant threat from both. Obedience to the Church and its dictates would help keep them safe.

For the people of Salem, Satan was alive and nearby in the dark forest. Miller allows the forest to act as a representation of hell, to be avoided at the cost of sin. The main sin is sex, which has been notoriously equated with the Devil by the Christian view of original sin. While godly folk stay at home at night, the girls dance illicitly in the woods around a fire (another hellish symbol), with Mercy naked and Abigail drinking blood to cast a spell on Elizabeth. Desire makes them wicked. Abigail's bedevilment is reinforced by the symbols that surround her: she has been initiated into the temptation of sex by her former employer through her 'sense for heat' and still feels Proctor 'burning' for her. He is described in his adulterous lust as a 'stallion', a beast that acts without self-control.

A central irony of the play is that by fixating so much on sin, the religious right, represented by Parris and Danforth, become sinful and 'turned' from God. Proctor accuses Parris of preaching too much 'hellfire and bloody damnation' and saying too little about God; this becomes a kind of prophesy as Parris and the judges become increasingly devilish in their treatment of others, condemning innocent people to death on spurious evidence. Signing the death warrants becomes an issue of pride rather than belief. As Proctor suggests when he is arrested, the fires of hell will consume the supposedly righteous for their 'black hearts' rather than the 'guilty' witches.

Gender and race

When people are treated by different standards in any society, dangers ensue. Both the gender and racial inequality are depicted in *The Crucible*, and without the confession of the slave Tituba and the outcry of the young girls, the subsequent horrors of the Salem witch trials might have been avoided. Therefore, what motivated these female figures becomes an important factor in our understanding of such occurrences.

The fact that most of the accused were female is dramatically significant. Women of that era were believed to be weaker and more lustful than men, and therefore more susceptible to temptation from the Devil. Although wives were given some authority in running the home, the husband was considered the undisputed head of the household. This is perhaps why Proctor resents the fact that his wife will not forgive him. Kept under double submission, both to men and God, strong-willed women would not have had easy lives. Growing up, boys had many more outlets beyond the home, being allowed to explore in order to fish and hunt. Girls were expected to tend the house, and were encouraged to be subservient. Disobedient children were swiftly disciplined and taught to obey. Even lower in the hierarchy than children would be anyone who was not white. Tituba is never allowed to defend herself from the accusations brought against her, but simply assumed to be guilty because of the colour of her skin, which her accusers believe automatically allies her with the Devil. They ignore her protestations of faith, and force her either to confess or die, which is little choice at all.

The girls of the town are similarly bullied. Several adults (including Proctor) suggest beating as a punishment for untoward behaviour – a common treatment at the time for any infringement of the rules. Young, unmarried servant girls are considered chattels rather than viable members of the community, ordered to and fro and chastised if they display any sign of independent thought. They were allowed to make no decisions for themselves, and were given no avenue to gain respect outside of marriage. The patriarchal Salem authorities may represent order and security, but such an arrangement comes at a heavy price. It is a price not all the girls are prepared to pay, hence their nocturnal visits to the forest, the place of the unknown and freedom from the town's restrictions.

In the forest the girls danced as their spirits and desires ran free; it is no wonder they found such escapades exciting. They carried this freedom forwards into the courtroom, where for the first time they are shown respect, as Abigail leads them to cry out against many of the town's elders. But such actions become a dangerous threat to the community. Introducing a form of chaos into a tightly ordered society, their actions go against everything this society holds sacred. Parris's fear that Abigail and her friends are going into the woods at night to dance naked and invoke the Devil is therefore justified, for by so doing they are attacking the foundations of their society: its religious beliefs, its social conventions and the sanctity of marriage (as Abigail plots to take Elizabeth's life and replace her). When a society consistently restricts an individual and will not allow a person to show independence or individuality, it effectively destroys the individual's spirit. The question arises as to whether or not we can condone the actions of an individual who tries to break a community's status quo.

It is hard to believe that Miller intends us to view Abigail – a young, orphaned girl who has been seduced by her boss (an older, family man and respected member of his society) and deflowered in an age when virginity was a prerequisite for marriage – as a villain. Indeed, from a feminist perspective she becomes increasingly sympathetic. After such treatment she is thrown out of the house on orders from the man's wife, and forced to live with her petulant and demanding uncle. She tries to win back Proctor's affection, resorting to casting spells on his wife to remove her from the competition. When she meets him again, she declares her love, but is ignored and rejected. He even threatens to disgrace her in the town. It is not until he publicly confesses their relationship that she finally attacks him, which could be viewed as an attempt to protect herself rather than a malicious act of revenge. Can we condemn such a girl, as the men of the play do, as a wanton whore? Even the wronged wife insists, 'There is a promise made in any bed', and admits the girl might indeed love her husband.

To view John Proctor as an innocent who has been seduced by an evil whore is too easy. Abigail is in love with Proctor, and it may be that he still harbours feelings for her. When she declares, 'You loved me, John Proctor, and whatever sin it is, you love me yet!' he does not deny the charge. Having been awakened by her affair from a slumbering servitude to see her potential as a human being, Abigail struggles to uncover a sense of self in a highly restrictive society. She creates for herself a position of respect outside of marriage by becoming the voice of accusation which all fear, a role more traditionally held by males who hold every position of authority. She refuses to accept a patriarchal society that silences and denounces independent, female vitality. She justifies the victimisation of her fellow women by calling them hypocrites who, like the men, have tried to keep her in her place. Her gulling of the judges, and eventual escape with the mercenary Parris's savings before the town turns against her, might depict her as victorious – a woman who refuses to be controlled and who wins her freedom through her own quick thinking. As a sad reflection of the lack of opportunities open to women in those times, however, we eventually learn that she ends up as a prostitute in Boston.

Key Elements of Style

While Miller never intended to present an historically accurate depiction of the Salem witch trials, having made several changes for 'dramatic purposes', he did view his depiction as an 'honest' one. He wanted his audience to be drawn into the world he created, but felt the archaic speech of the period might be off-putting. He developed his own poetic language for the play, based on the language he had read in Salem documents.

Wanting to make his audience feel they were witnessing events from an earlier time, yet not wanting to make the dialogue incomprehensible, he devised a form of speech for his characters that blended into present-day speech an earlier vocabulary and syntax. Incorporating more familiar archaic words like 'yea', 'nay', or 'goodly', Miller created the impression of a past era without distancing his audience from the action.

The play's language, however, is complex nonetheless, as it offers itself as a study in the power of the spoken and written word. It shows how accusations, once voiced in public, tend to stick, however much they are denied. We can view *The Crucible* as an exploration of how Salem performed its witch trials in the same way as we might watch a play. The trials were public events and, like the HUAC hearings, became show trials in which the guilt or innocence of those accused became less important than how the judges and accusers 'acted'. As Danforth complains when asked to delay the executions, 'Postponement now speaks a floundering on my part.' It is a performance in which those in power are in the director's seat and can chose how they wish to interpret what they hear. To write such things down gives them even greater power. Proctor recognises this when he is asked to write down his confession as well as voice it. There is an authority given to the written word that prevents ambiguity.

The fact that the first draft of the play was written in verse and later broken down into prose reflects in Miller's frequent use of poetic imagery within the deceptively simple speech patterns of his characters. Although this is one of Miller's more realistic plays, it is based on a central and controlling metaphor. A 'crucible' subjects items to great heat in order to purify their nature – the condition faced by the central characters of Proctor, Elizabeth and Hale. All ' endure intense suffering to emerge as more morally secure and more self-aware individuals. Miller also incorporates images of heat and light against cold and dark to play against our common concepts of heaven and hell and good and evil. Numerous references to cold and winter and the hardness of stone are used to indicate the harshness of Puritan life, trapped as it is in a cycle of toil unrelieved by leisure, as they strive to tame the hard landscape and their own natural impulses within the mandates of a restrictive religion. Abigail tells John that he is 'no wintry man', which is true in that he refuses to abide by many of the strictures of his community and is determined to have a mind of his own. It is partly this independent spirit that makes him such an obvious target. The network of symbolic elements within the play – from the 'crucible' of the title to the woods surrounding the township as well as the extended metaphors regarding blood, fire and ice – all contribute to the play's rich and unexpected lyricism.

The Characters

John Proctor

Although the original John Proctor was not a major figure in the Salem trials, Miller makes him the central protagonist. In his mid-thirties, Proctor is a straightforward man of common sense who is impatient with foolishness in others. This has at times led him into trouble with neighbours who dislike his bluntness, and will lead him into further trouble with the court, which views his scepticism as undermining their authority. A freer thinker than many of the townspeople, Proctor does not believe in witches and has a relatively egalitarian outlook for a Puritan, to the point where Parris accuses him of acting like a Quaker. Quakers were far less rigid than the Puritans and, to Parris's mind, less scrupulous in their religious devotion. Despite his relative openness, Proctor remains a strong disciplinarian – as most Puritan heads of family would have been – and is prepared to beat his servants. He expects his wife to forgive him once he has confessed. Despite his lapse with Abigail, he is a moral man, he works hard, values his friends and feels guilt over his shortcomings. Proctor's view of Reverend Parris as an ungodly materialist, and his subsequent refusal to attend church or have his third son baptised, show him as a man of principle. But this is exactly what works against him.

Miller describes Proctor as a sinner not just in the general sense 'but against his own vision of decent conduct' – in other words, he has become his own harshest critic. He fully repents of his weakness for Abigail, and Miller expects us to forgive him this lapse even if he cannot do so himself. Despite his adultery, he feels his commitment to his marriage deeply, which is why he confesses to Elizabeth and tries to make amends. Abigail has been sent away and he has vowed to have nothing more to do with her, a vow he has not found easy to uphold, but one he has kept. Elizabeth, we are told, is pregnant, which tells us that the couple continues to have sexual relations despite Elizabeth's disappointment in him. He tries hard to please his wife and be a better husband and father, and he does all he can to save her after her arrest, even going so far as to sacrifice himself.

Miller wants his hero to be realistic and he shows him with his human flaws. He is a man of deep passion, which not only led him into an affair with his servant, but can also be observed in the intensity of his frustration and anger. His rocky relationship with Elizabeth highlights this passion: one moment he is deeply solicitous, the next furiously angry. His attitude towards women often borders on the dictatorial; enlightened though he is, he is still a man of his time, and these were times in which the man was the head of his own household. There are moments when he seems unable to control his temper both verbally and physically. Shouting 'God is dead', and declaring the judges damned at his arrest, he also tears up the warrant for Elizabeth's arrest and makes physical threats against both Mary and Abigail. His anger seems rooted in an awareness that these events are partly his fault; if he had left Abigail alone, she might never have been driven to such lengths. Angry with himself for having betrayed his wife, he almost makes a false confession of witchcraft, in one sense to punish himself for what he has done. Once Proctor controls his anger, however, he is able to act in a far more positive fashion. His ultimate refusal to go along with the confession indicates his awareness that he has a responsibility to himself and his community. He would rather hang than participate in the false judgment of others. Through Proctor and the others who die with him, Miller acknowledges the heroism of these victims in order to recognise and celebrate the existence of such personal integrity even in the bleakest of worlds.

Elizabeth Proctor

Elizabeth begins the play hurt by and suspicious of her husband, having discovered his adultery seven months before. Though Abigail has been dismissed, they have all kept the real reason secret. Elizabeth's pregnancy could be as much the result of an adherence to a religious imperative to procreate as it is an indication of a fixed and renewed relationship. Indeed, she seems to have forgiven little and is both angry and distant, even while she performs her household duties. Elizabeth's apparent acceptance of events might lead us to judge her as merely a compliant wife, but she has both spirit and strength. Elizabeth acted decisively on hearing about her husband's affair, sending Abigail away and forcing Proctor to atone. It is also Elizabeth who pushes Proctor to denounce Abigail, as she fears that Abigail might act against her. Her forceful response on hearing that Abigail's 'poppet' has set the scene for her arrest ('She must be ripped out of the world') reminds us that she, too, has the human potential for violence.

Displaying great strength of character, she stands up to Hale on a number of occasions; even her husband's response is more deferential. Hurt by Hale's accusations, she denies that good people could become agents of the Devil and announces, 'If you think that I am [a witch], then I say there are none.' Bravely, she allows herself to be taken to jail rather than cause fruitless fighting. She quietly counters both Hale and Danforth as they try to manipulate her into forcing her husband to confess and promises 'nothing'. The dry eyes that Danforth takes as signs of her unnaturalness represent her strength and understanding in the face of their inflexibility. Although her pregnancy has saved her for the time being from being hanged with the rest, she is no less firm in her refusal to confess. Her dignity is further underlined by her acceptance of her husband's decision to be hanged at the play's close. Her love for Proctor is never greater than when she allows him to die.

Elizabeth's love and respect for her husband, although it has been severely tested by his adultery, is displayed when she lies for him in front of Danforth. She is a woman of staunch faith, to whom a lie would be a cardinal sin, yet she lies to save him embarrassment or worse. In Puritan times adultery carried harsh punishment for both participants. It is ironic that it is this lie that condemns him in the eyes of the judges. Her suffering in jail causes her to reflect on her former treatment of Proctor, and in their final meeting she confesses she has been cold towards him in the past. She recognises the part she has played in driving him into the arms of Abigail, and insists on her husband's essential goodness. It is this belief that strengthens Proctor to chose a dignified death rather than an ignoble betrayal by signing his name to a false document.

Abigail Williams

In her character description we are told that Abigail has 'an endless capacity for dissembling', which should prepare us for her vagrant allegiances and ability to manipulate others. We might have sympathy for a young orphaned girl whose parents were killed in front of her, whose only relative is a self-concerned minister, who lost her virginity to an older man while still in her teens and was then tossed aside. However, given the damage she causes to others in Salem it is difficult not to view Abigail as wicked, despite the circumstances that might have led her to behave in the way she does.

In the original Salem account Abigail was only eleven years old, but Miller increased her age to allow for her affair with Proctor. Abigail is the most complex of the girls of the town who cry out against their elders. Both clever and cunning, her cynicism about the so-called respectability of the town is partly supported by the way we see them act. Her understanding of people's darker sides – she sees no one as free of corruption and selfish motivation – allows her to be very manipulative, and she can even stand up to a figure like Danforth. While Danforth is an upholder of the rules, she is the exact opposite, a total anarchist who refuses to play by any other rules.

Abigail was awakened to her sexuality by her brief affair with Proctor, and is no longer content to play the role of meek serving girl. She sees in Proctor someone who treated her as a woman rather than a childish nuisance. Her desire for him seems to transcend the physical, and she has magnified the importance he holds in her life beyond any reasonable expectation. An additional scene, which Miller wrote to feature Abigail and Proctor, shows her uneasy psychological state, a result of her irrepressible desire for Proctor. She believes she is being attacked by the spirits of those she has had convicted. She quickly recovers her stability by Act Three, as she faces up to Danforth and forces the judges to overlook Proctor's charges of her corruption by manipulating Mary to accuse him of witchcraft.

Abigail uses the town's superstitious leanings to her own advantage, to claim greater respect in the community and revenge herself upon Elizabeth, who has 'blackened' her name with her dismissal and kept her from Proctor. The way she sacrifices former friends like Tituba to the court, without care, suggests her amorality. She will turn on her beloved Proctor in an act of self-preservation, and when the possibility of rebellion arises, she quickly flees, stealing Parris's savings on the way. Her fate as a prostitute in Boston seems almost inevitable.

Reverend Samuel Parris

In his mid-forties, Reverend Parris is the current minister of Salem, and anxious to keep his post. As the third minister Salem has hired in seven years, he wants to ensure he is not so easily dismissed, and ingratiates himself with those who have power, the Putnams and Danforth. Before being ordained he had been in business in Barbados, and this worldly background dictates how he now runs his ministry, wrangling for higher pay and the deeds to his house. He has estranged honest men like John Proctor because of his materialism and concentration on negative aspects of their common religion. He preaches so much 'hellfire and bloody damnation' that people are reluctant to bring their children to church. He considers any dissension from his views as both personal persecution and an attack on the Church itself.

There is no one in the play, including the judges, who respects Parris. Danforth has little patience with him and Hathorne considers him unbalanced. As a minister of God he strikes an ungodly figure, being petulant, selfish, unmerciful and awkward in his relationships with others, especially children. A widower, he has little interest in children and is clearly at a loss as to how to treat his own daughter. Parris's first thought on learning of his daughter's bewitching is how it affects him and his standing in the community. He would be prepared, also, to condemn his niece, Abigail, rather than allow her reputation to sully his by association. He is more reticent than the Putnams in bringing forward charges of witchcraft, even withholding information about what he saw the girls doing in the woods, but this is because of his own insecurity rather than any concern over endangering innocent lives.

Despite his initial doubts, it is Parris who brings in the witchfinders to ensure he keeps people like the Putnams content. He soon becomes a staunch advocate of condemning everyone the girls name, without allowing any proper defence. Indeed, he is the first to charge any defence as an attempt to undermine the court, including Proctor's efforts to defame Abigail, about whom he had previously had strong suspicions. His treatment of his slave, Tituba, who has raised his child for him and served him for many years, is savage in the extreme; threatening to whip her to death if she does not immediately confess, which allows her little option but to do so. Her declaration that the Devil has told her to cut his throat because he is 'no goodly man' but a 'mean man and no gentle man' indicates how he has most likely treated her for much of her service. As final proof of his self-regard, Parris turns against the idea of the witch trials only when his own life is threatened and he begins to fear rebellion. He helps Hale pray with the condemned to persuade them to confess, only to prove he was right – Hale, by contrast, is trying to save lives.

Reverend John Hale

The Reverend John Hale comes from Beverly, a nearby town, where in the previous year he thought he had found a witch who cast a spell over a young girl, but this turned out to be a mere case of neglect. Nearing forty, he is well-read, and has a reputation for understanding the demonic arts, so Parris has called him to Salem to investigate the rumours of witchcraft. Hale truly believes that witches exist and he is disturbed when the Proctors express their doubts. Beginning the play as a self-regarding, even a conceited, figure, Hale " sees himself as superior to the people of Salem; he is determined to uncover the villagers' evil spirits. As the girls' accusations begin to fall upon upright members of the community, Hale's convictions are eroded by doubt.

Once set in motion, the juggernaut of the trials cannot be stopped by Hale's growing concern for truth, yet his resistance helps to expose the flaws in the judges' closed logical system when he questions their motives. In contrast to the other judges, Hale shows himself to be more rational and conscientious by honestly considering the evidence. His private interviews with Rebecca and Elizabeth convey his growing doubts, while his assurance to the Proctors that Rebecca's goodness is self-evident just before we get news of her arrest shows us how little influence he actually has. Recognising the deception of the girls, he denounces the proceedings and tries to save the victims, but soon recognises the futility of his stance. Urging people he knows are innocent to confess in order to save their lives, he becomes a lost figure, not knowing what to believe, unable to understand the Proctors' noble behaviour in provoking the court to hang a truly innocent man.

The judges

One of the judges brought in from Boston, Judge Hathorne is described as a 'bitter, remorseless' man, and he is certainly more concerned with his own power than he is with uncovering the truth. His refusal to listen to others makes him contemptible. He has chosen to believe the girls and will allow nothing to shake that belief; any evidence brought to challenge this is viewed as necessarily false. He defers to Danforth, recognising his greater power, but insists on finding those accused guilty, even if it means harassing inconvenient witnesses like Mary to undermine their credibility. Giles's comment, 'You're not a Boston judge yet, Hathorne', suggests that Hathorne is an ambitious man whose involvement here is designed to advance his career on a higher court in Boston, rather than to uncover the truth in Salem.

However contemptible Hathorne appears to be, Deputy-Governor Danforth is even worse. He is more sophisticated than his fellow judges, which makes him more dangerous. Miller has described him as the 'rule-bearer' of the play who guards boundaries strictly because he cannot cope with the potential chaos caused by free thought. He is loath to relinquish control to anyone and forcefully dominates his fellow judges. Although he listens to counter-arguments, it is not with an open mind, and when he hangs the condemned with full knowledge of their innocence we should recognise him as an evil force. He places his own reputation above innocent lives and uses religion to justify the deceit. Danforth is as intelligent and strong-willed as Proctor, and becomes his main antagonist. Unlike Proctor, however, he is unwilling to change. He is responsible for putting four hundred people in jail throughout the area and he has sentenced seventy-two of them to hang. His proud announcement of these facts to Giles suggests he enjoys power and views himself as superior to those he judges.

Judges Stoughton and Sewall are mentioned as being in the court, but we never see them on stage. In the 1996 movie version Miller gives Judge Sewall a larger role, and portrays him as one judge who is less certain that what they are doing is right; this allows for an even greater case against Danforth.

Thomas and Ann Putnam

Although one of the richest men in the town, Thomas Putnam is a sour man filled with grievances against others, that have been created mostly by his own imagination and sense of self-importance. Greedy and argumentative, Putnam is not above manipulating truth and law to his own vindictive ends, and he may even have persuaded his daughter, Ruth, to cry out against men whose lands he covets. He argues with John Proctor over who owns a tract of land bearing timber, and he has had similar arguments with many other of the town's landowners, including the Nurses. A bitter man, he has even tried to break his father's will because he disagreed with the amount that had been left to a stepbrother. This was another public failure, which has embittered him further against the town. One genuine grievance, however, is against those Salemites who stood in the way of the appointment of his wife's brother-in-law, James Bradley, to the post of minister. Bradley had been well-qualified and had a majority of votes, but a small faction within the town, including the Nurses, managed to block his selection. Putnam believes his family honour has been belittled. In revenge, Putnam arranged for the minister who obtained the post, George Burroughs, to be sent to jail for debts he had not actually owed. It is little wonder that Parris wants to keep Putnam satisfied.

Ann Putnam is no less self-absorbed and vindictive, though for a religious woman she ascribes far too much value to superstition. Like her husband, she assumes that everyone else is plotting against her. It is she who sent her daughter into the woods to persuade Tituba to conjure a spell to explain why she has lost so many children. In Salem infant mortality was high and her loss of seven babies, although unfortunate, would not have been so unusual for the period. In their self-opinionated and self-serving rectitude, the Putnams represent the worst face of Puritanism.

Giles and Martha Corey

Eighty-three years old, but still a 'powerful' man, Giles Corey is an argumentative figure who fights with his neighbours and frequently takes them to court. Proctor tells us that he paid a fine to Giles for slandering him even though he had said nothing, but they remain friends, helping each other with the harder farmwork. Unlike Putnam, who appears malicious in his dealings, Giles's wrangling makes him comic and indicates his independent spirit. Giles has the courage and strength of the pioneer stock from which he sprang. He has married Martha late in life and only then became religious, so it is little wonder he stumbles over his prayers. At heart he is a good man, and he dies for his beliefs no less bravely than John Proctor. His refusal to speak as they weigh him down with rocks until he dies means that the authorities cannot confiscate his lands as they can those charged or condemned.

His wife, Martha, whom we briefly hear offstage but never see, seems a decent woman and is clearly no witch. Her interest in books indicates a lively mind rather than allegiance to the Devil. She is charged with witchcraft by a fellow townsperson to whom she had sold a pig which later died from neglect. The man has been unable to keep pigs since, most likely for the same reasons, but takes out his frustration by blaming Martha. Several townspeople vouch for her, but they too are arrested, and since she refuses to confess to being in league with the Devil, she is hanged alongside Proctor.

Francis and Rebecca Nurse

Town elders Rebecca and Francis Nurse offer a kinder picture of Puritanism than that depicted by the Putnams. Francis Nurse is the opposite of Thomas Putnam, being a man who puts others before himself, living a truly moral life. He is genuinely shocked by Danforth's reaction to the document he has had his friends sign in support of his wife, never wanting to bring trouble on anyone else. He has been the town's unofficial judge up to this point, evidence of his probity. He never sought this position, but it has made him and his family targets for those of a jealous nature. Many of the town's older families, such as the Putnams, resent the prosperity of the Nurses, seeing them as upstarts.

Francis's wife, Rebecca, is the ideal Puritan, who lives her faith, always showing kindness and compassion to others and displaying a gentleness in her life which is rightly respected – she can calm Betty by her mere presence. It is no wonder so many Salem people risk themselves by vouching for her. But she has a powerful enemy in Ann Putnam, who is jealous that Rebecca had eleven healthy children and lots of grandchildren, while seven of her own babies died. Ann accuses her of murder, and it is a sign of the times that the court even considers such a charge. It is her arrest and conviction that lead Hale to doubt the validity of the accusations. Rebecca is rightly horrified that Proctor endangers his soul by offering false testimony and never wavers in her refusal to co-operate with the court, going to her death with the same dignity with which she has lived.

Tituba and Sarah Good

Tituba and Sarah Good confess to witchcraft rather than hang, and they are readily believed, as neither has a good reputation in the town. The first people arrested were of a similar standing, which is why Salem went along with the judges' decisions. Sarah Good is a drunkard and a vagrant, and as a foreigner who is racially different Tituba has already been judged by the township to have an allegiance to dark forces. Tituba shows more personal concern for Betty Parris than Betty's father and she seems a decent woman. Though an adult, the colour of her skin and consequent low standing in the town have made her less of a threat to the girls, and they have been more open with her than with other adults. She has used her cultural knowledge to assist their requests for potions and charms, but with no sense of any allegiance to the Devil. However, her denials fall on deaf ears as Parris and Hale treat her as if she had already confessed. It is ironic that a woman who began the play asserting her allegiance to Christianity should end calling to the Devil. It is an indication of the true nature of the trials which have driven her to this, a connection Proctor makes when he asserts, 'I hear the boot of Lucifer, I see his filthy face.'

The girls

Mercy Lewis, Susanna Walcott, Betty Parris, Ruth Putnam and Mary Warren are among the young girls who follow Abigail's lead. All have led lives of limited possibility up until this point, as they have been bullied by employers, forced to be quiet and subservient. The only freedom they have had is sneaking off to the woods with the only person in town of a lower social standing than theirs: the black slave, Tituba. We see with Mary how harsh even good people like the Proctors are with their servant girls, restricting what they can do and whipping them when they fail in their service.

Mercy seems the closest in spirit to Abigail; she goes naked in the woods and is attracted by what she sees as Proctor's masculinity. She is clearly a girl who wants more than the quiet, restricted town of Salem can offer. Abigail allows the girls a chance to be at the centre of attention and treated as special. They are attracted to the power they see themselves holding over the townspeople when they offer the judges any names they like. We see Mary grow more independent with the understanding that her employers can no longer treat her with disdain.

Each girl is drawn into the plot for slightly different reasons, though many stay involved out of fear of what Abigail might do next. Ruth Putnam is doing this for her father, so he can grab the land of the accused, but Betty and Mary are simpler souls and seem drawn in against their wills by group hysteria. Betty's initial coma indicates her timid nature, literally paralysed as she is by having been caught doing something she knows is wrong. Mary, who has been used by Abigail to implicate Elizabeth with the possession of the 'voodoo' poppet, tries to tell the truth, but she is isolated and afraid once Abigail has the other girls gang up against her. Uneasy in conflict, Mary has been from the start the weakest of the group. She only watched in the woods and was not directly involved. The fact that Proctor could break her decision not to testify against Abigail prepares us for her reversal in Act Three when she caves in to accuse Proctor of witchcraft to save herself.

Major Productions

On stage

The Crucible opened on 22 January 1953 at the Martin Beck Theater on Broadway. Despite its later success, the play's initial reception was mixed, though this might have been partly the result of its being perceived as a work critical of current politics. Although it won Tony and Donaldson Awards for Best Play, some critics were quick to condemn both play and playwright. The production only ran for 197 performances, 545 fewer than *Death of a Salesman*. After the tremendous success of *Death of a Salesman*, some critics felt let down, and saw *The Crucible* as less innovative and therefore a step backwards. Walter Kerr said it was too mechanical and overtly polemic. Eric Bentley notably attacked the play, claiming that Miller's naive liberalism and depiction of innocence reduced it to melodrama. Even Miller's staunch ally at the *New York Times*, Brooks Atkinson, had reservations, concerned that the play was 'more like a tract than a drama about people'.

There were difficulties with the initial production. Unwilling to work with Elia Kazan, because of the director's friendly testimony before HUAC, Miller had to find someone else to produce his play. Despite a reputation for being difficult, Jed Harris took on the assignment. His working relationship with Miller was strained from the start. Harris disliked Miller's choice of Arthur Kennedy to play Proctor, and demanded a series of rewrites in an unsuccessful attempt to undermine the playwright's confidence so that he might gain full control of the production. His direction of the play was static; characters made speeches to the audience rather than to each other and Harris kept them frozen in tableaux while speaking their lines. This approach made critics view the play as cold and unemotional. After the initial reviews, Harris withdrew from the production and left Miller to try to salvage the show. Miller tightened the script and added a new scene at the close of the second act between Proctor and Abigail, recycled from an earlier draft of the play. Yet the New York production never captured the play's momentum.

In 1958 the Martinique Theatre was built out of an old hotel ballroom. The arena stage that resulted allowed for *The Crucible* to be presented in the round, which instantly made it more accessible. Henry Hewes felt it had 'more emotional impact' than the original Broadway production, and Lewis Funke admired its 'absorbing vitality', describing it as 'provocative' and 'stimulating'. Atkinson changed his mind about the play, praising its more vibrant staging, fluent pacing and the way the characters were presented with admirable modulation. Utilising moody lighting, Word Baker kept a fast directorial pace by having his actors change props.

Miller wrote additional background information inserted into the first act. Though rarely included in performances since, these notes were read aloud by an additional character, the Reader. Baker also placed a strong focus on Proctor, played with simplicity and vigour by Michael Higgins, making the role more clearly the play's centre. After several extensions, the production ran for 653 performances, proving the play's theatrical strength.

The play's emotional plot was nowhere better suggested than in Robert Ward's 1961 operatic version. Commissioned by the Ford Foundation for the New York City Opera, Ward was inspired by the 1958 Off-Broadway show. Drawn by what he saw as Miller's stylised rhetoric and a strong plot he felt was well-suited to the compression of a libretto, Ward persuaded an initially reluctant Miller to agree to this adaptation. Bernard Stambler's libretto cut a third of Miller's text, but changed very little of the play's essential nature. It eliminated Herrick and Hathorne, added more girls and a prison guard, and compressed the time-scale. Using a split-level set allowed individual singers to play key scenes above the chorus of townspeople, and it gave them greater prominence. The operatic format heightened its theatrical intensity, and Frank Merling suggested that 'the score adds something to the story: a non-topical sense of the development of the greatness of the human spirit'. John Rockwell would later call it 'one of the most powerfully affecting of all America's operas, capitalizing on the play's strength and adding a striking musical subtext'. Winthrop Sargeant declared it a 'smash hit' and a worthwhile occasion for 'thunderous and heartfelt applause'. It won a Pulitzer Prize for music in 1962.

Ten years later the Repertory Theater of Lincoln Center had a hit production, directed by John Berry. He was the first to emphasise the play's sexual rivalry and suggest sympathy for Abigail – perhaps a reflection of changing mores – as well as revealing contemporary connections to concerns about authority and truth during the Vietnam War. Pamela Payton-Wright's Abigail was portrayed as genuinely loving Proctor and highly aggrieved by his rejection, while Robert Foxworth's Proctor, spoken with a British North Country accent, became a representative of the working class when he spoke against the pompous magistrates and greedy landowners. Harold Clurman praised the 'unity' of the production and Clive Barnes its 'moral force' and 'great dramatic impact'.

Staged by Jo Mielziner, who designed the original set for *Death of a Salesman*, audiences saw a virtually empty stage on which projections and light changes were used to indicate the scene. The decision had been partly induced by the Center's need for a frugal production; they could not afford expensive sets and asked Mielziner to use existing lighting from a previous production. Mary Henderson describes Mielziner's stylised design as using only a few items of furniture and props, which were made slightly overscale to dwarf the characters and make them look like 'human pawns in a larger tragic game'. Set against two sloping planes that came to a point at the back, the concept allowed for greater focus on the actors. Emphasising Miller's references to light in the play, Mielziner lit Betty's bedroom from the outside. At the close of Act Two the cast appeared on the forestage singing a hymn, while an eerie light shone from below to suggest the flames of hell this community had unleashed. Act Three utilised a barred wooden partition through which light could stream over the magistrate's desk and oversized chair, as well as over the forestage where the accused would stand. In the final act Mielziner placed a large barred window high on the right wall to cast additional shafts of light across the entire stage.

After numerous Off-Broadway and regional productions, the play's fifth Broadway revival in 2002 emphasised the relationship between the Proctors rather than that between Proctor and Abigail and cast major stars – Liam Neeson and Laura Linney – in these roles. Directed by Richard Eyre, it won a Tony for Best Revival and several other nominations. The stars dominated the show, but this offered an interesting take on the Proctors' relationship. Neeson and Linney portrayed a more evident sexual relationship than usual, with Proctor purposefully stripping off his shirt to wash himself in front of his wife, while she struggled to control her emotional responses towards him. In this production Angela Bettis's Abigail was decidedly unsexy, played as a sullen teen. Though this made Proctor's adultery less credible, it focused the production on how a problematic marriage survives.

There have been just as many laudable British productions. The first, in 1954 at Bristol Old Vic, like the Broadway premiere, garnered mixed reviews and was considered melodramatic. But when Laurence Olivier directed Colin Blakely as Proctor at the Old Vic in 1965, the play, featuring strong ensemble acting, was well received by British critics. It raised the production above charges of melodrama. Though interested in the play's sexual themes and the relationship between Proctor and Abigail, Olivier deleted the additional scene between them in order to respect the rising dynamic of the play. Robert Brustein, who had originally disliked the play, felt that under Olivier it took 'on some of the proportions of a Shakespearian tragedy'. For Brustein, the English country accents of the cast gave the dialogue both vigour and authority.

In 1980 *The Crucible* was produced in the National Theatre's smaller theatre, the Cottesloe. Directed by Bill Bryden, with Mark McManus as Proctor, it garnered positive reviews and transferred to the Comedy Theatre in 1981. The National produced the play again, this time in its large Olivier Theatre, just ten years later, with Tom Wilkinson in the role of Proctor. This volatile production, directed by Howard Davies, received mixed reviews but had a generally positive response from large audiences. With fast pacing and strong acting, Davies tried to draw audiences into the group hysteria and make them feel the intensity of the domestic situation. In between the National productions, there was also a much lionised and fervent production at the Young Vic in 1985 directed by David Thacker, who would go on to direct the British premieres of several of Miller's later plays. Thacker paid close attention to individual characterisations and produced a finely detailed piece that Matt Wolf praised for 'bringing this drama's contemporary reverberations thrillingly, ringingly alive'.

Britain's 2006 revival at the Royal Shakespeare Company, on the main stage in Stratford, transferred to the West End to win the Olivier Award for Best Revival. The director Dominic Cooke also saw Shakespearean dimensions in the play and its relevance to a post-9/11 society in which politicians exploited public fear to destroy civil liberties and create scapegoats. The *Guardian* said that Cooke brought out 'the play's political urgency' and praised Iain Glen's Proctor as 'a figure of Lawrentian power and sensuality' pitted against Elaine Cassidy's Abigail, who was 'not the usual diabolical nymphet, but a young girl whose sexual stirrings find no outlet in this community'. This allowed Abigail to be as much a victim as those put on trial, a reflection, no doubt, of increased feminist awareness.

Hildegard Bechtler's set design for this production was faithful to the period but extremely austere, in order to focus attention on the actors and reflect the simplicity of the Puritan world. The production began with a view of the woods, eerily lit, before the back wall closed to form Betty's sparse bedroom. The trees remained visible through a large rear window in order to emphasise the ever-threatening mysteries faced by the early settlers. The courtroom scene emulated Mielziner's 1972 design, shooting shafts of light through high-barred windows on to the opposing wall. At the play's close the wall again parted as the condemned were led out into the woods to be hanged. This gave the impression of a lynching rather than anything resembling a regulated judicial system. The *Daily Telegraph* described this interpretation as a 'shatteringly powerful production that never releases its grip for a moment'.

On film

In 1957 the first film of Miller's play was produced in France, with a screenplay by the writer and philosopher Jean-Paul Sartre. He depicted the play as a conflict between capitalists and heroic Marxists. Retitled *Les Sorcières de Salem*, or *The Witches of Salem*, Miller felt that the

Marxist references Sartre included were too heavy-handed. Most critics agreed. Directed by Raymond Borderie and starring Yves Montand and Simone Signoret, the film met mixed reviews. Bosley Crowther called it a 'persistently absorbing film' with 'outstanding performances', while Stanley Kauffmann noted that Sartre's emphasis on socialist political agitation distorted the drama. In *Time* magazine Isabel Quigly saw the film as both forbidding and insightful, but sadly an 'appalling politically pointed tale' that missed the mark by identifying 'the witch burners as colonial capitalists and the hero as a son of the suffering masses'.

There have been several television versions of the play, including two in 1959: the Canadian Broadcasting Corporation production with Leslie Nielsen and Diana Maddox, and another by Granada TV in England, with Sean Connery and Susannah York. Alex Segal directed a version for CBS in 1967 with George C. Scott, but Jack Gould felt it lacked tension and seemed 'cold and remote'. None of these versions was highly acclaimed, although they served to introduce the play to a large number of viewers. More successful was Louis Marks' 1982 production for BBC television, which portrayed Proctor as a 'damaged man' who rises against injustice.

The film version of *The Crucible* with which Miller was most closely involved – and for which he rewrote scenes, added others and streamlined the rhetoric – was made in 1996 for Twentieth-Century Fox. While fastidious attention was paid to making the setting and costumes authentic, a national controversy contemporary with the film's production was the sexual scandal of President Clinton; this version emphasises the play's accent on the hypocrisy of religious zealots and the dangers of sexual repression and the political chaos to which this can lead. Such emphasis took it away from its increasingly less-known 1950s roots, but in the eyes of many critics made it more accessible. Directed by Nicholas Hytner, it starred Winona Ryder, Joan Allen, and Daniel Day Lewis. The sexual aspects of the story are evident from the opening sequence, one in which we see a group of Salem girls make love charms with Tituba in order to catch husbands for themselves. Sex is on everyone's mind, but it is something that can only be discussed in the dark woods. Abigail is teased by her friends for wanting Proctor, and Tituba objects to making a charm to bind a married man. Abigail's wild response is to smear her face with chicken blood and incite the girls into a raucous and sensual dance. The sexual tension between Proctor and Abigail is insistent from their first appearance together and continues in each subsequent encounter.

As a teenager passionately and fatally in love with a married man, the role of Abigail is presented with sympathy. When she and Proctor first talk together, their mutual attraction is evident. Proctor is clearly resisting temptation and trying to calm the fire between them. When Abigail kisses and gropes him, he lingers before turning away. Their second meeting takes place earlier in the timeline, before Elizabeth has even been charged, with Proctor asking Abigail not to name his wife. This acts as a goad for Abigail, the thwarted lover, to do just that. Before she leaves town near the close, Abigail visits Proctor in his chains and begs him to go with her, declaring 'I never dreamed any of this for you. I wanted you, that is all.' He refuses, saying they can only meet again in hell, where he sees both heading as a consequence of their past adultery. Yet Miller seems to want the audience to view the coupling of Proctor and Abigail more sympathetically. Proctor is depicted as a man caught between two passions, and his dealings with Abigail have been something more than mere casual sex.

Another major change is the addition of Judge Sewell, who offers a voice of reason. He warns the others from the start against the possibility of madness in their witnesses and therefore becomes a counterpoint to Danforth's stern insistence. Sewell wonders about the number of children involved, recognises the land-grabbing truth behind Putnam's accusations, and is uncertain about the accusations from the very first hanging. However, Danforth has a superior authority and dismisses his concerns, bullying him into compliance. Danforth seems less the rule-bearer than egoist; he thinks he knows best, demanding full control. When Abigail, worried that Hale might be about to interfere, accuses Hale's wife, Danforth refuses to listen, insisting she is mistaken because a minister's wife is inviolable.

The film shows the Salemites celebrating as the first group is hanged, but their hysteria dies down as the presence of death begins to pall. We see them beginning to spurn Abigail, provoking her departure, and when the time comes to hang Proctor, alongside Rebecca and Martha, the townspeople are far less enthusiastic. Several call 'God bless you' to the gallows as they pass, and they stand watching silently, weeping in disbelief as the three are hanged. Rebecca begins to recite the Lord's Prayer and Martha and Proctor join in for the closing 'for ever and ever'. But no one says 'Amen' as the film cuts to a tight shot on the hanging rope. This ending underlines who the godless truly are and it is little wonder that no one who witnesses the executions can sign off on the central prayer of their faith. Significantly, in this trinity of death, Proctor is central, thus reinforcing his connection to a beleaguered Christ, one made earlier in the film by his crucifixion pose when he is first arrested. Richard A. Blake saw the film 'as an incisive examination of the human condition', and Edward Guthmann as 'at once stunningly cinematic and perfectly faithful to Miller's text'. Jay Carr praised the film, announcing the drama to be 'more electrifying than ever, boldly focusing as much on repressed sexuality as on political paranoia and conflagration'.

Notes

The notes below explain words and phrases from the play, with page numbers referencing the Student Editions published by Bloomsbury Methuen Drama.

page

5   *An Overture*: in the original production Miller called Act One 'The Prologue' and did not start numbering the acts until the one that features Elizabeth and Proctor at home together. Both 'Prologue' and 'Overture' convey Miller's intent in this initial act to paint the social background against which the events of this play take place, as that is integral to what we witness. Just as in a musical overture, this act contains all of the refrains we will later hear repeated in the play: elements of materialism, superstition, selfish behaviour, insecurity and frustration that will combine to create the unfolding events. Given a different society, these atrocities could not have taken place, which is partly Miller's point.

5   *air of clean spareness*: Miller wishes to convey the austerity of Puritan culture. These are not necessarily evil people, but they are people who have reduced their lives to a spartan existence. It is a 'spareness' against which many in the township have begun to rebel, including the Reverend Parris himself with his desire for gold candlesticks and the deeds to his house.

5   *meeting house*: this was a large building at the centre of the town that was built collectively and paid for by the township. It was used for both religious worship and town business.

6   *would not have permitted anyone to read a novel if one were handy*: the town of Salem had a very restrictive outlook on what was considered proper behaviour. Little in the way of entertainment was condoned; reading, music and dance were all frowned upon. This is why Martha Corey's reading habit is considered to be suspicious and why even the idea that the girls had been dancing in the woods is scandalous, whether or not they were wearing any clothes.

6   *potent cider*: while the Puritans punished drunkenness, they were not against drinking alcohol in moderation, and actually considered alcohol a gift from God.

6	*time of the armed camp had almost passed*: the area at the mouth of the Naumkeag River was first settled in 1626 by a group of fishermen and became known as Salem in 1629. While the threat of an Indian attack had been there from the outset, given that they were settling on Native American lands, Salem had been relatively free from outside aggression, although people who came there from other settlements had been less fortunate. By the 1690s many townships had learned to exist peaceably with their indigenous neighbours. Fighting in Salem was mostly of a financial nature and was internally driven.
7	*parochial*: literally, of a parish, which would be a limited area, and here refers to the narrow-mindedness of those who live in Salem.
7	*been persecuted in England*: Puritanism was a Protestant movement that developed in England during the late 1500s. It called for a stronger commitment to Jesus Christ and greater levels of personal holiness. Objecting to what they felt was the growing decadence of the established Church in England, Puritans campaigned for social and political reform. Under Charles I, who had strong Catholic sympathies, Puritans were heavily persecuted and many fled to the American colonies. Charles's abusive suppression was a major factor leading to the English Civil War of the 1640s.
7	*But Virginia destroyed them*: Jamestown, Virginia, had been settled in 1607, but suffered from disease and starvation in its early years, as well as being victim of an Indian massacre in 1622 that killed 347 colonists. While the colony survived, it was not without great cost.
7	*autocracy*: a form of government in which one person has absolute power, to which everyone else defers. This is why Salem allows Danforth and his judges to make decisions for them, as they live in a culture in which obedience is encouraged.
7	*dedicated folk that arrived on the Mayflower*: a hundred and one Puritans had boarded *The Mayflower* in 1620 to escape persecution in England and to create their own society in which they would be free to live according to their religious beliefs. The passage took them a difficult sixty-five days, and they spent a month finding a suitable place to settle once they arrived, which they called Plymouth. Half of the colonists died within six months of the landing, and life in Plymouth was far more precarious than it was for the people in Salem more than seventy years later.

8   *a revolution had unseated the royal government and substituted
       a junta*: provoked by the oppressive rule of Charles I, whose
       religious and political aspirations were cause for alarm, in 1642
       the English Civil War broke out between Parliamentarians (on
       whose side the Puritans fought) and Royalists (who supported the
       monarchy). A series of conflicts took place during which Charles
       I was beheaded; the leader of the Parliamentarian forces, Oliver
       Cromwell, set up a Protectorate to rule what was now called
       the Commonwealth of England, but was in effective a military
       dictatorship. Cromwell died in 1658 and the resultant slide toward
       anarchy led to the re-establishment of the monarchy in 1660, with
       Charles II as the king, although with restricted powers.

8   *developed from a paradox*: this paradox, meaning something
       that appears contradictory but could be true, informs much
       of Miller's work. Here it is created by the tension between
       individual freedom and social responsibility. Both seem
       necessary; yet on the surface they appear to be in opposition.
       Miller's solution, as he suggests further on in the paragraph, is to
       find a 'balance . . . between order and freedom'.

9   *Lucifer*: the angel who led a rebellion against God and was cast
       out of Heaven with his supporters, to live in Hell, becoming the
       Devil.

9   *Negro slave*: the Puritans were not against slavery, seeing it as
       mandated by God. They were actively involved in the slave
       trade, taking both Africans and Native Americans they captured
       to the West Indies, and then bringing the more experienced and
       docile slaves to mainland America for work as servants. Tituba is
       one such slave who has been brought by Parris from Barbados,
       where he had previously worked.

9   *no longer bear to be barred from the sight of her beloved*: Tituba
       appears to care for Betty Parris, a detail that both highlights the
       father's insensibility and makes this character more sympathetic,
       even after she has been badgered into confessing herself a witch.

9   *be hearty*: be healthy.

9   *God help me!*: this indicates Parris's self-regard, as he should be
       praying for his ailing daughter but he is more concerned about
       how these events will affect his standing in the community.

10   *speak nothing of unnatural causes*: things unnatural are
       considered the realm of evil and the Devil, as anything that
       comes from God is part of nature and the natural way. Parris
       is fearful that his daughter's condition might be seen as devil's
       work; his reputation will be tainted by his family connection.

11   *you have not opened with me*: you have not told me the whole
      truth.

11   *There is a faction that is sworn to drive me from my pulpit*: the
      paranoia of Parris is depicted throughout the play and leads him
      to ally himself with whomever he feels is in power. Here he
      reveals a belief that there is a group of people in the township
      who are actively plotting to remove him from his ministry. Less
      a religious figure than a political entity, his presence in Salem is
      as divisive as it should be healing, given his profession.

12   *I cannot blink what I saw*: I cannot pretend that I did not see
      what I saw.

12   *it is entirely white, is it not?*: as in 'free from moral impurity'.
      In the kind of judgmental society Salem has become, one's
      reputation, or good name, is very important. Parris suspects that
      his unmarried niece, Abigail, may not be a virgin or, at the very
      least, does not always behave as properly as she should.

13   *Goody Proctor*: the term 'Goody', a contraction of 'goodwife',
      was used within this society's lower social level, in the same
      sense as we use Mrs today.

13   *How high did she fly*: determined to find scandal, Ann Putnam is
      convinced that Betty has flown, as all witches were suspected of
      being able to do.

14   *It is a providence*: related to the care and guidance of God,
      Putnam uses the term 'providence' to mean a 'godsend', literally,
      'it is fortunate'. Putnam feels that God has alerted them to the
      presence of witches in time for the town to do something to
      control their presence.

14   *forked and hoofed*: as in the pitchfork and cloven feet of the
      Devil.

15   *George Burroughs*: historically, George Burroughs, a former
      minister of Salem, was accused of witchcraft in the trials and
      hanged.

16   *I have laid seven babies unbaptized in the earth*: Puritans
      generally practised infant baptism. This was usually performed
      the first Sunday after birth, but Ann Putnam's children evidently
      did not live long enough to have the ceremony performed. It was
      common for Puritan women to be pregnant up to twenty-five
      times, especially as large families were strongly encouraged.
      Many infants would not survive, however.

16   *Tituba knows how to speak to the dead*: while Tituba declares
      herself to be a God-fearing Christian, given her colour and
      Barbados background, it is assumed by the townspeople that she

must dabble in some kind of witchcraft. The suggestion is that she has knowledge of voodoo, with its charms and powers of conjuring to raise spirits from the dead.

18   *Aye, mum*: 'Yes, madam'.

18   *If she starts for the window*: indicating a fear she might try to fly.

19   *What a grand peeping courage you have*: Mercy is pointing out that while Mary was too frightened to participate, she did not mind watching others perform the rituals.

20   *bring a pointy reckoning*: Abigail is threatening revenge if anyone dares to tell the truth of what the girls were doing in the woods.

20   *I have seen some reddish work done at night*: Abigail is connected to darkness and evil from the start, having experienced the deaths of her parents in an Indian attack. The colour red is used in the play to denote both death and sexual sin, both of which taint Abigail.

21   *calumny*: when someone makes false statements with malicious intent. Proctor is so marked because of his bluntness, which has offended people like Putnam and Parris and made them resentful.

21   *I'll show you a great doin' on your arse one of these days*: Proctor is threatening to beat her; one in a series of physical threats that are considered acceptable against a servant girl.

21   *strangely titillated*: though fearful of Proctor's manly strength, Mercy has a sexual response to his threat of violence. This shows her own secret urges in a restrictive society and her inability to suppress them.

22   *clapped in the stocks*: the stocks were wooden frames used for punishment. They were set up in a public place and held the culprit immobile by the feet or head and arms. Abuse and rubbish was then thrown at him or her.

23   *I may have looked up*: in this admission, Proctor could be confessing feelings for Abigail.

23   *You are no wintry man*: cold and without feeling.

23   *I know you*: Abigail means this in both the biblical sense, in that they have had sexual relations, and that she feels she knows what Proctor is really like as a person.

23   *We never touched Abby*: he is not denying they slept together but asserting that they should both act as if they never did.

24   *took me from my sleep and put knowledge in my heart*: a sleep of innocence from which she has woken up after she has had such an intense sexual experience with Proctor. She feels that the

township's rule against sex out of wedlock is wrong and unfairly restrictive.

25   *a prodigious sign*: in the sense of ominous.

26   *a charge that had more truth in it than Mrs Putnam could know*: the real iniquities to which Ann Putnam falls prey are her jealousy of Rebecca and her desire to make others a scapegoat for her losses.

26   *their silly seasons*: unexplainable but natural behaviour of children.

27   *My Ruth is bewildered*: in the sense of acting unnaturally because she is bewitched, rather than simply confused.

27   *This society will not be a bag to swing around your head*: Proctor asserts himself and warns Putnam that he will not allow him to manipulate the township for his own benefit.

27   *This will set us to arguin' again in the society and we thought to have peace this year*: Salem has evidently been a highly divided society for some time and has a history of grievances among its townspeople. It will be these grievances that feed the fire of the accusations.

28   *There are wheels within wheels in this village, and fires within fires*: these words convey Ann Putnam's belief that there are conspiracies in the village. Indeed, there are, but they seem to be caused by such people as the Putnams rather than created against them.

28   *We vote by name in this society not by acreage*: Proctor wants to live in a democratic community in which everyone has equal say, no matter how much property they own. There are others in town who think differently.

28   *many that quail to bring their children*: parents are fearful that Parris's sermons are too upsetting for their children, with his constant emphasis on sin and damnation. Puritan ministers could sometimes speak for up to four hours, and no one was allowed to leave or fall asleep.

29   *There is either obedience or the church will burn*: for Parris religion is not sustained through faith and caring for others, but through complete, unquestioning obedience.

30   *What, are we Quakers?*: in contrast to a strict Puritan society in which the minister held sway, the Quakers were more egalitarian, encouraging their members to experience spirituality on an individual level. They generally had a greater commitment to tolerance.

32   *beyond our ken*: outside of our knowledge.

33 *the necessity of the Devil may become evident as a weapon*:
    Miller asserts that the concept of the Devil is a human construct
    used in order to threaten people into behaving as the Church
    dictates.

33 *Inquisition*: from the twelfth century, the Catholic Church
    investigated heresy through the Inquisition, a body of monks and
    clerics who used torture to extract confessions. Heretics were
    burned to death at the stake.

33 *Luther*: Martin Luther (1483–1546) was the German theologian
    who initiated the Protestant Reformation.

33 *Erasmus*: Desiderius Erasmus (1466/9–1538) was a Dutch
    humanist and theologian. He steered a middle course over
    Reformation and was criticised by both Protestants and Catholics.

33 *the children of a history which still sucks at the Devil's teats*:
    Miller understood how modern society used the same technique
    of demonising anyone who did not agree with those in control
    in order to negate their influence. At the time he was writing
    the play this was a reference both to how communists viewed
    capitalists and how communists were being viewed and treated
    in the capital-driven United States. Both sides tended to set their
    political beliefs at a moral level, so to take an opposing stance
    would be equated to allying oneself with the Devil.

33 *succubi*: the plural for succubus, a female demon believed to
    have sexual intercourse with men while they were asleep.

34 *while there were no witches then, there are Communists and
    capitalists now*: Miller asserts that while there were people in
    Salem who probably called on the powers of the Devil, he never
    believed the Devil or real witches were involved. His play draws
    a sharp analogy between witch trials and the HUAC hearings.
    His disgust at HUAC was over the rationale behind the hearings,
    which to his mind unfairly demonised and destroyed those who
    might have been – or were – connected to communism.

34 *klatches*: informal social gatherings.

34 *Dionysiac*: Dionysus, the god of wine in Greek mythology, was
    noted for his drunken revels.

35 *yeomanry*: the common class who owned and cultivated their
    own land. Hale sees himself, with all of his book learning, as
    superior to the farming community that largely made up Salem.

38 *ncubi*: the plural for incubus, a male demon believed to have
    sexual intercourse with women while they were asleep.

40 *Perhaps some bird invisible to others comes to you*: witches
    were believed to be served by animal-shaped spirits. Hale

suggests an invisible bird, which Abigail uses later in the play to undercut Mary's testimony.

40   *In nomine Domini Sabaoth suifiliique ite ad infernos*: Latin for 'In the name of the Lord Sabaoth and of his son, depart to hell.' Hale calls on God and Christ to exorcise whatever evil spirit is afflicting Betty.

40   *any living thing in the kettle*: any cooking pot would be referred to as a kettle, and Hale's concern is that the girls were making a witches' potion in which living things were commonly placed.

41   *She makes me drink blood*: Abigail is connected to blood throughout the play, indicating her sexuality as well as the danger she represents to others. Betty tells us earlier that Abigail willingly drank blood as part of a charm to get rid of Elizabeth, and we know that her accusation here is calculated to divert attention from her own misdoings onto Tituba. Tituba, who has clearly had a trusting relationship with Abigail, is evidently upset by her betrayal.

42   *I don't truck with no Devil*: to 'truck' means to have dealings with or to be in league with someone, the double negative suggesting her lack of education rather than any affirmation.

44   *Did you ever see Sarah Good with him? Or Osburn?*: the interrogator puts words and ideas into the mouth of the interrogated, suggesting who is truly responsible for what happens. It is not the people who do the naming but those who cause the names to be spoken.

46   *The marshal, I'll call the marshal!*: it is Abigail who calls in the arm of the law to collect the people they name, suggesting how much control she has already acquired.

47   *takes a pinch of salt, and drops it in the pot*: a simple gesture that illustrates Proctor's dissatisfaction with his wife through his dissatisfaction with her cooking. He salts the stew behind her back, and then compliments her on it being well-seasoned, which also carries an implication of his ability to dissemble as well as his wish to please her.

48   *It's winter in here yet*: Proctor feels that his wife has been giving him the cold shoulder long enough for his lapse with Abigail.

50   *where she walks the crowd will part like the sea for Israel*: a reference to the biblical exodus, when the Jews fled from Egypt and Moses parted the sea for them to cross and make their escape. The image emphasises Abigail's power, as she takes on a prophet-like status in this religious community.

51   *You were alone with her?*: more evidence that Proctor does
      not tell his wife the full truth, albeit to forestall her suspicions.
      Instead, it makes her all the more suspicious.

52   *your justice would freeze beer*: Elizabeth is associated with
      images of frigidity throughout the play, and here Proctor accuses
      her of judging him too rigidly and destroying all possibility of
      pleasure.

53   *my wife not wholly well*: Elizabeth has been unwell for some
      time; partly the reason why they employed Abigail to help in the
      house. This might also be a reason Proctor turned to Abigail for
      sexual gratification.

53   *poppet*: archaic term for a small handmade doll. It was believed
      that witches used these to torture victims or make them sick by
      sticking pins into them.

53   *not Sarah Good. For Sarah Good confessed*: the irony of the
      witchtrials was that those who confessed were allowed to live on
      in jail, while those who refused to confess or denied the charges
      were found guilty and hanged. With such logic it is little wonder
      that it was near impossible to escape suspicion once named.

54   *Why I never heard you mention that before*: Elizabeth's comment
      is to assure us that what Mary is describing is a complete
      fabrication, however much Mary believes it to be true.

55   *commandments*: according to the Hebrew Bible, the Ten
      Commandments were a list of moral imperatives given by God
      to Moses. They later became part of Christian teaching.

56   *But she's safe, thank God, for they'll not hurt the innocent child*:
      not wishing to kill an innocent child, the court would not hang
      a woman known to be pregnant, but rather incarcerate her until
      after the baby was born.

56   *I would have you speak civilly to me, from this out*: Mary asserts
      authority over her employers here, given the status she has
      gained from being an official of the court. The comment also
      allows us to understand how poorly these young girls were
      usually treated by their employers.

57   *There is a promise made in any bed*: Elizabeth here seems more
      astute than her husband, recognising that when a man sleeps
      with a girl it engenders a relationship between them that cannot
      be easily ignored by either party.

59   *The promise that a stallion gives a mare I gave that girl*: Proctor
      sees his marital lapse as a bestial act without rational intent.
      The imagery here suggests his self-disgust as he compares his
      coupling with Abigail to the action of beasts in the field.

59   *She has an arrow in you yet, John Proctor*: Elizabeth believes
      that her husband still has feelings for Abigail, the arrow being a
      reference to that which Cupid fires into lovers' hearts. Given the
      extent of his guilt and the way he spoke to Abigail earlier in the
      play, she could be right, but he is clearly determined to fight this
      attraction and respect his marriage vows.

61   *Twenty-six time in seventeen month*: despite having farms to run,
      Puritans were expected to attend lengthy church services with
      the whole family every Sabbath, and so going to church less
      than twice a month would have been frowned upon by the entire
      community. The fact that Parris keeps an attendance record
      speaks of his petty nature and desire for control.

62   *there is a softness in your record*: meaning it is lax or negligent.
      The word choice also implies that it is preferable in this culture
      to be hard and rigid.

63   *Adultery, John*: it is significant that the single commandment that
      Proctor cannot recall is the one of which he is guilty of having
      broken.

65   *such a woman that never lied, and cannot*: an example of
      dramatic irony, as it will be Elizabeth's lie to save her husband's
      reputation that leads to his arrest.

65   *bound to Satan*: in service to.

67   *if Rebecca Nurse be tainted*: literally morally corrupt. The
      accusations against the kindly Rebecca seem to be what most
      cause Hale to doubt what is happening in Salem, especially after
      he has questioned her privately.

67   *an hour before the Devil fell, God thought him beautiful in
      Heaven*: refers to the belief that the Devil was originally one of
      God's favourite angels, but he was cast out of heaven for trying
      to rebel.

71   *Abby sat beside me when I made it*: suggests that Abigail
      has used her knowledge of the poppet to cast suspicion on
      Elizabeth.

72   *as clean as God's fingers*: pure or perfect, in the way that all
      parts of God were considered flawless.

72   *Pontius Pilate*: the Roman governor who could have prevented
      Christ's crucifixion but decided to wash his hands of the
      business and let others make the decision. Proctor feels that Hale
      has authority to intervene, but by allowing the courts to pass
      judgment is giving up responsibility.

74   *Think on cause, man, and let you help me discover it*: another
      example of dramatic irony, as Hale unwittingly provokes

Proctor's guilt over his adultery, thus making him feel the more responsible for the accusations taking place.

75   *God's icy wind, will blow!*: the Puritan God was not a kind and forgiving one, but a stern figure of justice. Proctor feels his own guilt deeply; realising that he cannot hide what he has done from God, he knows he will face punishment.

76   *the reading of fortunes*: even such apparently innocent activities as this were considered by strict Puritans to be the pastime of the Devil.

77   *Are you gone daft, Corey?*: the term in its historical context 150 The Crucible has a stronger connotation, implying insanity rather than foolishness.

78   *I have broke charity with the woman*: Giles feels that his questions about his wife's reading habits have brought these charges on her, and that he has betrayed her.

78   *in proper affidavit*: Danforth is a stickler for rules and expects Giles to submit what he wants to say in a formal, written statement that has been signed by someone who is authorised to administer oaths.

80   *I accept no depositions*: a deposition was a statement given under oath, but intended to be read aloud in court without the witness having to be present. Danforth's refusal indicates his suspicion that Proctor is trying to undermine his court, but also that he might prefer a live witness whom he can bully into submission if he dislikes what they say.

83   *He plow on Sunday*: Puritans were expected to keep the Sabbath holy and do no work from sundown the evening before through the whole of the Sabbath day. Most of that day would be spent in prayer.

83   *Cain were an upright man, and yet he did kill Abel*: the Book of Genesis relates how the previously devout Cain killed his brother Abel. It is unclear as to his motive, although jealousy is implied, as God had shown favouritism towards Abel.

83   *she is pregnant*: this means that they will not hang Elizabeth until after the baby is born, but also that, despite Proctor's adultery, he and his wife have resumed sexual relations.

84   *These are my friends, their wives are also accused*: despite being offered his wife's life for the time being, Proctor cannot back down. He feels responsibility towards his neighbours because his sin has partly caused these events.

86   *remember what the angel Raphael said to the boy Tobias*: Tobit suffered much for his good deeds and was blinded in an accident.

The angel Raphael assists Tobit's son Tobias in finding a cure for his father who has been a godly man and does not deserve to suffer. Proctor uses the angel's words to bolster Mary's resolve: however much she might fear doing the right thing, no harm will result.

91   *proof so immaculate*: Hale is asking for a higher standard of evidence than this court has so far required. He is beginning to doubt the unsubstantiated claims that have led him to agree that seventy-two people be hanged.

91   *for a man of such terrible learning you are most bewildered*: Danforth mocks Hale by pointing out that someone who has read so much should be less uncertain. He sees himself, with his unswerving determination, as the superior judge.

91   *ipso facto*: literally, as the result of a particular fact.

91   *Unless you doubt my probity?*: probity in the sense of absolute moral correctness. Danforth asks this rhetorically; he does not expect any dissent on the matter.

92–3   *you are either lying now, or you were lying in court, and in either case you have committed perjury and you will go to jail for it*: Danforth's harsh treatment of Mary indicates his reluctance to believe her. His words are meant to intimidate her into backing down rather than to elicit the truth.

93   *a very augur bit will now be turned into your souls*: an augur is a type of drill, and the image Danforth conjures up is a violent representation of how forcefully he intends to question them.

94   *We are here, Your Honour, precisely to discover what no one has ever seen*: the internal contradiction of Parris's words is an indication of his intrinsic foolishness.

95   *It is not a child*: Proctor's pronoun use indicates his disdain for Abigail; he no longer views her as human.

99   *a cold wind, has come*: Abigail's words echo Proctor's prediction from Act Two, connecting the couple and suggesting that their mutual sin is instrumental in these events.

100   *I have known her*: in the biblical sense, had sexual intercourse with her.

100   *In the proper place – where my beasts are bedded*: again Proctor describes his past relationship with Abigail in bestial terms.

101   *I have made a bell of my honor! I have rung the doom of my good name*: Proctor is pointing out that, having made such a public confession, his own reputation is ruined along with that of Abigail. Puritans viewed adultery as a capital offence for both the man and woman as they held marriage to be one of the highest sacraments.

103   *it is a natural lie to tell*: Hale asks them to consider that
Elizabeth has lied in order to save her husband's reputation,
but Danforth insists they take Proctor at his word that his wife
cannot lie, an ironic stance given that he next calls Proctor a
liar.

104   *Why do you come, yellow bird?*: while Abigail might have
got the idea of seeing a bird from Hale's earlier comments,
the choice of yellow as the colour has led some to wonder if
Miller intended this as an oblique reference to a 1947 Tennessee
Williams short story, entitled 'Yellow Bird'. Alma, the heroine
of this tale, is the daughter of a minister and descendant of
a woman who had been hanged as a witch during the Salem
witch trials. Her ancestor was reputed to have a yellow bird,
which attacked her enemies. During a long sermon given by
Alma's pompous father, she sees this bird and it inspires her to
embrace a life of drinking and sexual pleasure. If the allusion
is intentional it is clearly ironic, connecting Abigail to both a
witch and a hedonist. In the transcripts of the actual examination
of Tituba, she speaks of having seen a little yellow bird as a
familiar of the devil.

106   *They're gulling you, Mister*: Proctor recognises this is a trick
to discredit Mary and calls it such. The fact that he refers to
Danforth as 'Mister', rather than 'Your Honour', is a sign of his
bluntness and refusal to see any man as his superior, as well as
his disdain for Danforth's authority, especially when it is based
on what he views as foolish beliefs.

107   *as though infected*: Hathorne had earlier asked Mary to show
him how the girls created their performances; she had been
unable to do so, given the lack of atmosphere. Ironically, here we
see exactly how each girl's growing hysteria infects the rest, but
the judges seem convinced that this performance is genuine.

107   *You're the Devil's man!*: Mary desperately turns on Proctor to
protect herself, as it is he alone who pressures her to go against
the other girls. When she bemoans being forced to sign her
name, it is Parris who supplies the idea of her having signed the
Devil's book rather than the deposition she no doubt means.

108   *I say – I say – God is dead!*: a blasphemy in any circumstance
but perhaps an understandable one given Proctor's level of
frustration at the way his good intentions have been turned
against him, belying the words of Raphael to Tobias. He feels
at this point that justice itself must be dead, and equates that to
God, whom Puritans viewed as the fount of all justice.

108   *I hear the boot of Lucifer, I see his filthy face! And it is my
       face, and yours, Danforth!*: Proctor thinks that by hiding his
       adultery with Abigail he has helped cause these events, but he
       sees Danforth and the rest as partners in crime as they, too, do
       not allow the truth to be heard. All, therefore, will be damned
       together. It is such understanding that makes Proctor a tragic
       hero in that he takes responsibility for what occurs.

109   *I denounce these proceedings*: this is a turning point for Hale as
       he has been made to realise the injustice of the trials, and now
       refuses to have any more to do with them.

110   *He is nearly drunk*: Marshal Herrick entering the jail cell drunk
       and jangling his keys seems to recall the drunken gatekeeper
       from another famous play about witches, *Macbeth*. It is also
       evidence of Herrick's distaste for what he has been reduced to
       doing to his neighbours.

112   *I should not be surprised he have been preaching in Andover
       lately*: although Danforth denies the reports, rumours that the
       people of Andover are in rebellion against the authority of the
       courts have reached Salem. Associating Hale with Andover
       indicates Hathorne's suspicion that Hale is working against the
       court.

114   *we might think on whether it be not wise, to –*: Parris's desire
       to postpone the hangings results from selfish motives, but his
       hesitation to say what he wants indicates his fear of Danforth as
       well as his uneasiness to name what they are about to do.

114   *my strongbox is broke into*: we might ask, why should a minister
       be hoarding money? That Parris has been robbed has a sense of
       justice to it, since it hits him where it hurts most.

115   *it were another sort that hanged till now*: one reason the courts
       were initially supported was that they generally arrested and
       hanged undesirables whom the townspeople were thankful to see
       go: vagrants, loose women and drunkards. Rebecca and Martha
       had far higher standing in society; their deaths could call into
       question the court's standing.

115   *gibbet*: the structure on which people were hanged.

117   *Postponement now speaks a floundering on my part; reprieve or
       pardon must cast doubt upon the guilt of them that died till now*:
       such an argument highlights Danforth's self-concern. He is not
       worried about sentencing innocent people to death, but about
       preserving his reputation and justifying his decisions regarding
       those already killed.

118	*like Joshua to stop this sun from rising*: see Joshua 1:15 and 10:24. Joshua asked God to stop the sun from rising in order to spread terror among his enemies while fighting them in battle.
118	*There is blood on my head!*: Hale has lost all belief in what the court is doing and sees himself as a murderer.
118	*Her clothes are dirty; her face is pale and gaunt*: the descriptions of both Elizabeth and Proctor after their time in jail are meant to shock, to show how this court has seriously harmed those already in its clutches.
120	*I tell you true, woman, had I no other proof of your unnatural life, your dry eyes now would be sufficient evidence that you delivered up your soul to Hell! A very ape would weep at such calamity!*: Has Elizabeth been numbed by events, or does she not view Proctor's impending death as worthy of tears? Her demeanour at this point, given her situation, is extremely stoic, and suggests an inner strength this court can neither break nor understand.
123	*It is a pretense, Elizabeth*: Proctor recognises that the deaths of Rebecca and Martha are unjustified; death will make them martyrs. The 'pretense' is that he is actually unworthy of dying alongside them, since he views himself as a sinner. He plans to confess as a form of self-punishment, to show Salem that he is an evil man.
124	*It needs a cold wife to prompt lechery*: Elizabeth blames herself for her husband's adultery, reflecting that she held herself back and drove him into the arms of another woman.
124	*I never knew such goodness in the world!*: having asked for forgiveness and to transfer his feelings of guilt on to herself, Elizabeth offers a valuation of her husband designed to bolster him against his impending death. She hopes to give him the strength to do what is right. She will not tell him what to do, but her assertion of his goodness implies that it would be wrong for him to confess.
127	*I am not empowered to trade your life for a lie*: Danforth is not satisfied with Proctor's confession; he needs him to name names, to implicate the others they plan to hang. This is the way in which HUAC also operated, and the aspect of the hearings that Miller found the most despicable.
128	*I speak my own sins; I cannot judge another . . . I have no tongue for it*: Proctor is not confessing to witchcraft but his adultery, and this is a crime of which only he is guilty. When Miller was brought to testify before HUAC three years later, he told the

committee: 'I take the responsibility for everything I have ever done, but I cannot take responsibility for another human being.'

130   *I have given you my soul; leave me my name!*: this concern with holding on to one's name is noticeable in Miller's plays of this period. Eddie Carbone, from 1956's *A View from the Bridge*, also tries to defend the integrity of his name. During the Red Scare of the 1950s, people whose names were given to HUAC often lost their careers and their livelihoods. But the idea of a 'name' also seems to evoke for Miller the essence of a person, an essence that must be held on to by any individual who wishes to maintain a sense of his or her own selfhood.

130   *I do think I see some shred of goodness in John Proctor*: Proctor has come to recognise the truth of his wife's recent declaration.

131   *It is pride, it is vanity . . . what profit him to bleed*: Hale cannot see the nobility of what Proctor is doing and views his self-sacrifice as an act of pride, a stubborn refusal to give the court what they want. He fails to acknowledge the moral implications of Proctor's false confession and the value of what he stands for.

131   *He have his goodness now. God forbid I take it from him!*: Elizabeth fully endorses Proctor's decision.

131   *the new sun is pouring in upon her face*: the lighting reference emphasises the transcendent aspects of Proctor's death against its cold reality.

Appendix

132   *I thought you would come a good time sooner*: Abigail's softness toward Proctor suggests that she truly is in love with him, and sincerely thinks that he loves her too.

132   *I had thought to come many times*: Proctor's meaning here is ambivalent. Is he saying he thought to come to her to ask for help with Elizabeth or as a sometime lover? She clearly takes him to mean the latter (which also may be his intention, in order to flatter her into compliance). As the scene progresses, Proctor, finding himself unable to persuade her with words, again resorts to violence by shaking her roughly, though such violence continues to be ineffective.

132   *I hear only that you go to the tavern every night, and play shovelboard with the Deputy Governor, and they give you cider*: Abigail's position in the township has been greatly elevated. She is now treated as an honorary man, allowed in the tavern to drink and play games.

133   *I'm holes all over*: this suggests that Abigail is psychologically distressed, believing that spirits torture her. Given that we are meant to believe there are no witches in Salem, she must be inflicting these injuries upon herself. It could be that she is doing this consciously in order to give greater credibility to her claims, but the stage directions imply that this may be part of her madness.

134   *you burned my ignorance away*: the references to burning and fire between Abigail and Proctor suggest that their coupling was aligned to hell. It also relates their affair to the play's title. A crucible is a container in which materials are heated to high temperatures in order to change their basic properties.

134   *hypocrites in their hearts*: Abigail is right to view some of the townspeople as hypocrites, but she casts her net too widely, asserting that even such as Rebecca could be counted among these.

134   *How – ruin me?*: more evidence of Abigail's pride and psychological state, as she seems to believe that despite her adultery she remains nonetheless in an unassailable position of right.

136   *Fear naught. I will save you tomorrow . . . From yourself I will save you*: Abigail still hopes that she can win Proctor for herself.

Questions for Further Study

1 In what ways can you view John Proctor as a tragic hero?
2 Who do you see as the most evil character in the play and why?
3 What do you believe causes the girls of Salem to cry out in the way that they do?
4 How far does Tituba's race affect how the people of Salem treat her?
5 In the play who do you think changes the most and who changes the least?
6 In what ways does *The Crucible* represent morality in conflict with the law?
7 The appeal of the play cannot be attributed only to the Salem witch trials or the Red Scare of the 1950s. Why has *The Crucible* held up so well? What makes it still worth reading and performing?
8 How does *The Crucible* reflect the day-to-day life of seventeenth-century Salem?
9 Analyse the ways in which gender influences the action and relationships presented in *The Crucible*.
10 What is the importance of poetic and stage imagery in *The Crucible?*
11 What insights are gained by the characters of Elizabeth Proctor, Reverend Hale and John Proctor, and what leads them to embrace these new understandings?
12 Assess Miller's claims that *The Crucible* is a companion piece to *Death of a Salesman* in the way that both plays explore the role of the individual in conflict with the dictates of society.
13 To what extent can *The Crucible* be considered an example of stage realism?
14 How far are we meant to accept Elizabeth taking on the blame for her husband's adultery?
15 What does the play suggest about the nature and challenge of marriage?
16 Compare Danforth and Proctor as characters, outlining their motives for action and the way they value and relate to other people.
17 Is sex and sexuality the underlying cause of what happens in Salem?
18 If you were directing a production of *The Crucible*, how would you have the character of Abigail Williams played?
19 In what ways have visual and non-verbal stage effects been used to communicate meaning in the play?
20 To what extent is *The Crucible* a criticism of American society past and present? In what ways is it a critique of other societies?

21 In his hearing before HUAC Miller declared, 'I will protect my sense of myself. I could not use the name of another person and bring trouble on him.' How does this statement parallel John Proctor's stance? What does a 'name' represent to Miller?

22 What are the dangers of interpreting this play in a narrow political sense?

A View from the Bridge

commentary and notes by
STEPHEN MARINO

Plot

Act One

The play begins with the narrator, the lawyer Alfieri, directly addressing the audience from his office. His speeches punctuate many of the scenes, and he is also a participant in the action. Alfieri's opening speech directly relates the events that will unfold during the play, set in Brooklyn, to the attitudes of the Italian-Americans and their forebears in Sicily. As narrator, he tells how they consider meeting a priest or a lawyer 'unlucky', associating these figures with impending disasters. He thinks that this attitude lies in 'three thousand years of distrust'. He proclaims that: 'Justice is very important here.' Finally, he explains that in his legal practice he deals mostly with longshoremen and their wives, fathers and grandfathers in compensation cases, evictions and petty squabbles. Yet every few years a case comes along that is different from the petty troubles of these poor people, and as he listens to it, he surmises that some lawyer thousands of years ago heard the same complaint, 'powerless as I, and watched it run its bloody course'. He concludes with 'This one's name was Eddie Carbone, a longshoreman . . .'.

The first scene takes place in the Red Hook apartment of Eddie Carbone and his wife, Beatrice, who have raised her niece, Catherine, since she was a child. Catherine is seventeen and on the verge of becoming a woman. Eddie has just come home from work and Catherine greets him excitedly. He notices that she is 'dressed up', in a new skirt and with a different hairdo, and he wants to know where she is going. Catherine has some news for him, but wants to wait for Beatrice to come into the room. Eddie thinks Catherine's skirt is too short and expresses concern that she gives him the 'willies' when she walks 'wavy' down the street. Moreover, he does not like the looks that men give her at the candy store and when she wears her new high heels. Eddie's criticism almost brings Catherine to tears; he explains that he promised Catherine's mother on her deathbed that he would be responsible for her. He calls her a 'baby', and admonishes her for waving at a neighbour called Louis out of the apartment window. He tells Catherine that she is getting to be a 'big girl' and cannot be so friendly with men.

He then asks Catherine to call Beatrice from the kitchen because he has news that her cousins – illegal immigrants also known as 'submarines' – have landed in New York harbour. The two men will be staying with the Carbones. Beatrice is overjoyed at their impending arrival; but not expecting them so soon, she worries about feeding them and about the condition of the apartment. Eddie assures her that the men will think they are in a millionaire's house compared to their circumstances in Italy. Eddie teases Beatrice about her generosity. Beatrice is concerned that Eddie will be angry with her if the living situation turns unpleasant, but Eddie cautions that if they all keep quiet about the presence of the illegal relatives, nothing can happen.

Catherine returns to the exciting news that she wanted to tell Eddie at the beginning of the scene. The principal of her school has arranged for her to get a job as a stenographer at a plumbing company. Eddie is reluctant to let her accept because he wants her to finish her secretarial school training. But Catherine explains that the principal advises that she should take the job, and that he will allow her to sit the examination for a certificate at the end of the year because she is the best student in the class. Eddie is still uneasy. He does not like the neighbourhood near the Brooklyn Navy Yard where the company is located and where she will be exposed to unsavoury men like plumbers and sailors. Beatrice explains to Eddie that Catherine is not a baby any longer, saying: 'She's seventeen years old, you gonna keep her in the house all her life?' When Catherine returns to the room, Eddie looks at her with tears in his eyes and tells her she looks 'like a madonna'. He agrees to allow her to work, but warns her: 'Don't trust nobody.'

Their conversation then returns to the imminent arrival of Beatrice's cousins. Eddie reiterates to Catherine and Beatrice the importance of not speaking about their status as illegal immigrants. He tells them: 'You don't see nothin' and you don't know nothin'.' He warns them that there are 'stool pigeons' all over the neighbourhood who would inform the Immigration Bureau. Eddie and Beatrice both recall an incident that occurred in the neighbourhood years ago. A family had an uncle whom they were hiding in their house and their fourteen-year-old son snitched to Immigration. The boy was punished by his father and five brothers who dragged him down the stairs in their house and spat on him in the street in front of the entire neighbourhood. When Catherine asks what happened to him, Eddie says, 'You'll never see him no more, a guy do a thing like that? How's he gonna show his face?'

Their conversation again returns to Catherine's job when Eddie says, 'So you gonna start Monday, heh, Madonna?' and he is moved to tears as he expresses that he never thought she 'would ever grow up'. When Catherine leaves to get Eddie his cigar, Beatrice and Eddie are alone for a minute and Eddie asks Beatrice if she is 'mad' at him: Beatrice retorts with, 'You're the one is mad.' The scene ends and the lights come up on Alfieri, who describes Eddie as 'a good man as he had to be in a life that was hard and even'; then he announces the arrival of the cousins.

When the two cousins arrive, Catherine is struck by the physical differences between the two brothers. The older, married man, Marco, is dark-complexioned while the younger, unmarried man is light with blond hair. Beatrice and Eddie are interested in the living and working conditions in post-war Sicily, and the men explain the occasional construction and field work they do. Marco is particularly interested in working regularly on the docks so he can send money back to his wife, who will then be able to feed the three children better and buy medicine for the eldest child, who is ill. He eventually wants to return home. Catherine focuses her attention on Rodolpho who, in contrast to his brother, wants to become an American and stay forever. Rodolpho has an exuberant spirit and dreams about returning to Italy as a rich man with a motorcycle. Rodolpho reveals that he is also a singer who took the place of a sick baritone one night and sang to great acclaim in the garden of a local hotel. Marco affectionately mocks the youthful bravado of his brother, but Catherine is enthralled and coaxes Rodolpho to perform his version of the song 'Paper Doll'. Eddie is not happy about the performance and warns that his singing might attract unwanted attention to the illegal submarines. Then he turns to criticise Catherine for wearing high heels, and the scene ends with Eddie sizing up Rodolpho, whom he regards suspiciously.

The next scene begins with brief commentary by the narrator Alfieri, who tells the audience that 'Eddie never expected to have a destiny'. A couple of weeks have passed and trouble has come to the Carbones. The first part of the scene takes place in front of the Carbone apartment where Eddie is standing at the doorway. Beatrice comes along and Eddie is worried because it is after eight o'clock and Catherine and Rodolpho are not yet home from the movies. Although he seems to be concerned about Rodolpho being picked up by the immigration authorities, actually Eddie does not like the romantic relationship that has grown between Catherine and Rodolpho. He transfers his jealousy into an assault on Rodolpho's masculinity. He tells Beatrice that Rodolpho gives him the 'heebie-jeebies', explaining that he is not the kind of man who should be Catherine's husband. He does not like the fact that Rodolpho sings on the ships, that his blond hair makes him look like a chorus girl, and that other longshoreman call him 'Paper Doll' and 'Canary'. When Eddie expresses frustration that Beatrice apparently does not understand the problem, she explains that she has 'other worries' and asks Eddie when she is 'gonna be a wife again'. Beatrice and Eddie have not slept together in almost three months; Eddie refuses to discuss the issue further, claiming he is worried that Rodolpho is taking Catherine 'for a ride'. Beatrice retreats into the house and Eddie encounters three neighbourhood longshoremen on the street who talk about how Marco works like a bull when off-loading ships and Rodolpho's sense of humour.

When Catherine and Rodolpho return home from their date, Eddie's anger, especially with Rodolpho, is apparent. He dismisses Rodolpho so he can talk to Catherine alone. Catherine attempts to explain to Eddie that Rodolpho 'blesses' him, but Eddie counters that Rodolpho does not respect Catherine because, if she were not an orphan, Rodolpho would have to ask the permission of her father to date her. When Catherine explains to Eddie the proper respect which Rodolpho exhibits, Eddie proclaims that Rodolpho is just 'bowin' to his passport', i.e. merely using the ploy of marriage to obtain American citizenship. They take their argument into the apartment where Eddie asks Beatrice to 'straighten' Catherine out, and then he storms out of the apartment. Beatrice explains to Catherine that Eddie would not be satisfied with any beau of Catherine's and that she cannot be taking orders from him any more because she is no longer a girl now but a woman. Beatrice tells her that, 'If you act like a baby, he'll treat you like a baby.' Beatrice displays both awareness and sensitivity to the relationship between Eddie and Catherine. She tells her niece that she should not walk around the apartment in her slip, or sit and watch Eddie shave while he is in his underwear. Beatrice says that she has previously tried to tell her about this inappropriate behaviour, but Catherine now has to realise that she is a grown woman and Eddie is a man.

The next scene begins with brief commentary by Alfieri about a 'passion' which he perceived had moved into Eddie's body. Eddie has come to Alfieri's law office to seek advice about finding legal recourse to stop Catherine's relationship with Rodolpho. Alfieri explains that there is nothing illegal about a girl falling in love with an immigrant, but Eddie's frustration over Rodolpho's spending habits, his masculinity, his high singing voice and his sewing ability is evident. He says, 'The guy ain't right.' When Alfieri explains that the only legal question is the manner in which Marco and Rodolpho entered the country, Eddie explains that he wouldn't do anything about that. Alfieri gently tries to explain to Eddie that sometimes there is 'too much love' from a father to a daughter or niece – as Alfieri and the audience clearly understand is so in Eddie's case. Eddie does not completely understand and continues to object to Rodolpho's stealing Catherine from him. Even when Alfieri is more candid, saying, 'She can't marry you, can she?' Eddie says, 'What the hell you talkin' about, marry me?' After Eddie leaves the office, Alfieri again addresses the audience, explaining that after that meeting with Eddie, he realised the situation would end badly and that he was powerless to prevent it.

The final scene of Act One takes place in the Carbone apartment one evening a short time later. Beatrice and Catherine are clearing the dinner table and Eddie, Marco and Rodolpho are in the living room. Catherine initiates conversation about Marco and Rodolpho's life in Italy, fishing and sailing. Eddie is in a particularly surly and contradictory mood. When Beatrice enquires of Marco whether his wife is receiving the money he is sending, Eddie takes the opportunity to ask if there are any 'surprise' children when the fathers eventually return home. After Marco explains that the women wait, Rodolpho adds that their town is 'more strict'. Eddie uses this as an opening to tell Rodopho that the States are not so free – an obvious objection to Rodolpho's freedom with Catherine and his risking arrest by Immigration. Marco attempts to alleviate Eddie's concerns. After an awkward silence, Catherine asks Rodolpho to dance to a new record they have bought – 'Paper Doll', the same song that Rodolpho sang on the night of his arrival. While Rodolpho and Catherine dance, Beatrice, Eddie and Marco talk about how Rodolpho cooks for the crew on the fishing excursions the men take. To Eddie this is another example – along with the singing and sewing – of Rodolpho's lack of masculinity. During this scene, Eddie has been twisting his newspaper in frustration as Catherine and Rodolpho continue dancing. Eddie then suggests that Rodolpho and Marco should go to the fights next Saturday night. When the men agree, Eddie offers to teach Rodolpho how to box. He proceeds to show him a few punches, ultimately landing a blow that staggers Rodolpho. After this obvious and planned humiliation, Rodolpho initiates the resumption of dancing with Catherine. The previously polite and deferential Marco, now challenges Eddie to pick up a chair by one leg. Eddie attempts this, but is unable to perform the task. Marco then kneels, grasps the leg, picks up the chair and lifts it high, facing Eddie with the chair raised menacingly over his head.

Act Two

The second act begins with a brief set-up by Alfieri: it is 23 December, a case of Scotch whisky had 'slipped' while being unloaded on the docks, Beatrice is shopping, Marco is working. Rodolpho had not been hired that day; consequently, he and Catherine are alone in the Carbone apartment.

Clearly upset about the conflict that their relationship is causing and perhaps aroused by Eddie's accusation, Catherine asks Rodolpho if he would consider living in Italy after they marry. Rodolpho absolutely refuses to consider this, explaining to Catherine that there is nothing in Italy for them to go to: 'How can I bring you from a rich country to suffer in a poor country?' He is adamant; he knows that Eddie has raised these doubts in Catherine, and he is insulted. Catherine explains her complicated feelings for Eddie: she feels indebted to him for his goodness in having raised her and she is torn about rejecting him. She reveals considerable awareness of Eddie's needs as a man and husband. But Rodolpho's and Catherine's love is genuine, and Rodolpho convinces her that she must grow and, like a little bird, fly away. They retreat into the bedroom.

At that moment Eddie comes home drunk. When he calls for Beatrice in the apartment, Catherine, followed by Rodolpho, emerges from the bedroom. Eddie is furious and tells Rodolpho to pack his things and leave. When Catherine proclaims her intention to leave as well, Eddie tells her that she is going nowhere. But Catherine proclaims, 'I'm not gonna be a baby any more!' Eddie suddenly reaches out to her and kisses her on the mouth. When Rodolpho tries to stop him, Eddie in turn attacks, pinning Rodolpho's arms, laughing and suddenly kissing Rodolpho, humiliating him. Eddie then orders Rodolpho to leave the apartment, threatening to kill him if he ever lays a hand on Catherine again.

The next scene begins with Alfieri's narration about another visit by Eddie to his office a few days after the confrontation in the apartment. Alfieri recalls the fixed look in Eddie's eyes, which he compares to tunnels. Eddie tells Alfieri that Beatrice will be moving Marco and Rodolpho to a room in an upstairs apartment. In discussing Eddie's attack on Rodolpho, Alfieri judges that Rodolpho was just not strong enough to break Eddie's grip on him. However, Eddie insists that Rodolpho did not fight back because the 'guy ain't right'. When Alflieri asks Eddie why he humiliated Rodolpho, Eddie claims that he wanted Catherine to see what Rodolpho really is. But Eddie again asks Alfieri what legal recourse he has to stop the marriage that is soon to take place between his wife's niece and the 'submarine'. Alfieri explains to Eddie that morally and legally he has no rights whatsoever. Alfieri warns him further that the law is nature and 'a river will drown him if he tries to buck it'. Eddie leaves in dismay.

The lights come up on Eddie at a public telephone, making a call to the Immigration Bureau. He reports illegal immigrants living at his address, the same heinous act he scorned earlier in the play.

The next scene is in the Carbone apartment, where Beatrice is taking down Christmas decorations. Eddie enters and discovers that Marco and Rodolpho have already moved to an upstairs apartment. Eddie and Beatrice argue. She regrets that she ever agreed to have her cousins to stay in their apartment, but she wants to know why he humiliated Rodolpho in front of Catherine. Now that they are gone, Eddie asserts command of his home and demands his 'respect' back from Beatrice, especially about references to their sex life. Beatrice tells him that Rodolpho and Catherine plan to marry the next week because her niece is concerned about him getting picked up by the immigration authorities; if they marry, he can begin the process of applying for citizenship. Beatrice tells Eddie that despite what has occurred, Catherine would still like his blessing at the wedding.

Catherine comes down from the apartment upstairs as Beatrice attempts a reconciliation between them. However, Eddie is resolute and tries to convince Catherine not to marry; she is equally determined to go ahead with her plans. When Catherine asks Beatrice's permission to take a few pillowcases upstairs, Eddie discovers that there are additional illegal boarders in the apartment where Rodolpho and Marco are now lodged. Eddie panics and, without revealing that he has informed, demands that Catherine move Rodolpho and Marco out of the apartment on the grounds that mixing with other illegals will attract attention. At that moment the immigration officers arrive and both Beatrice and Catherine realise what Eddie has done. As the group of submarines is arrested and brought out on the street in front of the apartment house, Marco lunges for Eddie, accusing him of betraying him and his brother to the authorities. The crowd of neighbours gather one by one and shun Eddie, who screams that Marco is 'gonna take that back'.

The next scene is set in the reception room of a prison where Alfieri serves as legal counsel to Marco and Rodolpho. He will be able to bail out Marco if he promises not to take revenge on Eddie. Alfieri explains that Marco will be deported in any case, but that Rodolpho, because he is going to marry Catherine, can become an American citizen. Marco and Alfieri discuss what 'honorable' action is. Marco explains that in his country Eddie would already be dead for his action; and Alfieri explains that to promise not to kill is not dishonourable. Marco wants to know where the law is that governs the despicable degradation which Eddie has brought upon Marco's blood and kin. Alfieri counters with, 'Only God makes justice.'

The final scene takes place in the Carbone apartment the afternoon of Catherine and Rodolpho's wedding. Beatrice is dressed to leave for the nuptials and Eddie tells her not to come back home if she goes. Eddie still wants his 'respect' back and demands that Marco apologise to him before any wedding takes place. Catherine yells at Eddie calling him a rat who belongs in the sewer; Eddie moves to attack her, but Beatrice intervenes, then decides not to attend the wedding. At that moment Rodolpho rushes into the apartment warning that Marco is coming to avenge himself on Eddie. Rodolpho wants Eddie to avoid this confrontation and attempts a reconciliation by kissing his hand and apologising. Eddie rejects his overture because he wants nothing but Marco to give him back his 'name', which he has besmirched in the neighbourhood. Beatrice says to Eddie: 'You want somethin' else, Eddie and you can never have her', finally stating the truth of what has been obvious all along to everyone but Eddie.

Eddie is horrified, but at that moment Marco arrives in the street in front of the apartment and calls out Eddie's name. The whole neighbourhood has gathered to witness this final confrontation. Eddie goes out to the street, where Marco calls him an animal as he strikes him and demands that Eddie get down on his knees before him. Eddie pulls a knife on Marco, but in the ensuing struggle, Marco turns the knife on Eddie, mortally wounding him.

The play ends with final commentary by Alfieri, who acknowledges how wrong Eddie was and that his death was useless but inevitable. Nevertheless, he mourns him with 'a certain alarm', searching for the meaning that might be found in the tragedy of his death.

Commentary

Literary, Historical and Social Context

A View from the Bridge ended a remarkably productive time in Arthur Miller's career when he stood, along with Tennessee Williams, as one of America's most distinguished play-wrights. The plays he wrote during this period – *All My Sons* (1947), *Death of Salesman* (1949), *An Enemy of the People* (1950), *The Crucible* (1953), *A View from the Bridge* (one act, 1955) and *A View from the Bridge* (two acts, 1956) – are dramas upon which his lasting critical reputation will undoubtedly be judged. After the London production of *View from the Bridge* in 1956, Miller did not have another original play produced on either the New York or London stages until *After the Fall* in 1964. Miller first wrote *A View from the Bridge* as a one-act play with a companion piece, *A Memory of Two Mondays,* which premiered in New York in 1955. Miller wrote the two-act version in 1956, which premiered in London. Miller considered the two-act play the definitive version, including it in the first edition of his *Collected Plays* in 1957.

A View from the Bridge had a long period of gestation. In 1947, after his success with *All My Sons*, Miller became intrigued with writing about the Italian immigrant society of the Brooklyn docks. He had noticed graffiti during his walks across the Brooklyn Bridge that read: 'Dovè Pete Panto?' which translates from the Italian as: 'Where is Pete Panto?' The message also began appearing on subway stations and on office buildings at the Court Street Civic Center in downtown Brooklyn. Miller learned from newspaper coverage that Pete Panto was a young longshoreman who had challenged the powerful Mafia leadership of the seamen's union and had mysteriously disappeared, effectively ending the threat of an investigation of the union's corruption. Miller was fascinated by the idea of writing about the tragic end of this heroic man. He began researching the criminal underworld of the Brooklyn docksides by visiting the piers and attempting to find out the truth behind Panto's fate. However, Miller was stymied by the intimidated silence of the longshoremen, who feared speaking out against their bosses and the hiring traditions transported from their native Sicily.

Nearly deciding to give up his project, Miller unexpectedly received a phone call from Mitch Berenson, a union organiser, and Vinny Longhi, a lawyer, who were attempting to continue Pete Panto's resistance to the longshoremen union's power structure. After Miller offered to write about their plight, they gave him the opportunity to enter the mysterious underbelly of this corrupt world. He learned about the lives and culture of the longshoremen, many of whom he befriended, often visiting their homes in their Red Hook neighbourhood. In 1947 to 1948 Miller even accompanied Longhi on a trip to Sicily where he hoped to solicit support for his cause in an upcoming union election. In Italy Miller absorbed Sicilian society and came to understand the cultural connection between the American immigrants and their native land.

During this time, Longhi told Miller the story of another longshoreman who had informed the Immigration Bureau about two brothers who were related to him and living illegally in his house. In order to break up the relationship between his niece and one of the cousins, the longshoreman had informed the immigration authorities, an action which made him a pariah in his neighbourhood. Local gossip said that he was killed by one of the brothers. In an essay, 'On Social Plays', which Miller wrote as an introduction to the published one-act play, Miller explained that when he first heard the tale in his Brooklyn neighbourhood, he thought he had heard it before as 'some re-enactment of a Greek myth'. To Miller, it seemed the two illegal immigrants set out from Italy as if it were two thousand years ago; he was awed by the destiny of the immigrants and their informer, as though this was almost the work of Fate. Miller fiddled with a screenplay about the story, but then, not quite ready to dramatise the tale fully, dropped it after his trip to Sicily and eventually became consumed with writing *Death of a Salesman* in 1948 and with the production of that masterpiece in 1949.

During the run of *Salesman*, Miller wrote a screenplay, *The Hook*, about his experience on the docks, focusing on Pete Panto's doomed attempt to overthrow the Mafia gangsters who ruled the New York waterfront. After he read the script, Elia Kazan, the renowned film and stage director of *All My Sons* and *Death of a Salesman*, thought the film was a viable project for him to direct. Consequently, in 1951 Miller and Kazan took a trip to Hollywood to obtain the backing from a major studio. The negotiations for the film broke down when the Hollywood producers were reluctant to make a film critical of the unions and demanded unrealistic changes such as depicting the union crooks as communists, which Miller refused to do. The studios also performed background checks on Miller and Kazan – an indication of the coming hysteria about communism just beginning. In Hollywood, Miller also met the starlet Marilyn Monroe for the first time.

After his trip, disappointed at the commercial failure of his rewrite of Henrik Ibsen's *An Enemy of the People* (1950), Miller returned to the tale of the Italian longshoreman who had snitched on his relatives, working on the play for several months under the title 'An Italian

Tragedy', before abandoning it again. It was not until 1954 that Miller would complete the play.

After his frustration with the critical reception of *The Crucible* in 1953, his controversial play about the Salem Witch Trials, Miller received a phone call from the actor Martin Ritt, who asked him to write a one-act play for a group of actors who had a theatre available for use on Sunday evenings and wanted to act in a play without any commercial restraints. Miller agreed and wrote his one-act *A Memory of Two Mondays*, which is based on his own life –the dramatised recollection of the summer he spent working as a clerk in an auto-parts factory in Manhattan before he attended the University of Michigan. Ritt loved the play, and asked Miller if he had another one-act play to begin the evening, a so-called 'curtain raiser'. Thus, Miller returned to 'An Italian Tragedy' which suddenly 'seemed to fall into place as a one-act with a single rising line of intensity leading inevitably to an explosive climax' (*Timebends*, 353). Miller realised that his difficulty in dramatising the story of the longshoreman was that he had worried too much over making it a full-length play for the Broadway theatre. He transformed 'An Italian Tragedy' into the drama of Eddie Carbone and his niece Catherine, writing the one-act version of what he now called *A View from the Bridge* in ten days. The title refers to the famous Brooklyn Bridge which spans the East River between Manhattan and Brooklyn at the foot of Brooklyn Heights, and not far from the Red Hook neighbourhood. However, when the original theatre for the Sunday performances was no longer available, Kermit Bloomgarden, the producer oi *Death of a Salesman*, became enthusiastic about both one-act plays being performed by the same cast, and he offered a fully fledged Broadway production.

Miller originally wanted to dramatise the story of the informer without embellishment, exactly in 'its exposed skeleton' because he did not want to interfere with the 'myth-like march of the tale' toward its tragic ending. At this stage in his career, Miller was interested in writing modern American tragedies. For example, a few weeks after the production *of Death of a Salesman* opened, Miller wrote an op-ed piece for the *New York Times* entitled 'Tragedy and the Common Man', in which he made the case for Willy Loman as a modern tragic hero. Miller maintained that modern literature does not require characters to be royalty or leaders, as in the tragedies of other eras, and therefore fall from some great height. Rather he insisted: 'I think that the tragic feeling is evoked when we are in the presence of a character who is ready to lay down his life, if need be, to secure one thing – his sense of personal dignity. From Orestes to Hamlet, Medea to Macbeth, the underlying struggle is that of the individual attempting to gain his "rightful" position in his society.' Thus, Miller argues that a lowly man like Willy Loman could be considered a tragic hero. He clearly set his dramatic sights on achieving this in *A View from the Bridge*. Of course, the original attraction to him of Pete Panto's story was that he seemed a modern hero whose demise was a tragedy. Miller had also explored this notion in *The Crucible* with his hero John Proctor, and he aimed at a similar depiction for Eddie Carbone.

At this time in 1955, Miller was also clearly interested in exploring further the themes of betrayal, informing and adultery, which he had illustrated in *The Crucible*. For by the time he was writing the one-act version of *A View from the Bridge*, he had embarked on his affair with Marilyn Monroe, was about to divorce his wife, and was becoming a target of the House Un-American Activities Committee (HUAC). In 1950 the United States had begun a period of political and social upheaval that would have a lasting effect on Miller's career and personal life. During this time, Miller witnessed the rise of the Army/McCarthy hearings, conducted by the Wisconsin Senator, Joseph McCarthy, and the establishment of HUAC, which was revived after the Second World War in response to the 'Red Scare' from the Soviet Union and the fall of China to a Communist government. Citizens were called before the committee in order to admit to radical pasts, and its targets were often high-profile celebrities, especially in the entertainment world, whose appearance would guarantee major publicity for the committee. Miller and Kazan had discovered this in Hollywood with their attempt to get *The Hook* made, but during his writing of *The Crucible* and *A View from the Bridge* Miller would see his friends and colleagues – and eventually himself – targeted.

In fact, in April 1952 Miller decided to write *The Crucible* because he saw a 'living connection between myself and Salem, and between Salem and Washington'. Miller had planned an exploratory trip to Salem to research the original court records. Coincidentally, the day before he was to leave for Massachusetts he received a phone call from Elia Kazan who had been subpoenaed by HUAC. Kazan and Miller met in Connecticut where Kazan told Miller that he had decided to cooperate and testify about the names of other celebrities he had encountered at Communist Party meetings years earlier. Kazan's decision would cause a breach in his personal and professional relationship with Miller that would last until the next decade, when, in 1964, Kazan directed *After the Fall*. When Miller left Salem, he heard on his car radio a news report of Kazan's testimony before HUAC: he had 'named names'. In the next few months, the playwright Clifford Odets, whose work had had a major influence on Miller, would be called before the committee; he too named names. Lee J. Cobb, the original Willy Loman, was called, and he too succumbed to the power of the committee. Miller was struck by the political forces which cause men to inform on others. This became a central focus in *The Crucible* and one which he also carried over into *A View from the Bridge.*

Miller wanted *A View from the Bridge* to follow very closely the tale Vinny Longhi had told him, trying not to change its original shape. He hoped the audience would feel as he felt when he heard it for the first time – not with sympathy but with wonder. Miller admits that the meaning of Eddie's fate remained a mystery to him during and after writing the one-act play. But he was dissatisfied with the final result. The reviews were mixed and the production consequently had a disappointing run, closing after 149 performances, though Miller won his third Drama Critics' Circle Award. In *Timebends* he acknowledges that personal and professional distractions in his life caused him not to focus fully on writing the play as the Broadway hit which Bloomgarden wanted. Miller was deeply involved in his relationship with Marilyn Monroe at this time and was contemplating the painful divorce from his wife. Moreover, he continued to be distracted by personal attacks on him brought by his political views. In 1954, the American government refused to grant Miller a passport and visa for the European premiere of *The Crucible*, and his break with Kazan over his testimony received wide press coverage. In addition, while casting and rehearsing the one-act *A View from the Bridge*, Miller had been researching and writing a screenplay for the New York Youth Board about juvenile delinquents. An investigator from HUAC warned the city administration about being associated with Miller because of his political opinions. In turn, the American Legion and the Catholic War Veterans applied pressure to stop the film because of Miller's 'Communist ties'. The project was stopped.

Miller had the opportunity to revise the play in 1956, a tumultuous year for him: committed to Monroe, he spent six weeks in April in Nevada to establish residency for a 'quickie' divorce. After filing for divorce, Miller had his celebrated hearing before HUAC. Following this, he and Monroe were married in late June, then the famous couple flew to England where Monroe was to star with Laurence Olivier in *The Prince and the Showgirl*, and where Miller revised the play into a two-act for the London production directed by Peter Brook.

The seemingly unlikely marriage between Miller and Monroe caused a media sensation, with headlines like 'Pinko Playwright Weds Sex Goddess'. Miller perceived that his relationship with Monroe would bring needed attention to the HUAC, whose influence had been waning. In May 1956, Miller was subpoenaed, and the hypocrisy of the committee was evident to him when his lawyer told him that the Pennsylvania Representative Francis E. Walter, chairman of the committee, proposed that the hearing could be cancelled if Monroe agreed to be photographed shaking hands with him. In Miller's testimony, he answered cordially the committee's questions about his association with political groups, and gave his opinions on freedom of speech, communist conspiracies, and figures like Elia Kazan and the poet Ezra Pound. At the end of his testimony, Miller was asked about his attendance at a meeting of communist writers a decade earlier. Miller freely admitted his presence, but refused to give the names of others in attendance. The committee already knew the names of attendees; they were concerned with Miller's compliance to their power and his betrayal of friends and colleagues. Miller was warned that he would be in contempt of Congress for refusing to answer, since he had chosen not to claim the Fifth Amendment's constitutional protection against self-incrimination. Miller still refused and, therefore, was cited. Eventually he was tried for contempt of Congress and was found guilty on two counts. His sentencing was deferred for an appeal and in 1958 the US Court of Appeals overturned his conviction.

In revising *A View from the Bridge* for the London production, Miller responded to criticism of the sketchiness of the characters in the one-act play. He enlarged the psychological motivations of the principal characters – Eddie Carbone, his wife Beatrice and their niece Catherine – in order to emphasise the social consequences of the play's central action: Eddie's desire for Catherine. The London production received rave reviews and ran for 220 performances; a subsequent production in Paris ran for two years.

Structure

In addition to the 1955 one-act version of *A View from the Bridge* and the 1956 two-act version which premiered in London, there is also a third version: Miller rewrote the end for the 1957 Paris production because he was advised that a French audience would not accept that Eddie and Catherine could be unaware of the emotions between them. Ostracised by his society, Eddie kills himself.

In the writing and production of the first version of *A View from the Bridge*, Miller decided on the one-act form to 'recreate my own feeling toward this tale – namely wonderment. It is not designed primarily to draw tears or laughter from an audience, but to strike a particular note of astonishment at the way in which, and the reasons for which, a man will endanger and risk and lose his very life' ('On Social Plays', 68). Miller explained that, 'Nothing was permitted which did not advance the progress of Eddie's catastrophe in a most direct way . . . [I felt] that I ought to deliver it onto the stage as fact; that interpretation was inherent in the very existence of the tale in the first place' (*A View from the Bridge*, Introduction). Thus, the one-act version consists often scenes, performed without a break or intermission. Although the play is practically full-length in its running time, when writing it Miller said he 'did not know how to pull a curtain down anywhere before its end . . . I kept looking for an act curtain, a point of pause, but none ever developed' ('On Social Plays', 65). The New York production used sparse staging to achieve the 'skeletal' quality of the mythic story because, as Miller wrote, 'nothing existed but the purpose of the tale'. Even the character development was limited to advancing the tale, thus restricting the naturalistic acting style that still dominated the American stage.

When writing the two-act version, Miller enlarged the psychological motivations of the principal characters – Eddie, Beatrice and Catherine. He believed Eddie's action was made more understandable because he no longer concentrated only on the factual events of the tale. With the inclusion of additional dialogue to round out the characterisations of the three principal roles, the expanded version demanded two acts. Miller wrote in the Introduction to the two-act play that

> I felt it could now afford to include elements of simple human motivation – specifically the viewpoints of Eddie's wife, and *her* dilemma in relation to him. This in fact accounts for almost all the added material, which made it necessary to break the play in the middle for an intermission.

Miller decided to end Act One with the dramatic confrontation between Marco and Eddie when the once-compliant Marco shows his awareness of Eddie's threat to Rodolpho by holding the chair over Eddie's head. Act Two begins with the explosive scene when Eddie discovers Rodolpho and Catherine in the bedroom.

In revising the play, Miller also tried to show Eddie more closely in relation to the Sicilian-American society. He realised that 'The mind of Eddie Carbone is not comprehensible apart from its relation to his neighborhood, his fellow workers, his social situation. His self-esteem depends upon their estimate of him, and his value is created largely by his fidelity to the code of his culture.' In this production the set was more realistic. The pay-scale of the London theatre also allowed Miller to have several more actors playing Eddie's neighbours. Miller explained that in the New York production, there had only been four strategically placed actors to represent Eddie's community. In London, at least twenty men and women surrounded the main action. Miller ultimately judged that 'once Eddie had been placed squarely in his social context, among his people, the mythlike feeling of the story emerged of itself, and he could be made more human and less a figure, a force'. Moreover, 'the importance of his interior psychological dilemma was magnified to the size it would have in life. What had seemed like a mere aberration had now risen to a fatal violation of ancient law.' Twenty years later, in *Timebends*, Miller commented on how the revised staging also emphasised Eddie's universal destiny:

> The play began on a Red Hook street against the exterior brick wall of a tenement, which soon split open to show a basement apartment and above it a maze of fire escapes winding back and forth across the face of the building in the background. On those fire escapes the neighbors appeared at the end like a chorus, and Eddie could call up to them, to his society and his conscience for their support of his cause. Somehow, the splitting in half of the whole three-story tenement was awesome, and it opened the mind to the size of the mythic story. (431)

In the two-act version, Miller expanded the characterisation of Beatrice by focusing on her relationships with Eddie and Catherine. For example, there are substantial differences between the one-act and two-act versions of the play regarding the nature of Eddie and Beatrice's sexual relationship. The one-act version downplays Eddie's impotence, something that is central in the two-act version. The two-act version more vividly portrays Eddie and Beatrice's sex life when she asks him, 'When am I going to be a wife again, Eddie?', which heightens the sexual conflicts of the play. In Act Two, Miller also includes dialogue in which Eddie speaks about his sex life: 'I want my respect, Beatrice, and you know what I am talkin' about . . . What I feel like doin' in the bed and what I don't feel like doin' . . . I don't want no more conversations about that.'

Miller also added a scene in Act One which includes a conversation between Beatrice and Catherine about her relationship with Eddie. Miller portrays Beatrice as aware of both Catherine's and Eddie's complex feelings. She realises much more consciously than Catherine or Eddie does that Catherine is a woman, and Beatrice tries to convey that to her. Beatrice encourages Catherine to leave the house, to marry Rodolpho and for them to find a place of their own. She says, 'You're a woman, that's all, and you got a nice boy, and now the time came when you said good-bye.' When Catherine hesitates, Beatrice is firm: 'Honey . . . you gotta.' Beatrice's action in this additional scene displays her own complicated situation: torn between her devotion to her husband, her own desires as a wife and the responsibility for the girl she has raised as a daughter.

In *A View from the Bridge* Miller created the role of a narrator, the lawyer Alfieri, who functions like a Greek chorus: he is both a character and a commentator. Although his original intention was to use Alfieri to convey his own wonder when he first heard the tale of the longshoreman, he clearly uses Alfieri's speeches to the audience to connect Eddie to what Miller sees as the mythic level of the play: Eddie's larger universal fate and his destiny to enact the tragedy. Alfieri is also crucial in showing the audience the significance of Eddie's actions to himself, his family and his society. Miller's decision to use a narrator in *A View from the Bridge* was perhaps influenced by Thornton Wilder's use of the Stage Manager in *Our Town* in 1938, and Tennessee Williams's successful use of Tom Wingfield as the narrator in *The Glass Menagerie* in 1945. Miller acknowledged the influence that both Wilder and Williams had on the development of his stagecraft.

Themes

In *A View from the Bridge* sexuality, responsibility, betrayal and the law are intertwined with the psychological and social forces operating in the play.

Sexuality

The most provocative sexual issues *A View from the Bridge* raises are incest and homosexuality. Eddie's desire for his niece Catherine is at the centre of all the play's action. From the outset his attention to Catherine is depicted as more than fatherly affection. There are a number of intriguing twists to Eddie's desire for Catherine. Catherine is really Beatrice's niece whom Eddie has raised as his own daughter. And the fact that she is not his niece by blood further complicates Eddie's attraction to her. His need to protect her childhood innocence and virginity, first portrayed as fatherly affection, is put into a different light when he becomes enraged by her relationship with Rodolpho. His desire is evident when he reveals his disgust at Rodolpho putting his hands on her. Yet twice in the play Eddie is portrayed as unconscious of his desires. When he goes to see Alfieri for legal advice, the lawyer voices his concern for Eddie's inner turmoil. And at the end of the play Beatrice will similarly confront her husband by forcing him to face the reality he is unwilling or unable to acknowledge.

Catherine's interest in Rodolpho is obvious on the first night of their arrival. When Catherine and Rodolpho begin their relationship, Eddie's paternal concern turns into jealousy, which he uses to attack Rodolpho. Eddie is repulsed by what he perceives to be Rodolpho's effeminate nature, an unfamiliar form of masculinity. Eddie is especially alarmed that Catherine finds Rodolpho sexually attractive. Eddie tries to convince Catherine that Rodolpho is merely using her as a means to achieve American citizenship but his argument is actually a mask for Eddie's own desire for her.

Eddie's conflicted sexual impulses remain one of the most intriguing aspects of the play. There are substantial differences between the original one-act version of the play and the revised two-act version regarding the nature of Eddie and Beatrice's physical relationship. Although he is unable to perform with Beatrice, he clearly desires Catherine, but at the same time he does not want her virginity violated. Furthermore, Eddie seems to be similarly attracted to Rodolpho, whose masculinity he assaults because he is both confused and repulsed by Rodolpho's behaviour. Nevertheless, Eddie perceives Rodolpho as a sexual threat. Eddie confuses sexual potency with a macho form of masculinity. He discovers that, in addition to singing and sewing, Rodolpho also cooks. Although he is told about the male chefs in European hotels, he does not appreciate a European view of what constitutes masculine behaviour. As a recently assimilated American, Eddie is uneasy about his own immigrant Italian culture. For him, masculinity is only physical strength and he challenges Rodolpho to a boxing match, knowing that he can overpower him.

Responsibility

Miller's plays concern themselves with the issue of characters accepting responsibility for their actions. Joe Keller in *All My Sons*, Willy Loman in *Death of a Salesman* and John Proctor in *The Crucible* struggle to accept and understand the consequences of their actions on themselves and others. At its core *A View from the Bridge* illustrates the complexity of accepting – or denying – full responsibility for one's actions and the effect this has on oneself, one's family and society. Eddie declares that Catherine 'is my niece and I'm responsible for her'. But Eddie perverts his responsibility to her and in the process violates the codes that bind him to his community. The consequences are tragic.

One of the most shocking aspects of Eddie's failure to fulfill his responsibility is that the play initially depicts him as fully aware of his role as surrogate father to Catherine, husband to Beatrice, willing host to Marco and Rodolpho, and member of his immigrant community. Although Miller was intrigued by the events of the story on which he based the play and wanted to illustrate the events as the work of fate, the playwright in Miller wanted to show that human beings are not merely victims of forces beyond their control. His characters determine their own destinies. Most of Eddie's actions are indeed purposeful – his attack on Rodolpho, the passionate kissing of Catherine, the demeaning kiss on Rodolpho's lips, the information he delivers to the Immigration Bureau. His failure is that he is never truly aware of the part he has played in the unfolding of these terrible events. Refusing to accept blame, he displays no guilt and accepts no responsibility, even when the catastrophe he has caused is pointed out to him. In contrast, Beatrice and Rodolpho clearly take full responsibility for the choices they have made.

Betrayal and informing

From the perspective of Eddie's society, informing on Marco and Rodolpho to the immigration authorities is a heinous act. Although Eddie snitches for personal motives – to have Rodolpho deported and therefore eliminated from Catherine's life – he unwittingly commits an act of betrayal not only of his family but also of the larger circle of the immigrant society in which he lives. He makes his telephone call without knowing that Beatrice has arranged to move Marco and Rodolpho to an upstairs neighbour's apartment where other illegal immigrants are housed. His violation of what is in fact taboo becomes public when Marco accuses him before the gathered neighbours. As a result, Eddie becomes obsessed with his reputation. And it is his mania to maintain his dignity before his society that ultimately causes his death.

In *A View from the Bridge* Miller was also interested in exploring further the themes of betrayal and informing that he had previously illustrated in *The Crucible* in his response to McCarthyism and the naming of names before the House Committee on Un-American Activities. However, between writing the one-act version in 1955 and his revisions for the two-act version, Miller himself experienced the pressure to inform and betray when he, too, was called before HUAC in 1956 to 'name names'. Thus, his depiction of those who would 'call out' others in order to protect themselves is perhaps even more complicated than it is in *The Crucible*. Eddie Carbone is an amalgam of motives, emotions and unreconciled conflicts. Miller structures his play for us to witness and consider its multiple resonances. And as we do so, it is difficult to condemn Eddie without sympathy.

Law

A View from the Bridge represents a world in which legal, moral, ethical and social issues are in conflict with one another. Although Alfieri, as a lawyer, provides the interpretation of civil law, from his very first monologue he also shows that such law is not always a cultural precedent followed in the context of a Sicilian neighbourhood in Brooklyn. The law is not always clear nor does it satisfy basic instincts. Alfieri has witnessed men 'justly shot by unjust men'. The longshoremen of the play operate outside technical legality and sometimes consider illegal action 'just' in their code: harbouring illegal aliens is a sanctioned activity; the act of informing is abhorrent, a crime against the clan. Alfieri gives voice to these contradictions to both Eddie and Marco but he is powerless to prevent the law of the tribe from being enacted. As the play moves to its conclusion, we see how moral law is far more persuasive than civil law.

The scenes in Act One and Act Two when Eddie visits Alfieri's office forcefully present the contrast between the social, moral and legal codes that operate in the play. Eddie wants to prevent Catherine and Rodolpho's marriage because 'the guy ain't right'. But Alfieri tells him that 'morally and legally you have no rights'. Eddie fails to understand how Alfieri's explanation of civil law interprets natural law. As a lawyer, Alfieri functions under a code of modern American society which he describes in his very first commentary in the play as 'more civilized'. However, in Alfieri's own words, Eddie is not connected to this civilised law; his nature harks back to his roots in the old world. Because Eddie has no legal recourse to stop Catherine and Rodolpho's relationship, he chooses to act according to his own code. Alfieri points out to him that he will drown if he violates the social and moral codes so powerful in his neighbourhood, especially the ethnic code he breaches by reporting Marco and Rodolpho. It is ironic that according to the code operating in Red Hook, Eddie is technically committing a crime by harbouring illegal aliens, but this action is permissible, even sanctioned in the community. Making the phone call to report illegal immigrants, according to civil law, is the proper action; however, the play illustrates that the moral law of the Italian society supersedes civil law – an action which makes Eddie an outcast.

The violation of this ethnic code is enforced in the scene between Alfieri and Marco after his arrest by immigration officials. Marco seeks revenge on Eddie because he has violated the Sicilian code based on loyalty to one's blood and family, and the violation exacts terrible consequences. As Marco says, 'In my country he would be dead now.' Alfieri is reluctant to bail out Marco unless he promises not to exact this revenge: 'To promise not to kill is not dishonourable.' Ironically, Marco has the same difficulty as Eddie in understanding how the civil law conflicts with his moral code:

Marco   Then what is to be done with such a man?

Alfieri   Nothing. If he obeys the law, he lives. That's all.

Marco (*rises, turns to* **Alfieri**)   The law? All the law is not in a book.

Alfieri   Yes. In a book. There is no other law.

Marco (*his anger rising*)   He degraded my brother – my blood. He robbed my children, he mocks my work. I work to come here, mister!

Alfieri   I know, Marco –

Marco   There is no law for that? Where is the law for that?

Alfieri   There is none.

Marco (*shaking his head, sitting*)   I don't understand this country. (73)

Marco's frustration at the law not punishing Eddie shows how the law is at odds with Marco's sense of justice. Here 'civilised' America undermines the ethnic code of Marco's land, which abhors the violation of 'blood'. For Sicilians this violation must be avenged, offering us another 'view' of how justice has its say in different worlds.

Language

Miller wrote the one-act version in an intriguing mixture of prose and verse; the expanded two-act version eliminated the verse, but retained the characters speaking in a colloquial idiom that actually disguises Miller's use of metaphor.

Although Miller eliminated the verse lines in rewriting the play, he retained a sophisticated use of poetic language. Very little critical attention has been paid to the language of Miller's dialogue. Throughout his career, Miller was subject to reviews critical of the language of his plays. For example, in a review in the *Nation* of the original production of *Death of a Salesman*, Joseph Wood Krutch criticised the play for 'its failure to go beyond literal meaning and its undistinguished dialogue'. As a language stylist, Miller has been under-appreciated, too often overshadowed by his contemporary, Tennessee Williams, whose major strength as a dramatist for many critics lies in the lyricism of his plays. Because Miller was so often pigeonholed as a social dramatist, most criticism focuses on the cultural relevance of his plays. Most critics are content to regard his dialogue as 'colloquial', judging that Miller used best what Leonard Moss described as 'the common man's language' to reflect the social concerns of his characters. The assumption is that most of Miller's characters speak a realistic prose – a style that by implication seems at first glance antithetical to poetic language. However, Miller created a unique dramatic idiom which undoubtedly marks him as a significant stylist nonetheless.

Although Miller works mostly in a form of colloquial prose, there are moments in his plays when the dialogue reaches for something more. He often takes the colloquialisms, clichés and idioms of everyday language and reveals the eloquence it can contain, especially in shifting words from their denotative to connotative meanings. Moreover, he employs the figurative devices of metaphor, symbol and imagery to give poetic significance to prose dialect. In many texts he embeds a series of metaphors – many are extended – which possess particular connotations in the societies in which individual plays are set. Most importantly, such figurative devices serve to support the tragic conflicts of the social themes that are the central focus of Miller's plays.

Indeed, poetic elements pervade the Miller canon. For example, in *All My Sons*, allusions, symbols and images place the themes of sacrifice and redemption in a religious context. In *Death of a Salesman* the extended metaphors of sports and business convey Willy Loman's struggle to achieve the American Dream in a capitalist economic system. In *The Crucible* poetic language illustrates the conflicts polarising the Salem community; images, symbols and metaphors, conceived in series of opposites, signify the Salemites' polarised view of a world of extremes. Heat and cold, white and black, light and dark, soft and hard connote the existence of the ultimate opposites: good and evil. In fact, Miller acknowledged that he was 'up to his neck' in writing many of his early full-length and radio plays in verse. When he graduated from the University of Michigan and started his work with the Federal Theatre Project in 1938, he wrote *The Golden Tears*, a verse play about Montezuma. Later he explained that his first drafts for *Death of a Salesman* and all of *The Crucible* were written in verse. Miller regretted his failure to do this in *The American Clock*.

A View from the Bridge contains several poetic devices that heighten the conflicts and themes of the play. Consistent with Miller's use of language throughout his work, these poetic devices rely heavily on the tension between literal and figurative meanings, and they often include a high level of dramatic irony. Many of Alfieri's speeches to the audience at the beginning and end of scenes use figurative devices. In his opening monologue in Act One, he uses images of the sea and blood to connect the Brooklyn immigrant society to its roots in Sicily – especially Sicily of the past. He uses the sea of New York harbour to make this connection:

> But this is Red Hook, not Sicily. This is the slum that faces the bay
> on the seaward side of Brooklyn Bridge. This is the gullet of New
> York swallowing the tonnage of the world. And now we are quite
> civilized, quite American. (4)

Alfieri speaks of a case coming every few years that goes beyond the petty legal squabbles he usually arbitrates, and when he hears this kind of trouble

The flat air in my office suddenly washes in with the green scent
of the sea, the dust in this air is blown away and the thought comes
that in some Caesar's year, in Calabria perhaps or on the cliff at
Syracuse, another lawyer, quite differently dressed, heard the same
complaint and sat there as powerless as I, and watched it run its
bloody course. (4)

The images of sea and blood in this speech establish a number of parallels
between the old and new worlds: the green scent of the sea in New York
harbour echoes the Mediterranean sea surrounding Italy. And such images
emblematise just how deeply rooted Eddie's fate is in a mythic past.

Alfieri's monologue ends with another sea image that reinforces Eddie's
connection to an older world: 'This one's name was Eddie Carbone, a
longshoreman working the docks from Brooklyn Bridge to the breakwater
where the open sea begins.' Thus, the 'bridge' of the play's title gives us the
'view' for this story. From the Brooklyn Bridge one can see all the docks
in Red Hook where Eddie works as a longshoreman. The metaphoric view,
however, extends beyond the breakwater – because Eddie's destiny comes
from Italy across the same luminous sea. The destiny of his ancestors
spans a bridge between the old and new worlds. The span here further
suggests the bridge of a ship, the lookout from which a ship is commanded
as it sails between the two worlds.

Alfieri conveys that Eddie's case must run its 'bloody' course, an
image that has a powerful literal and figurative meaning in the play.
Miller emphasises this by repeating the narrator's statement a number of
times, heightening the figurative use of language through the device of
repetition. For Sicilians blood is the unifying factor in society, connecting
the individual to his immediate family, as well as to his societal family.
Eddie violates such blood relationships: he violates his paternal relation to
Catherine; he violates his conjugal relationship with Beatrice; he violates
Rodolpho's masculinity; and he fatally violates his immigrant society by
informing on 'illegals' to the authorities. Both Marco and Eddie want to
avenge their 'blood' and their vengeance operates literally and figuratively.
As Marco says to Alfieri, 'He degraded my brother. My blood.'

At the play's climax, the image of blood is particularly effective.
Rodolpho tries to make peace with Eddie before Marco comes for revenge,
but Eddie refuses because he is furious at Marco for having sullied his
name in front of the neighbourhood. When Eddie rebuffs Rodolpho,
Beatrice says: 'Only blood is good? He kissed your hand!' Of course,
Beatrice refers to the literal shedding of blood, the vendetta which may be
avoided only by Eddie, Rodolpho and Marco's rapprochement. However,
in the ensuing dialogue blood assumes an additional symbolic meaning:

Beatrice   You want somethin' else, Eddie, and you can never have her!

Catherine (*in horror*)   B!

Eddie (*shocked, horrified, his fists clenching*)   Beatrice! *Marco appears outside, walking toward the door from a distant point.*

Beatrice (*crying out, weeping*)   The truth is not as bad as blood, Eddie! I'm tellin' you the truth – and tell her goodbye for ever!

Eddie (*crying out in agony*)   That's what you think of me – that I would have such thoughts? (77)

In this scene Beatrice refers to blood as 'bloodshed'. However, because she juxtaposes blood with the truth of Eddie's desire for Catherine, it assumes a figurative meaning as well. For Eddie's desire for Catherine is a violation of the blood that courses through his relationships with his family. His violation tragically severs the responsibility to his own blood.

The image of 'tunnels' is also significant, and Alfieri uses this more than once. In his commentary at the end of Act One, he describes Eddie's eyes 'like tunnels; my first thought was that he had committed a crime'. As Eddie moves towards his tragic fate, the light of his eyes indicates the tunnel in which he is trapped. Alfieri describes a passion which 'had moved into his body, like a stranger'. Of course, this passion has many meanings for Eddie: his desire for Catherine, his jealousy, his hatred – even attraction – for Rodolpho.

When Eddie returns to Alfieri's office in Act Two, the imagery of a tunnel stresses Eddie's march toward his fate. In his commentary Alfieri says: 'I will never forget how dark the room became when he looked at me; his eyes were like tunnels. I kept wanting to call the police, but nothing had happened.' This is a crucial scene because Alfieri's mention of a possible crime shows how the law works on several levels in the play: natural law, the Sicilian code and civil law. Eddie is about to snitch: the very act at the end of the dark tunnel when his tale has run its bloody course. Eddie's real tragedy is that he does not recognise the tunnel he is walking through.

In addition to the figurative language that Alfieri uses in his speeches, other images, symbols and metaphors are scattered throughout the play. These devices are rooted in the language of Sicilian-American society, a unique idiom expressing personal, familial, social, religious and cultural codes dictating an individual's behaviour and with which Eddie is in perilous conflict. Images, symbols and metaphors, among them the Madonna, angels and the innocence of a child appear throughout the play to indicate Eddie's struggle with these moral codes.

Eddie's awareness of Catherine's sexuality is often expressed by the iconic female image of the Madonna, the mother of Jesus. In Act One, Eddie first uses this religious allusion to convey his awe at Catherine's beauty:

> With your hair that way you look like a madonna, you know that? You're the madonna type. (*She doesn't look at him, but continues ladling out food onto the plates.*) You wanna go to work, heh, Madonna? (13)

The allusion works on many complicated levels in the text. The Madonna, as the mother of Jesus, possesses a purity, chastity and virginity that contrasts with the immoral sexual attractiveness which Eddie associates with high-heeled shoes and actresses. Eddie would like to preserve Catherine's chastity, which could be threatened by young men if she flaunts her physical beauty by wearing high heels and calling out of windows. In Act One, Eddie repeats his concern for Catherine's chastity when he warns Rodolpho that he does not want her to go to Times Square because 'it's full of tramps over there'. Yet Eddie's wish to keep Catherine's virginity intact is juxtaposed by his physical desire for her, which ironically would destroy her purity. His physical urge is clearly indicated later in the play when he kisses her passionately in Act Two. The Madonna image has powerful religious connections for Italians, which expands Eddie's violation of his cultural codes still further. For not only does Eddie's violation of Catherine, as her surrogate father, border on incest, his violation of her as a Madonna figure is also a grievous sin.

The Madonna image also has powerful psychological connotations in the play. Normally applied to a husband's feelings for his wife, the so-called 'Madonna Complex' operates in an intriguing manner in *A View from the Bridge*. Eddie obviously possesses potent feelings for Catherine that resemble the Madonna complex; however, Eddie and Beatrice's marriage bears scrutiny in this vein. Eddie's inability to sleep with Beatrice may be explained easily by the Madonna complex, but his sexual feelings are complicated. Moreover, the Madonna complex maintains that a husband's sexual inadequacy with his wife occurs as a result of her becoming a mother. The one-act and two-act plays offer different versions of this. In the one-act play, Eddie and Beatrice have two children; in the two-act play, references to the children have been cut. This editing has a powerful effect on how we read the images. Because Beatrice and Eddie are childless in the two-act version, they have put all their parental feelings into Catherine. In a sense, this magnifies Eddie's incestuous attraction. And because Eddie is so consumed with Rodolpho's masculinity, his own infertility somehow magnifies his inadequacy, especially for a man from a macho Italian culture.

Another image, used both literally and figuratively, is that of riding. In Act One, Rodolpho romantically and humorously describes how he pushes taxis and horse carriages up the hill in his Italian home town, and how he desires to own a motorcycle so he can become a messenger. Such modes of transport become figurative in the next scene when Eddie and Beatrice await Rodolpho and Catherine's return from a date. Eddie is worried that 'he's takin' her for a ride', a slang term for taking advantage of her that includes significant sexual connotations. Moreover, Beatrice's response, 'All right, that's her ride', is ironic since she senses Eddie's desire for her niece. Eddie's sexual feelings for Catherine are challenged by Rodolpho, and for Catherine to become Rodolpho's, he must take her for the metaphorical ride, not Eddie.

The image of riding continues in the same context later in the play when Eddie tells Catherine his suspicion that Rodolpho is only 'bowin' to his passport'. Eddie describes him as 'a hit-and-run guy, baby; he's got bright lights in his head, Broadway'. With the 'hit-and-run guy' image, Eddie vividly depicts Rodolpho as a driver intent on running down Catherine's chastity, then leaving the scene. However, when Catherine denies this, Eddie says, 'He could be picked up any day here and he's back pushin' taxis up the hill.' Ironically Eddie applies the literal meaning to the image, exhibiting how Miller can create significant tension between the denotative and connotative meaning of his words.

Eddie's conversation with Alfieri in his law office in Act One contains many images with various negative and positive connotations about women, all of which connect to indicate Eddie's growing crisis and conflicted feelings towards Catherine and Rodolpho. Early in the play Eddie has made references to actresses, chorus girls, high-heeled shoes, stereotypical blondes and the film star Greta Garbo to describe the types of women he does not want Catherine to emulate because of the way they flaunt their sexuality. His desire to preserve Catherine's chastity is clear from the outset of the play. He does not like Catherine to wear high-heeled shoes because he associates high-heeled shoes with the kind of shoes worn by actresses in the movies and, perhaps, with whores in Sicily. Eddie obviously associates movie actresses with female immorality. The image of shoes reveals his actual concern with the sexual allure they give, and Eddie's desire for Catherine is at the core of this allure. Eddie does not want Catherine desired by other men like some Garbo-esque, screen-star icon. He does not want her to attract sexual attention, as he says, 'You're walkin' wavy.' Eddie attempts to suppress Catherine's budding sexuality; ironically, he not only notices it, but is enticed by it. Yet his physical attraction to her is a violation of one of the supreme moral codes at the centre of this play.

In his attempt to feminise Rodolpho, Eddie describes Rodolpho's blond hair as 'platinum', which echoes his previous descriptions of women. Eddie also says about Rodolpho: 'I mean if you close the paper fast – you could blow him over.' This recalls Rodolpho's rendition of 'Paper Doll' and his previous complaint to Beatrice about the dockworkers' nickname. In emasculating Rodolpho, Eddie figuratively attempts to make him into a paper doll.

Eddie uses a particularly revealing image when he describes Rodolpho sewing a dress for Catherine: 'I mean he looked so sweet there, like an angel – you could kiss him he was so sweet.' The angel comparison echoes many of the previous images and allusions. Certainly an angel recalls the Madonna image, for an angel typically possesses the same whiteness and purity. Moreover, traditionally angels are often depicted as blonde and sexless. Yet the angel imagery also shows the complicated nature of Eddie's feelings for Rodolpho. Eddie ironically reveals the same attraction to Rodolpho as he does towards Catherine. The angel image connotes the same sanctity as the Madonna image, both of which are juxtaposed with the physical desire, culminating in a kiss. Although he attempts to emasculate Rodolpho, Eddie paradoxically perceives him as a sexual threat, as when he says, 'When I think ofthat guy layin' his hands on her I could –.' However, Eddie has confused sexuality and masculinity. Blind to his own desires, he merely sees Rodolpho as a criminal: 'He takes and puts his dirty filthy hands on her like a goddam thief Eddie's blindness is indicated when Alfieri says, 'She can't marry you, can she?' and he furiously replies, 'What are you talkin' about, marry me! I don't know what the hell you're talkin' about!' Ironically, the initial use of 'angel' in the play is when Beatrice describes Eddie in the very first scene as an 'angel' for agreeing to take her cousins in as illegal boarders.

Finally, the play consistently uses terms like 'baby', 'little girl' and 'big girl' to describe Catherine. In the first scene of the play, Eddie tells Catherine, 'You're a baby, you don't understand these things.' He then says, 'You're gettin' to be a big girl now.' Beatrice repeatedly addresses her niece as 'baby', but argues with Eddie when he is reluctant to allow her to take the secretarial job, saying 'She's no baby no more' – indicating the essence of the conflict. Eddie, almost in tears after giving her permission to work, laments, 'I guess I just never figured on one thing . . . That you would ever grow up.'

Characters

Eddie

Eddie Carbone is one of Arthur Miller's more complicated and puzzling protagonists. After writing the one-act version of the play Miller said that the meaning of Eddie's fate still remained a mystery to him. Concerned about telling the 'myth-like march of the tale' without embellishment, Miller remained unsettled by Eddie's tragedy. In revising the play for its two-act version, Miller thought that the addition of significant psychological and behavioural details, including Beatrice's and Catherine's viewpoints, would render the play not only more human, warmer and less remote, but also provide a 'clearer statement'. Miller noted that the two-act play made it 'more possible now to relate [Eddie's] actions to our own and thus to understand ourselves a little better not only as psychological entities, but as we connect to our fellows and our long past together.'

Eddie's complex personality manifests itself in a series of contradictory actions that violate the codes by which he lives. We are shocked and appalled by much of what he does: his feelings for Catherine are nothing if not incestuous, and his disregard for Beatrice violates their marriage vows. His attack on Rodolpho involves several motives, and his betrayal of the cousins to the immigration authorities is inexcusable.

Yet Alfieri clearly judges that 'he was a good a man as he had to be in a life that was hard and even'. This goodness must be considered in any evaluation of his character. He has raised Catherine, he agrees to put up the 'submarines' who are, after all, Beatrice's cousins not his, just as Catherine is Beatrice's biological niece. He is a decent provider and a hard worker. There is even a reference to Beatrice having taken in relatives after her father's house burned down, causing Eddie to sleep on the floor. He is genuinely moved by the prospect of taking in the 'submarines', even while acknowledging the substantial legal risks this involves.

All of his actions in the play are motivated by what he believes are the best interests of Catherine. His concern about her safety in a new job and her attractiveness to young men seems initially appropriate and paternal. Nor is he portrayed as intractable: he gives in to Beatrice's and Catherine's pleas and allows her to take the job she is offered. His sense of duty is laudable: he promised Catherine's mother on her deathbed to raise her and he has. All of this kindness is compromised when he is unwilling, indeed unable, to see any other point of view once he sets himself the task of protecting Catherine.

Alfieri describes a passion that 'had moved into his body, like a stranger'. Eddie Carbone is a man in whom passion outweighs reason.

He does not understand his desire, even when it is pointed out to him. When Alfieri suspects that Eddie is on the verge of an act of betrayal, he warns him of the consequences: 'You won't have a friend in the world, Eddie! Even those who understand will turn against you . . . Put it out of your mind!' Despite the warning, Eddie makes his fateful telephone call. He doesn't even seem to recognise the impulse that leads to his kissing Rodolpho.

One way to understand Eddie is to see him in the context of his culture. Revising the play for the London version, Miller sought to place Eddie squarely in relation to the cultural codes of his Sicilian-American environment of Red Hook in the mid-1950s. Eddie's world is insular, personal, familial, social and religious. For the transplanted Sicilians, these are the unifying factors that determine their relationship to the docks and the streets of their neighbourhood, even to their own homes. When Eddie crosses these boundaries he is doomed.

Eddie belongs to a long line of Miller characters who want to protect the dignity of their names. In Miller's first Broadway hit *All My Sons* (1947), Joe Keller's pride as a self-made businessman is proclaimed in the sign over his warehouse. In *Death of a Salesman*, Willy Loman's search for dignity is part of the play's climax: 'I am Willy Loman and you are Biff Loman.' In *The Crucible*, John Proctor refuses to let his signed confession be posted on the Salem church door: 'Because it is my name.' In *A View from the Bridge*, Eddie Carbone similarly wants his good name back. Although Alfieri's final monologue mourns him, 'I admit it – with a certain . . . alarm', Miller said that 'Eddie is still not a man to weep over'.

Eddie's situation in the play can be tied to Miller's original intention of telling the tale as a Greek myth, linking the protagonist's story to ancient, even savage, roots. Are not myth and legend our struggle to explain inexplicable dark human desires and instincts? Aristotle tells us to pity and fear, pity out of human compassion and fear because the same fate can happen to all of us. Miller believed that the two-act play made it 'more possible now to relate [Eddie's] actions to our own and thus to understand ourselves a little better not only as psychological entities, but as we connect to our fellows and our long past together'. As a tragic figure Eddie cries out for personal dignity, even though he is in wrongful pursuit of a dignity he has himself never really understood.

Beatrice

Beatrice is depicted as the devoted wife of Eddie and mother figure to Catherine. Her genuine goodness and generosity is shown by how she has raised Catherine, her sister's child. Initially in the play, Beatrice's character seems stereotypical: she is concerned about the cooking and the cleanliness of the apartment. She exhibits the appropriate deference to Eddie as husband and man of the house, seeking his permission and approval for Catherine's job and her cousins' stay in the apartment. She genuinely means it when she calls him an angel and proclaims that he will be blessed for his good deeds.

However, this is not to suggest that Beatrice is a flat, one-dimensional character. She has considerable depth and complexity and the ability to respond sensibly to the conflicts that erupt when her cousins arrive. Beatrice is often a mediator. At the beginning of the play she successfully convinces Eddie that Catherine, now seventeen, is no longer a child and that he must let her grow up. When Eddie objects to Catherine and Rodolpho's growing relationship, Beatrice tries to persuade him that it is time he let her go. In the final scene of Act One, she is particularly adept at reading the tension between Eddie, Rodolpho and Catherine; she encourages Rodolpho and Catherine to dance, gently probes Marco about his wife, moderates Eddie's scoffing at Rodolpho and questions why Eddie needs to teach Rodolpho to box. In Act Two she makes the arrangements to move Rodolpho and Marco to another apartment.

Beatrice is perceptive about the complexity of Eddie and Catherine's relationship. She is aware of both Catherine's and Eddie's complex feelings for one another. Her dimension as a character is also evident in the way Miller depicts Beatrice and Eddie's sexual relationship in the two-act play. Beatrice has needs and desires of her own. She needs Catherine out of the household in order to preserve her own marriage. Catherine's sexual maturity coincides with Eddie's apparent impotence. Beatrice wants her husband back as a lover but Eddie's physical attraction to Catherine interferes with Beatrice's sex life.

Ultimately Beatrice chooses to side with her husband when Eddie won't allow her to attend Catherine's wedding. However, in the climactic scene when Catherine tells Eddie that he belongs in the garbage, Beatrice shows enormous awareness of the role they all share in the tragedy, declaring: 'Then we all belong in the garbage. You and me, too. Don't say that. Whatever happened we all done it, and don't you ever forget it, Catherine.' She is the only one who understands the responsibility they all share in the events that unfold.

Catherine

Catherine is a character who develops her own strength during the course of the play. In the first scenes, she conveys an innocence that belies her seventeen years. She is compliant and deferential, particularly to Eddie.

Yet the play begins exactly at the moment when Catherine is coming of age, and she is aware of her budding femininity and womanhood. Her desire to take a secretarial job indicates her search for the independence of adulthood. She is clearly devoted to Eddie, her surrogate father, and still seeks his permission, approval and affirmation in most aspects of her life.

Her change from child to adult is swift. Initially her innocence is evident in her awe at Rodolpho's blond hair and her naive questions about life in Italy. She is immediately attracted to him but once they establish a serious relationship, she begins her separation from Eddie, the centre of the play's conflict. In the scene when Eddie suggests that Rodolpho is only using her to obtain a passport, she rejects his suggestion: 'I don't believe it and I wish to hell you'd stop it.' The final scene of Act One, when Catherine purposefully and provocatively dances with Rodolpho, is the final physical manifestation of her selfhood as a woman.

The first scene of Act Two is crucial. In Catherine's conversation with Rodolpho she shows a sensitivity to Eddie's needs as a man, and a remarkable perception that Beatrice does not provide for them. Underlying Catherine's speech is the suggestion of sexual awareness. Her own sexual needs will be fulfilled by Rodolpho. Catherine is even complicit in the loss of her virginity; she initiates their lovemaking when she says to Rodolpho 'teach me . . . I don't know anything', underlining also her inexperience. Catherine and Rodolpho's awareness of their own sexuality magnifies even further the shock of Eddie's kiss, which occurs moments later. Just before this occurs, Catherine expresses an awareness of her newly found maturity when she says, 'Eddie, I'm not gonna be a baby any more.' The image of her as a baby contrasts sharply with her physical experience as a woman. Eddie's kiss is therefore dramatic – the physical sign of his struggle to love her as a child/baby and desire her as a woman.

Rodolpho

Rodolpho is the younger of the two 'submarines' and his role in the play is in contrast to that of his brother Marco in many ways. With no family in Italy to support, he has no responsibilities and has come to indulge himself in the American dream of opportunity. He has the idealism and spirit of youth and sees possibilities in all things. He enjoys life and loves to share his joy with others. The playwright details the generous spirit of this blond Italian: his singing in the hotel in Italy, cooking for the men at sea, singing on the Red Hook docks – all of which Eddie neither appreciates nor understands. Rodolpho proclaims his intention to become an American citizen and return to Italy a rich man. Catherine is immediately attracted to Rodolpho's *joie de vivre* and he is equally attracted to her. Their young love is genuine – a result of his awe at this new world of New York with its movies, theatres and night life, and her wonder at the cultural difference of Rodolpho's life in Italy, with its lemons, fountains and old-world charm.

Like Catherine, Rodolpho is subject to change. He possesses a seriousness which tempers his natural inclination to be fun-loving, and he exhibits appropriate deference to and respect for Eddie, who has taken him in. The turning point in Rodolpho's development comes in the final scene of Act One which occurs late one evening after dinner. Eddie questions Marco about the sexual fidelity of wives back in Italy; he does this to emphasise to both Marco and Rodolpho that American girls like Catherine are not sexually 'easy'. He again complains about Rodolpho's lack of respect in keeping Catherine out late. Marco initially reinforces Eddie's position by telling Rodolpho that he must obey his host. When Catherine asks Rodolpho to dance, he agrees to do so only reluctantly, for he fears Eddie's reaction. Eddie seethes as he watches the couple engage in this most basic of mating rituals. Eddie reacts by coaxing Rodolpho into a boxing match, intended as an aggressive display of his superior physical strength in his own territory. Eddie strikes a staggering blow. The fight ends and Eddie seems satisfied – for the moment. But then a defiant Rodolpho immediately turns to Catherine and asks her to dance, a direct challenge to Eddie's authority as well as his perceived physical strength.

Rodolpho's true character emerges in the final scene of the play. Despite the way Eddie has treated him, he warns him that Marco is coming to wreak vengeance. Rodolpho takes responsibility for his wrongdoing, wishes to apologise and even goes so far as to kiss Eddie's hand in deference, proclaiming, 'I have made all our troubles.' Clearly, Rodolpho, steeped in the Italian mores more than Eddie, understands the coming confrontation with Marco can only result in bloodshed.

Marco

As opposed to the younger Rodolpho, Marco is the serious, dark and brooding brother. He has come to America because the poor economic conditions of post-war Italy have made it difficult for him to support his wife and three children, one of whom is seriously ill. Marco is grateful and appropriately deferential to Eddie, and he often reminds Rodolpho to display the same respect. Marco's situation is made clear on the first night he arrives. He is moved to tears when he realises that he will immediately find work on the docks and can begin to send money back to his wife right away. He offers his hand in thanks to Eddie. In contrast to the entertainment Rodolpho provides on the piers (according to his fellow longshoremen), Marco works like a bull unloading cargo ships.

Marco is nonetheless a force to be reckoned with, especially when crossed. This is exhibited at the conclusion of Act One when Eddie defeats Rodolpho in the boxing match. Eddie has his own tactic turned on him when Marco challenges him to life one leg of a chair with a single hand and Eddie is unable to do so. By raising the chair over Eddie's head, Marco conveys a threat to Eddie: that he will protect his brother, his blood, should Eddie overstep the line again. His action foreshadows his challenge to Eddie at the end of the play.

Alfieri

Miller's plays are full of references to jail, crime and the law. Several of his plays contain lawyers either as major or minor characters. The most notable examples are George Deever in *All My Sons*, Bernard in *Death of a Salesman*, Danforth in *The Crucible*, Quentin in *After the Fall* and Tom Wilson in *The Ride Down Mount Morgan*. In Miller such figures often serve to elevate the moral crisis at the heart of a particular play.

Alfieri in *A View from the Bridge* is the moral arbiter of the law. He plays a dual role, functioning as both narrator and participant in the action. As the narrator of the play, he comments on the action and the audience is meant to view the events through Alfieri's eyes. Alfieri could be said to establish the 'view' to which the play's title refers. His opening monologue indicates that he acts in many ways as a 'bridge': he is a bridge between the old and new worlds, a bridge between the audience and the action, and a bridge between the various characters.

However, this is not meant to suggest that we should make the same judgments as Alfieri does. For he, too, clearly must be seen as a member of the Sicilian-American culture in which he lives. He readily acknowledges the status that his legal profession gives him in the Brooklyn neighbourhood. Unlike Eddie, Beatrice and Catherine, he was born in Italy: he is a genuine immigrant who truly understands the connections between the old and new world. As narrator he signals the importance and dimension of Eddie Carbone's story and he struggles hard to understand Eddie's actions and fate. Eddie is more than a client – for Alfieri he represents something almost larger than life itself.

As a participant in the action of the play, Alfieri is both father-confessor and arbiter of the law. Miller gives him three important scenes: with Eddie in his office in Act One, again with Eddie in his office in Act Two and in the detention centre offering advice to Marco. In his role as a lawyer, Alfieri represents American civil law, but he is also crucial in showing how civil law and its justice conflict with the morals operating in the Sicilian-American society.

Productions

American and English stage productions

The one-act version of *A View from the Bridge* opened on Broadway on 29 September 1955 at the Coronet Theatre (now the Eugene O'Neill Theatre) in a double-bill with *A Memory of Two Mondays*. Directed by Martin Ritt, the cast included Van Heflin as Eddie, Eileen Heckart as Beatrice, Gloria Marlowe as Catherine, Jack Warden as Marco and Richard Davalos as Rodolpho. The set was designed by Boris Aronson and the production ran for 149 performances.

The relatively short run for *A View from the Bridge* was disappointment for Miller, following the equally short run of *The Crucible* in 1953. The reviews were mixed. Brooks Atkinson recognised that the play had enough powerful material for a 'forceful drama', but concluded that it did not quite measure up to the level of tragedy. Despite such reviews, Miller won his third Drama Desk Award.

Miller recognised that he was not fully focused on the production. Distracted by his relationship with Marilyn Monroe and his impending divorce, he remembered that he could not concentrate during the casting calls. He assumed that good actors could play most of the roles; he realised later that some of the actors were miscast. Van Hefm's preoccupation with conveying the mannerisms and speaking in accents of an Italian longshoreman kept him from 'feeling' his part as Eddie. J. Carrol Nash was equally troubled with portraying Alfieri. Miller also recognised that he had not fully explored the roles Eddie, Catherine and Beatrice play and, their parts underwritten, they seemed to appear in an 'academic and irrelevant story of revenge' (*Timebends*, 354).

Miller revised the play into its two-act for the London production where it was first performed at the New Watergate Club at the Comedy Theatre on 11 October 1956. The cast featured Anthony Quayle as Eddie, Mary Ure as Catherine, Megs Jenkins as Beatrice, Brian Bedford as Rodolpho, Ian Bannen as Marco, Richard Harris as Louis and Michael Gwynn as Alfieri. The play opened only after some considerable controversy. The Lord Chamberlain refused to grant permission for *A View from the Bridge* to be performed because he considered a homosexual theme was inappropriate for the public good. The producers came up with the solution of making the audience members of the Comedy Theatre's New Watergate Club as part of their ticket price. The production was therefore considered private and could be performed without any restrictions.

The reviews of the London production were enthusiastic. The *Guardian's* Philip Hope-Wallace called it 'deathly earnest'. Kenneth Tynan declared the play 'just short of being a masterpiece', and he found Peter Brook's production 'uncannily good'. The *Daily Mail's* Cecil Wilson said that the play was 'savage, searing and spellbinding', Quayle giving 'the performance of his life'.

In casting for the London production, Miller was concerned, as he was in New York, with the ability of the actors, this time British, to speak with the deep Sicilian-American accents required for realistic characterisation. Quayle and Ure worked out an accent which Miller described as 'never heard on earth before', but they did convince London audiences that they were speaking Brooklynese. Under Peter Brooks's direction, *A View from Bridge* became in Miller's words, 'a heroic play of great emotional force, the working-class characters larger than life, grand and rather strange' (*Timebends*, 431).

The American premiere of the two-act version took place in 1965 in a successful off-Broadway production at the Sheridan Square Playhouse in New York. The play opened on 28 January and ran for 780 performances. Robert Duvall starred as Eddie Carbone and Jon Voight played Rodolpho. The show was produced and directed by Ulu Grosbard, and Dustin Hoffman, who played Willy Loman in the 1984 Broadway revival of *Death of a Salesman*, was the assistant director. The play won two Obie Awards, for Distinguished Performance by Duvall and Best Direction by Grosbard.

Miller felt that this production 'magically' caught the play's 'spirit'. Duvall said that Eddie Carbone was his favourite role and *A View from the Bridge* the 'greatest play': 'People tend to overlook it. It's my Othello – as great a part, to me, as Othello.' The reviews were enthusiastic: 'Robert Duvall realizes the role of Eddie, the longshoreman whose protective love of his niece turns incestuous, more completely, I think, than any actor who's ever played it,' wrote Norman Nadel in the *New York World-Telegram and Sun* (29 January 1965). In the *New York Post* of the same date Richard Watts wrote, 'In the crucial role of the embittered Eddie, Robert Duvall is especially fine in suggesting the attempted sense of fun in a man totally without it.'

The two-act version of *A View from the Bridge* did not have its Broadway premiere until 1983. Directed by Arvin Brown and starring Tony LoBianco as Eddie, the play opened on 3 February 1983 at the Ambassador Theater, where it repeated the 1955 run of the one-act version of 149 performances before closing on 12 June. The reviews were glowing. Frank Rich in the *New York Times* described it as a 'stunning revival . . . a much-needed evening of electric American drama'. He praised 'the shrewd and forceful direction of Arvin Brown and the tumultuous star performance of Tony LoBianco'. The production won the 1983 Tony Award for Best Revival of a Play.

In 1987 Alan Ayckbourn directed a major London revival at the National Theatre. The play opened on 12 February 1987 Cottesloe, and transferred to the Aldwych Theatre in London's West End on 3 November 1987, closing its year-long run on 20 February 1988.

Michael Gambon's portrayal of Eddie Carbone and Ayckbourn's direction received universal praise among the London critics. 'In any critic's life there are certain red-letter nights. The new production of *A View from the Bridge* at the Gottesloe is empathetically one of them. In the first place it shows Michael Gambon shaking hands with greatness. But Alan Ayckbourn's immaculately detailed production also banishes any doubts about Arthur Miller's play and vindicates its claim to be a modern tragedy' (*Guardian*, 14 February 1987). 'It remains one of the great productions of our time not only because of Michael Gambon's towering central performance but because Ayckbourn establishes the vital Miller connection between the tragic hero and the moral laws of the tribal community' (*Guardian*, 5 November 1987). 'It is hard to believe that there ever has been, or perhaps ever will be, a better production of Arthur Miller's *A View from the Bridge*' (*Punch*, 18 November 1987). Gambon won the 1983 Olivier Award for Best Actor.

Another major Broadway revival opened on 14 December 1997 at the Criterion Center Stage Right in a Roundabout Theatre Company production that later transferred to the Neil Simon Theatre. Directed by Michael Mayer, the cast included Anthony LaPaglia as Eddie, Allison Janney as Beatrice, Brittany Murphy as Catherine and Stephen Spinella as Alfieri. The production ran for 239 performances and won the Tony Award for Best Revival of a Play; LaPaglia won the Tony Award for Best Actor in a Play. The production also received the Drama Desk Award for Outstanding Revival of a Play, Outstanding Featured Actress in a Play for Janney, and Outstanding Direction of a Play for Mayer. The reviews were enthusiastic. Ben Brantley in the *New York Times* described the production as a 'first-rate new revival . . . with a cast that approaches perfection . . . Under Mr Mayer's finely calibrated direction, this production seems to meet every requisite Mr Miller might desire. The correlation with classical tragedy is directly evoked by David Gallo's amphitheatre-inspired set, with curved tiers of steps overlooking the circle where the principal action takes place. The sense of a judgmental community, which Mr Miller insists is central to the play, is vividly embodied by the large ensemble of extras who fill the stage between scenes. And Kenneth Posner's shadowy lighting seems to locate the emotions the characters often don't dare express.'

Another major London revival opened on 5 February 2009 at the Duke of York's Theatre, directed by Lindsay Posner. The production featured Ken Stott as Eddie, Mary Elizabeth Mastrantonio as Beatrice, Hayley

Atwell as Catherine and Harry Lloyd as Rodolpho. It closed on 16 May 2009. Michael Billington in the *Guardian* described it as a 'perfectly decent production' but noted that Posner 'treats the play as the tragedy of a doomed individual', rather than 'a portrait of a community'. He took issue with Christopher Oram's design, 'dominated by a massive tenement providing little space for the teeming street life of Red Hook'. Lizzie Loveridge (*Curtain Up*) was, however, more favourably impressed: 'With the experience of Lindsay Posner and talented actors Ken Stott and Mary Elizabeth Mastrantonio in the lead roles, there is very little that can go wrong.' She, too, saw this production as focusing on the tragedy of an individual: 'Here Eddie Carbone is an isolated figure, head of his own family rather than a member of the wider Italian American community.' Benedict Nightingale of *The Times* wrote that, 'Lindsay Posner's fine revival goes far towards convincing me that Miller was right to believe he'd written a tragedy, complete with a flawed protagonist.'

A much anticipated Broadway revival of *A View from the Bridge* opened on 24 January 2010 at New York's Gort Theatre, directed by the veteran Gregory Mosher. Tony Award-winner and film star Liev Schreiber returned to the Broadway stage as Eddie, the accomplished Jessica Hecht was cast as Beatrice, and movie star Scarlett Johansson made her Broadway debut as Catherine. The production received universal rave reviews. John Lahr of *The New Yorker* described the production as 'a singular astonishment: a kind of theatrical lightning bolt that sizzles and startles . . . one of the best productions of [Miller's] work that I've ever seen.' Ben Brantley of the *New York Times* judged that Schreiber's conception of Eddie 'registers changes in emotional temperature with organic physical precision.' He also noted that Johansson 'melts into her character so thoroughly that her nimbus of celebrity disappears.' Joe Dziemianowicz of the *New York Daily News* singled out Hecht as giving a 'performance of quiet anguish that ultimately erupts into something shattering.'

Film adaptations

Luchino Visconti directed a stage version of *A View from the Bridge* in Italy in 1958. At the same time, he was working on his film *Rocco and his Brothers*, shot in 1960 and released the next year. The film is about an impoverished widow and her five sons, who migrate from a small southern Italian village in search of a better life in Milan. Critics at once recognised the strong influence of *A View from the Bridge* on Visconti's film.

A film directly based on *A View from the Bridge*, titled *Vu du pont*, was released in February 1961. The two-year run of the French stage production convinced the producer Paul Graetz that a movie version would be successful in the so-called 'art-house circuit' popular in the United States and Western Europe. Graetz shot the film simultaneously in English and French. He chose an American, Sidney Lumet, to direct. Exterior scenes were filmed on the streets of New York, and interior scenes in a Paris studio. The film featured a notable cast: Raf Vallone, who starred in the Paris stage production, reprised his role as Eddie. Maureen Stapleton, the renowned stage and screen actress, played Beatrice; Carol Lawrence, widely known for her role as Maria in the original Broadway production of *West Side Story*, was Catherine. Miller's friend, Michigan classmate and fellow playwright Norman Rosten wrote the screenplay. The film, however, opened to mixed reviews, some praising Lumet's superb direction and others describing it as bankrupt of vision. Some felt that the film was unclear on whether the events were naturalistic or tragic.

Opera

In 1999 an opera of *A View from the Bridge* with music by William Bolcom and libretto by Arnold Weinstein and Arthur Miller premiered at the Lyric Opera of Chicago.

The gestation for the opera version of *A View from the Bridge* began with Weinstein, who had taught the play in his classes at Columbia University. After Bolcom wrote the music for Miller's play *Broken Glass* in 1994, Weinstein, with Miller's approval, encouraged him to make *A View from the Bridge* his next operatic project.

The work was performed in New York at the Metropolitan Opera in 2002. Bolcom made changes for the New York version, most notably adding two new arias, one each for the characters of Eddie and Beatrice. The New York production premiered on 5 December and received strong reviews. Howard Kissel of the *New York Daily News* judged it as 'one of those rare times when opera is great theater'. Anthony Tommasini of the *New York Times* called it an 'involving and significant work'. The New York production was given a total of eight performances and the final performance on 28 December 2002 was broadcast live over the Chevron Texaco Metropolitan Opera International Radio Network to more than 360 stations in the United States and forty countries around the world.

The production was widely praised for its strong performances: Kim Josephson's robust portrayal of Eddie strongly conveyed his tragic downfall; Catherine Malfitano's vocal range was particularly effective in capturing Beatrice's conflict between her niece and her husband; Isabel Bayrakdarian, in her Met debut, convincingly expressed Catherine's growth from girl to woman. Gregory Turay was outstanding as Rodolpho; his tenor voice frequently moved the audience to applause. His performance of 'New York Lights', when Rodolpho sings a paean about his love for New York City in the first act, is one of the more dramatic moments in the opera. The song received particular notice from music critics as a melody that could be attractive to popular music listeners. Bolcom explained that he conceived the piece as a fusion of Broadway melody and early-twentieth-century Neapolitan songs and the lyrics also mix images from Sicily and New York.

The massive set, designed by Santo Loquasto, who had previously designed the sets and costumes for Miller's 1994 play *Broken Glass*, merged the interior and exterior settings without clear delineation. Steel girders and platforms evoked both the docks where Eddie plied his trade as a longshoreman and the Brooklyn Bridge, with its literal and figurative importance in the work. Brick and wood suggested the tenement buildings of the Red Hook neighbourhood. Scrims and projection screens on the back walls of the stage showed images of Sicily, Brooklyn. Manhattan and the Red Hook docks. The set provided the necessary space for the production's large chorus. The chorus, of course, fits Miller's grand scheme to place Eddie among his neighbours in the large Sicilian-American community.

In writing the libretto, Miller incorporated a significant amount of the prose poetry belonging to the original one-act version of *View*, adapting lyrical dialogue to the conventions of operatic music. Since its premiere *A View from the Bridge* has become a regular part of the American operatic repertoire, playing at the Washington National Opera in 2007.

Notes

The notes below explain words and phrases from the play, with page numbers referencing the Student Editions published by Bloomsbury Methuen Drama.

6	*I promised your mother on her deathbed*: Catherine is the daughter of Nancy, Beatrice's sister. The play is unclear about how she died, but Eddie and Beatrice have raised Catherine since she was a baby.
7	*North River*: another name for the Hudson River on the west of Manhattan.
7	*That's fixed*: Beatrice means this as 'set' or 'determined', but the term also has the connotation of meaning as arranged through illegal activity as 'putting the fix in'.
10	*Stenographer*: a boss dictated letters to a stenographer, who wrote them down in shorthand and would then type them up. The stenographer had fewer duties and responsibilities than a secretary.
11	*Navy Yard*: the Brooklyn Navy Yard was the famous shipbuilding yard located on the East River. Arthur Miller worked there during the Second World War before his successful career as a playwright.
13	*Madonna*: Mary the mother of Jesus Christ. Eddie's description of Catherine as a Madonna has many significant meanings (see 'Language' in Commentary).
14	*We'll bust a bag tomorrow*. Eddie means that a sack of coffee will 'accidentally' get damaged while being unloaded from the ship, enabling him to bring home some of its contents.
14	*Buick*: an American automobile characterised by its large size.
16	*The kid snitched?*: slang for informing. The story about Vinny Bolzano, who informed to immigration authorities, foreshadows Eddie's action.
17	*Captain's pieced off*: slang term for an illegal payment to keep silent.
17	*the Syndicate*: another term for organised crime such as the Mafia. Illegal immigrants like Marco and Rodolpho must work off the price the Syndicate paid for smuggling them into the country
20	*Danes invaded Sicily*: Sicily located at the crossroads of the Mediterranean, has been one of the most invaded lands in Europe. The Viking invasions of Sicily occurred during the Middle Ages. This is often used as an explanation for the physical appearance of blond, blue-eyed Sicilians.
22	*He trusts his wife*: A reference to the sexual fidelity of Italian women. Later in Act One, Eddie implies otherwise.
22	*I understand it's not too good here, either*: A reference to the economic conditions and the availability of work in America

25   *Napolidan*: popular Neapolitan songs. *Bel canto*, literally
      'beautiful singing', was a style of singing much favoured in
      mid-nineteenth-century Italy; it emphasised beauty of tone in the
      delivery of highly florid music.

25   *Paper Doll*: the famous hit song by the Mills Brothers.

26   *Garbo*: the Hollywood movie star Greta Garbo.

27   *Paramount*: at the time in which the play is set, New York had
      two movie theatres named the Paramount, one in downtown
      Brooklyn and one in Manhattan.

28   *sump'm*: something.

29   *When am I gonna be a wife again?*: Beatrice and Eddie have not
      had sexual relations in three months.

30   *submarines*: slang for illegal immigrants who have arrived by
      ship, implying the stealthlike way they have arrived in America.

30   *Matson Line . . . Moore-MacCormack Line*: names of shipping
      companies.

32   *Times Square*: the famous entertainment centre of New York,
      where Broadway meets Seventh Avenue just north of 42nd
      Street. Tramps in this instance are prostitutes.

32   *Broadway*: the main thoroughfare through Times Square; it is the
      generic name for theatre district in New York.

34   *if you wasn't an orphan, wouldn't he ask your father's
      permission before he run around with you like this?*: Eddie
      makes a number of references to the promise he made to
      Catherine's mother on her deathbed. Note that no mention is
      made in the play to Catherine's father. Patriarchal authority
      remained strong in the 1950s Sicilian-American culture depicted
      by Miller, and Eddie assumes this role.

34   *Katie, he's only bowin' to his passport*: Eddie insists that
      Rodolpho only wants to obtain American citizenship, which
      would be easier for him to achieve if he married an American
      citizen.

41   *I mean he looked so sweet there, like an angel – you could
      kiss him he was so sweet*: this line foreshadows the kiss Eddie
      delivers in Act Two.

41   *There's only one legal question here . . . The manner in which
      they entered the country. But I don't think you want to do
      anything about that, do you?*: this foreshadows Eddie's snitching
      to the immigration authorities, the very act he abhorred earlier in
      the play

45   *Coney Island*: the famous amusement park and beach in
      Brooklyn.

46   *I betcha there's plenty surprises sometimes when those guys get back there, heh?*: Eddie insinuates that many Italian wives are unfaithful to their husbands; consequently, upon his return, a husband may find a child not fathered by him

50   *Danish*: Eddie calls Rodolpho by this name to bring attention again to his unusual blond hair.

55   *This is your question or his question?*: Rodolpho is aware of the doubts which Eddie has placed in Catherine's mind.

56   *razzes*: criticises with the intention of annoying someone.

66   *Bari*: a city on the Adriatic coast in southern Italy.

69   *Andiamo*: 'let's go' in Italian.

70   *Marco spits into Eddie's face* in Italian culture a particularly insulting act.

71   *That one! I accuse that one!* Marco's public accusation humiliates Eddie in front of his neighbours, causing him to be ostracised.

72   *In my country he would be dead now*: Marco seeks the vengeance on Eddie that would be exacted in Italy

73   *The law? All the law is not in a book*: Marco is frustrated that civil law in America provides no justice for him against Eddie, just as earlier Eddie was frustrated that the law could not help him stop Rodolpho and Catherine's relationship.

Questions for Further Study

1 Discuss Catherine's growing awareness of herself as a woman. Do you think she recognises Eddie's desire for her?

2 How important are Alfieri's roles as lawyer and narrator?

3 Is Eddie a tragic hero? Do we sympathise with him at the play's end?

4 When Miller first heard the tale upon which he based *A View from the Bridge*, he thought it was 'some re-enactment of a Greek myth'. To Miller, the events seemed almost the work of fate. Gould Eddie have prevented his fate?

5 Discuss why Alfieri uses the words 'a passion which had moved into Eddie's body'.

6 Rodolpho refuses to go to Italy when he and Catherine marry. Does this give credence to Eddie's claim that Rodolpho is 'bowin' to his passport'?

7 What does the play suggest about immigration issues and illegal aliens?

8 Discuss whether Marco wants to exact justice or revenge on Eddie.

9 Why does Eddie knowingly inform to the immigration authorities when Alfieri has told him the consequences of such an action?

10 Analyse Eddie's apparent lack of awareness of his desire for Catherine.

11 Discuss Eddie's violation of the codes of his society.

12 Explain Eddie's state of mind in wanting his name back. How does he expect to retain his honour in front of his neighbours when he has knowingly informed?

13 How does civil law operate in the play? How does social law operate in the play?

14 The play ends with Eddie crying out, 'My B'. Discuss Beatrice's devotion to Eddie.

15 Discuss the characters in the play who take responsibility for their actions.

16 Analyse Miller's use of symbolic and metaphorical language in the dialogue.

17 Why is the stage presence of the neighbours in the Red Hook community so important to the effect of the play?

18 At the end of the play, Alfieri tells the audience that he mourns Eddie with a 'certain alarm'. Arthur Miller said that Eddie is 'not a man to weep over'. How do you ultimately judge Eddie? What do his actions suggest about the human condition?

19 Discuss how the casting of the play with additional actors affects the production and ultimately the meaning of the play in performance.

20 In the 1956 production of *A View from the Bridge*, the set was more realistic than the skeletal set of the original New York production. Other recent productions of the play have used a scrim of the Brooklyn Bridge and the Brooklyn Navy Yard as backgrounds. Discuss how the set of a particular production can affect the performance of *A View from the Bridge*. How would you design a set for the play?

21 There is significant argument about the meaning of Eddie kissing both Catherine and Rodolpho in Act Two. As a director, how would you block this scene?

22 At the climax of the play, Marco comes to take revenge on Eddie, but it is Eddie who springs the knife on Marco. How does the staging of this scene affect the audience's perception of Eddie's tragedy?

Broken Glass

commentary and notes by
ALAN ACKERMAN

Plot

It is November 1938. News from Germany has reached New York of the anti-Jewish pogroms known as *Kristallnacht* or 'the Night of Broken Glass'. In Brooklyn, a Jewish-American housewife Sylvia Gellburg, who is obsessed with the newspaper reports, has become paralysed from the waist down. Doctors can find nothing wrong with her. Her condition appears to be psychosomatic. She is emotionally repressed, unhappily married to a 'self-hating Jew' and she identifies with the victims of violence.

In *Broken Glass*, Arthur Miller digs beneath the respectable veneer of family life to explore the destructive impulses that individuals turn upon themselves and the social pressures they internalise. Onstage, the neighbourhood doctor Harry Hyman leads the excavation through a series of conversations. He probes the psychological sources of both Sylvia's paralysis and her failed marriage. The domestic drama coincides with her husband Phillip's disintegration at Brooklyn Guarantee and Trust, where he heads the Mortgage Department. He makes a costly mistake, then cringing before his anti-Semitic boss, collapses of a heart attack. In the end Phillip and Sylvia are both invalids at home, where Phillip recognises the destructive power of self-hatred and suffers a second heart attack. Sylvia, in an effort to help him, manages to rise to her feet, creating an ambiguous final image of alarm and hope.

Scene One

The office and home of Dr Harry Hyman. This scene provides an exposition or background information. Phillip Gellburg waits to enquire about the condition of his wife, Sylvia. He is middle-aged, intense and dressed in black. The doctor's wife, Margaret, tells him that Hyman has been delayed because of a strike at the hospital and because his horse went lame. The image of him riding a lame horse suggests Sylvia's paralysis and foreshadows Hyman's relation to her. Margaret's lusty energy contrasts with Gellburg's limpness. She is 'fair', not Jewish, and makes the common mistake of calling him Goldberg, which reinforces his sense of being stereotyped. When the handsome, Heidelberg-educated Hyman arrives, Margaret exits. The two men trade clichés about women, and Hyman's attempt at male bonding reinforces the impression of his masculinity and Gellburg's anxiety about his own. It contributes to the stereotype of the emasculated Jewish man and associates masculinity with power. The conversation turns to Sylvia, at home in a wheelchair, as well as to news of Hitler and the smashing of Jewish stores in Berlin. Gellburg thinks that nothing can be done about anti-Semitism and that Jews bring persecution on themselves.

Hyman wants to learn more about the Gellburgs. He and other physicians have been unable to find any explanation for Sylvia's paralysis. They believe that she suffers from a 'hysterical paralysis', an affliction rooted in an unconscious trauma. Gellburg recounts the onset of the paralysis: they had been going to the movies, and suddenly her legs 'turned to butter'. Hyman probes with personal questions because 'sex could be connected'. Gellburg tensely replies that they have a healthy sex life; the physical problem started with the newspaper pictures of *Kristallnacht*. He boasts that he is the only Jew at Brooklyn Guarantee, where he heads the Mortgage Department. Finally, Hyman advises Phillip to give his wife 'a lot of loving'. After Gellburg departs, Hyman and Margaret discuss the case. They agree that Sylvia is a beautiful woman. The scene ends with him describing a fantasy with his wife on a desert island, exciting her before the blackout.

Scene Two

Next evening in the Gellburg bedroom, the 'buxom' Sylvia in a wheelchair reads a newspaper and chats to her sister Harriet, who tidies up. Harriet expresses bewilderment at her sister's condition. They discuss Harriet's son David, who has decided not to go to college in these Depression years because it wouldn't help him to get a job. Sylvia laments the fact that she never went to college. She is curious about the world and explains why she has been riveted by the recent newspaper accounts of old Jewish men forced by Germans to clean sidewalks with toothbrushes. Harriet says it is not her business. Sylvia must stop thinking about the Germans. Sylvia returns to the paper, and Harriet leaves. Gellburg enters and surprises his wife. Following Hyman's advice and hoping to please her, he brings pickles from Flatbush Avenue, where he went to foreclose on a property. Sylvia wants to know if the tenants were nice people. Gellburg doesn't care, setting up a moral contrast between his failure to empathise and Sylvia's sympathy with strangers. Nonetheless, Sylvia feels guilty and apologises for her condition. They discuss a letter from their son Jerome, who has progressed to the rank of army captain and inspires his father with pride. Gellburg thinks it's an honour to be a West Point graduate and hopes that his son will become the first Jewish general. They bicker. Then, as the doctor ordered, Gellburg displays affection. He says he wants her to be happy. He suggests talking 'everything' out with Hyman, hinting at something traumatic in their past. There follows an elliptical conversation about trying to overcome a longstanding problem in their marriage which goes nowhere.

Scene Three

A conversation between Harriet and Dr Hyman, who is dressed in riding clothes, in his office. Harriet has come at Hyman's request to talk about her sister. She mentions that Hyman had dated her cousin twenty-five years earlier. Hyman probes to learn if Sylvia experienced any shock before her paralysis; he asks intimate questions about her marriage and her fascination with the Nazis. They discuss the oppressive character of Gellburg, who is a Republican, afflicted by Jewish self-hatred. Harriet tells a story about how Gellburg hit his wife with a steak she had overcooked, an episode that Gellburg patched up with expensive gifts. Sylvia is an innocent victim who has done nothing but love everybody. The conversation leads to speculation that, though Gellburg adores his wife, he is sexually impotent.

Scene Four

Stanton Case's office. Donning his blazer and a captain's cap, Stanton Case, President of Brooklyn Guarantee, prepares to go yachting. Gellburg comes in to discuss a property on Broadway that Case hopes to buy and renovate as an annexe for the Harvard Club. Case takes no personal interest in the obsequious Gellburg and makes a few broadly anti-Semitic remarks. Getting down to business, Gellburg explains that Case's project for the Harvard Club is dubious. Over-analysing it, Gellburg interprets recent maintenance decisions by the neighbouring retail giant, Wanamaker's Department Store, as a sign that Wanamaker's will be moving or going out of business. He concludes that the neighbourhood will depreciate in value. Case thanks him for the research, heads off to sail, and Gellburg remains with a 'self-satisfied toss of his head'.

Scene Five

Sylvia at home in bed. Hyman lets himself in, fresh from a ride on Brighton beach, suggesting interrelated themes of freedom and paralysis and analogies between the relationships of rider/horse, doctor/patient and man/woman. He sits on the bed, draws up the covers and looks appraisingly at Sylvia's legs. He compliments her strong, beautiful body. Hyman acknowledges his attraction and his own vanity. He then urges her to talk about what's bothering her and to take responsibility for herself. Sylvia wishes she could; she loves talking with the charming doctor. They recollect the days when he drove girls crazy doing acrobatics on the beach. Sylvia also expresses her attraction to Hyman. The conversation turns to Phillip, who insisted that she should stop working when they married, though she loved her job as a bookkeeper. Hyman urges her to move; it doesn't work. They talk about his experience as a medical student in Germany and about recent pictures of *Kristallnacht* in the *New York Times*. Hyman concludes by advising Sylvia to imagine that they have made love and that she is telling him 'secret things'. He departs, and Sylvia remains, knees spread, paralysed in bed.

Scene Six

Hyman's office. As Hyman finishes with another patient, Gellburg waits and chats over cocoa with Margaret, but they irritate each other. Margaret exits. When Hyman arrives, Gellburg says that he has followed his advice about having sex with his wife. Hyman speculates that Sylvia's fear of the Nazis is a product of feeling vulnerable and unloved. Gellburg expresses his own feeling of persecution and anxiety that Sylvia is pretending paralysis to hurt him. He explains to the sexually confident Hyman that he has problems with sex. The conversation becomes more intimate. Gellburg says that he got a 'big yen' for Sylvia one night when she was sleeping and made love to her. She responded physically but the next morning claimed that she didn't remember it. He believes that his wife is trying to nullify him. According to Gellburg, she told him that he'd imagined the sex. Gellburg becomes increasingly worked up. Hyman asks abruptly if Sylvia has said anything about him. Gellburg wants to know what Hyman is up to: 'Are you a doctor or what!' He storms out. Hyman remains, guilty and alarmed. Margaret comes in and also becomes suspicious. She thinks that it might be best if Sylvia saw an actual psychiatrist. Hyman believes that Sylvia really 'knows something'. Margaret, a sensible and ironic woman, finds her husband exasperatingly self-absorbed.

Scene Seven

The office of Stanton Case. Case, in a dark mood, is angry with Gellburg for having lost him the property on Broadway. Gellburg misread the signs. Rather than going out of business, Wanamaker's had simply hired another plumber. To make matters worse, a Jewish investor has bought the property, prompting Case to suspect Gellburg of collusion because he, too, is Jewish. Gellburg insists that he is loyal to Case and begs forgiveness for his mistake. But Case remains cold, which only heightens Gellburg's anxiety.

Scene Eight

Sylvia, in a wheelchair by her bed, listens to the popular Jewish singer Eddie Cantor on the radio. Hyman arrives, and they chat about music. Hyman lifts her on to the bed, raising the sexual tension. He talks of psychoanalysis: he would need to deal with her dreams and deepest feelings, and he is not trained in psychotherapy. Nonetheless, Sylvia wants to tell him her dreams. She describes a nightmare in which a crowd of Germans are hunting for her, as in the newspaper pictures of *Kristallnacht*. She tries to run but is captured, raped and mutilated by a faceless man she identifies as her husband. Sylvia connects the dream to Gellburg's Jewish self-hatred. Hyman concludes that she is frightened of her husband; she draws the doctor to her and kisses him on the mouth. She becomes ashamed. Hyman asks if she and her husband have had sex and discovers that Gellburg lied. They haven't had sexual relations for almost twenty years, since the birth of their son. There is no clear explanation, only that Gellburg suddenly became impotent. When they were young, Sylvia's father suggested that Gellburg see a doctor, and he was so humiliated and felt so emasculated that he stopped having sex with his wife. Hyman explains that Margaret thinks there is something between himself and Sylvia, and Sylvia is pleased. She says that Phillip once hit her, drawing a connection between her husband and the Nazis. She points out that, though Hyman has said that the Germans were such nice people, they too suddenly turned violent. She wants to know what will become of 'us'. Hyman says she's confusing two things. He's out of his depth and can't help. She takes a step off the bed in an attempt to reach him and 'the power he represents' but collapses on the floor before he can help her.

Gellburg arrives and demands to know what has happened and what Hyman is doing there. Hyman says he was worried and came to see her because Sylvia is 'desperate to be loved'. This statement is a revelation to Gellburg. After Hyman's departure, Gellburg and Sylvia discuss her conflation of attacks on Jews with their self-destructive marriage, implying the complicity of the victim. Sylvia accuses him of being a 'little liar' (like Biff to Willy in *Death of a Salesman*) for telling Hyman that they slept together, and this is followed by a moment of recognition. Sylvia exclaims: 'What I did with my life! Out of ignorance. Out of not wanting to shame you in front of other people. A whole life. Gave it away like a couple of pennies.' For Gellburg, the turning point was when she wanted to go back to work after having the baby and he insisted that she stay at home. He feels that she never forgave him for making her a housewife. But he feared that she 'didn't want him to be the man', and when she did not want more children, he dried up. He never knew why she married him because he finds his Jewish face unattractive. Gellburg insists that they have to sleep together. She says no. Weeping, he shouts that she is trying to kill him. She begins to reach out in pity before the blackout.

Scene Nine

Case's office. Gellburg, still distraught by the Wanamaker's business, has asked for a meeting to prove his dedication to the company (another scene with a parallel in *Death of a Salesman*). His whole life is there. He is more proud of his work at the company than anything except his own son. Radically insecure, he expresses his anxiety at losing Case's confidence and his sense of unfairness. Case coldly replies that he hopes his old confidence will return as time goes by, but he refuses to reassure Gellburg, who becomes hysterical, accuses Case of anti-Semitism and collapses of a heart attack.

Scene Ten

Sylvia is at home in bed, Margaret and Harriet are with her. This scene was a late addition, which Miller wrote at the request of the British director David Thacker, who wanted to see the women together before a final confrontation between the men. They discuss Gellburg's condition. Margaret and Harriet worry that Sylvia blames herself. She does, but she also acknowledges that she has always been the stronger partner, despite the pretences, and she wants to help her man. Harriet insists that Sylvia should not blame herself and that no marriage would survive if people started to say what they know. Margaret expresses the fatalistic view that a person's character is determined from infancy by genetics. The scene sets out a basic opposition between free will and determinism: each person does the best she can with the cards she's been dealt. It concludes on a note of moral ambiguity with Sylvia expressing the desire to go to her husband.

Scene Eleven

Gellburg's bedroom. Hyman examines him and urges him to go to hospital. Gellburg resists. His job, he believes, is over. He feels that his boss made a fool of him, and he is convinced that he has been unfairly treated. He also comes to the realisation that what Sylvia fears most is him. Finally, Gellburg wants to talk about being Jewish with Hyman, whom he knows is also Jewish, but someone who is not obsessed with identity. The anti-religious Hyman says that he has never pretended that he wasn't Jewish. He is a socialist. Gellberg wonders how there can be Jews if there is no God, and Hyman expresses the belief that groups will simply worship different consumer items. The scene raises the question of what it means to be a Jew and whether that identity is important. Gellburg says, 'I wouldn't know you were Jewish except for your name.' But he has also turned from his pride at being the only Jew employed at his company to the awareness that he has been exploited: 'You got some lousy rotten job to do, get Gellburg, send in the Yid.'

Building to a conclusion, Gellburg claims that 'they will never destroy us'. He wants his wife back. Hyman tells him to look in the mirror and recognise that he hates himself; that is what is scaring Sylvia to death. He concludes that Gellburg 'helped paralyse her with this "Jew, Jew, Jew" coming out of your mouth and the same time she reads it in the paper and it's coming out of the radio day and night'. Gellburg expresses a near-tragic paradox: he wants to be an Old-World Jew *and* he wants to be an assimilated American. Hyman believes that Jews don't have to be different from anybody else, and 'Everybody's persecuted'. Even Hitler has a persecution complex. There is no solution, but Gellburg should forgive Sylvia, forgive himself, forgive the Jews and forgive the goyim. Hyman leaves. Margaret pushes Sylvia in her wheelchair into Gellburg's bedroom. In their final conversation, Phillip acknowledges his fears and begs her forgiveness. On realising that he has harmed her, he seems to have another, perhaps fatal, heart attack. Sylvia struggles to break free of the wheelchair and rises to her feet. With a combination of hope and alarm she takes a faltering step towards her husband.

Commentary

The Holocaust gained enormous prominence in American culture during the 1990s, when Arthur Miller wrote his play. In 1993 the United States Memorial Holocaust Museum was dedicated on the National Mall in Washington DC, with speeches by President Bill Clinton and Nobel Peace Prize-winner Elie Wiesel, making it the dominant symbolic representation of Jewishness in America. In that same year, *Schindler's List*, which centres on the efforts of a German industrialist to save Polish Jews, became the most critically acclaimed film of Steven Spielberg's career. It won seven Oscars, including Best Picture and Best Director. On 1 March 1994, Miller's *Broken Glass*, a play that takes its title from the 1938 anti-Jewish pogrom known as *Kristallnacht*, or 'Night of Broken Glass', opened at the Long Wharf Theatre in New Haven. The play relates the failed marriage of a middle-aged Jewish couple in Brooklyn to those world-historical events. It underscores the characters' kinship to both the perpetrators and the Jewish victims of Nazi terror. It explores the theme of 'Jewish self-hatred', a term whose history dates back to the nineteenth century, and raises questions about whether identity derives from the choices people make or from something essential in their nature.

For a moralistic playwright such as Miller, anti-Semitism and the Holocaust had long been important subjects, but, unlike Clifford Odets, Saul Bellow or Philip Roth, he is not well known for making Jewish themes the focus of his major works. Critics have debated, therefore, whether Miller ought to be called a 'Jewish writer'. Christopher Bigsby, a leading scholar of his work, thinks he should. At the conclusion of *Arthur Miller: A Critical Study*, Bigsby draws a picture of Miller's Jewish origins in mystical terms: to be a Jew was to 'draw down lightning'. Jews have been the victims of numerous persecutions, and Miller made the Holocaust his subject more than any other American dramatist. Bigsby cites references in his plays to this 'Jewish trauma' as key evidence that Miller is a Jewish writer, dating Miller to a historical moment when the Holocaust appeared to deeply inform Jewishness, at least in America. This defence of Miller's Jewish identity echoes the rhetoric of *Broken Glass*. 'I never pretended I wasn't Jewish,' says Dr Hyman, perhaps reflecting the author's point of view in the play. *Broken Glass* shows that it is impossible to locate a precise source of Jewishness and highlights the fact that many assimilationist Jews of Miller's generation erased, evaded, or worried about their Jewish origins in America. But it is less important to establish whether Miller was or wasn't a Jewish writer than to appreciate why this question came up in the first place. Written late in Miller's career, yet contemporary with the rise of 'identity politics' in America, *Broken Glass* illuminates this historical debate.

In a 1969 interview, Miller responded to a series of questions about 'Jewishness' in his work and life by saying, 'I take all this as an accusation that somehow I'm "passing" for non-Jewish. Well, I happen to have written the first book about anti-Semitism in this country in recent time. I've written numerous stories about Jews as Jews.'[1] Miller's reaction recalls a crucial theme in *Broken Glass* and in several of his other works, which represent characters that attempt to pass as non-Jews or express anxiety at being associated with Jews. The protagonist of the 1945 novel *Focus*, to which he refers, is an anti-Semitic non-Jew who is mistaken for being Jewish. The novel climaxes with a vicious attack by a racist organisation in a residential neighbourhood in Queens, New York, in which the gentile protagonist Lawrence Newman, who resembles Phillip Gellburg in *Broken Glass*, fights back-to-back with the Jewish shopkeeper Finkelstein and finally recognises a responsibility to combat a world of prejudice in which he had been complicit. It also represents a model of Jewish identity that is fundamentally oppositional, a struggle against stereotype.

The Holocaust – the very term Holocaust – only began to penetrate the broader American consciousness in the 1960s, after the capture and trial of the Nazi war criminal Adolf Eichmann. Although *Kristallnacht* was widely publicised and ran on the front page of the *New York Times* for nearly two weeks in 1938, the Holocaust was not central to American Jewish culture in the 1940s and 1950s. There was a reluctance to portray Jews as victims in the post-war years. Miller's plays from those decades – *All My Sons*, *Death of a Salesman*, *The Crucible*, *A View from the Bridge* – did not feature explicitly Jewish characters. The plays turned away from the author's origins, but they also typified the assimilationist values of that time, which are central to *Broken Glass*. In the 1930s, many Jewish immigrants' children (of which Miller was one), eager to assimilate, left behind most of the ritual practices of traditional Judaism. Eichmann's trial and execution, which attached the word 'Holocaust' to the murder of European Jews, occurred in 1962. Hannah Arendt's *Eichmann in Jerusalem: A Report on the Banality of Evil* appeared in 1963, prompting an enormous controversy because she depicted Eichmann as an ordinary bureaucrat who just followed orders and was not even particularly anti-Semitic; she noted that Jewish victims had been largely submissive; and she critiqued the role of Jewish leaders who had co-operated with the Nazis. These views led many critics to label her a self-hating Jew. Arthur

---

1   Robert A. Martin, 'Arthur Miller: Tragedy and Commitment' (1969), in Roudané, ed., *Conversations with Arthur Miller*, 184.

Miller's first two Holocaust plays, *After the Fall* and *Incident at Vichy*, were produced the following year.

For two decades after the war, American Jews de-emphasised the idea of special Jewish victimhood. They aimed to show not simply that the Nazis were enemies of the Jews, which was common knowledge, but that they were *everyone's* enemy. The central figure of Miller's ensemble play *Incident at Vichy* is an Austrian prince, Von Berg, who, like Lawrence Newman in *Focus*, ultimately allies himself with the victims of anti-Semitism. Miller turned to the Holocaust in his 1964 plays after visiting the Mauthausen Concentration Camp in Austria and attending the Auschwitz trials in Frankfurt with his third wife, Inge Morath. (Morath had been born in Austria and had grown up in Hitler's Germany. Her brothers had fought in the regular German army or *Werhmacht*, and her uncle had been a general.) *After the Fall* dramatises the inner life of a character named Quentin who closely resembles Miller. The drama is enacted in the shadow of a concentration camp, and when Quentin's thoughts turn to the Jewish cemetery there, he realises that he is less moved by thoughts of the murdered Jews than is his German lover, Holga. The play suggests that humanity in general was guilty of the Holocaust, not just the Germans. In 1994, approaching the fiftieth anniversary of the liberation of the concentration camps, the Holocaust also spoke to other, more recent genocides, a connection Miller himself was quick to draw: 'Look at the Second World War. Look at Vietnam, Korea, Rwanda, the Balkans . . . We're savages.'[2] Miller's pessimistic message reflects the universalising outlook that makes everyone a victim (and a victimiser). Far from suggesting a particularly Jewish tragedy, Miller taps into the post-war view that we are basically all the same and that anti-Semitism is only one form of hatred, essentially no different from others.

Context

Kristallnacht

Within twenty-four hours on 9–10 November 1938, the Nazi Reich unleashed a massive wave of violence against the Jews of Germany. The National Socialists (Nazis) had taken power in Germany in 1933 with an explicitly anti-Semitic agenda under the leadership of Adolf Hitler. Between 1935 and 1938, the situation of Jews in Germany grew increasingly desperate. In

---

2   Interview with Michael March. 29 October 2001. http://www.guardian.co.uk/
books/2001/oct/29/stage.arthurmiller.

1935, the Nuremberg Laws classified who was Jewish and made it easier
to pass further legislation restricting human rights for its Jewish citizens.
The Nuremberg Laws deprived assimilated Jews of German citizenship
and prohibited marriage between Jews and other Germans. They restricted
the professions Jews could enter and deprived them of numerous other civil
and political rights. In the United States, the Neutrality Acts of 1935 and
1937 passed by an isolationist Congress prevented the administration of
President Franklin Delano Roosevelt from intervening in conflicts overseas.
In *Broken Glass*, Sylvia's paralysis evokes America's neutrality as the
Nazis annexed Austria and Czechoslovakia, perpetrated *Kristallnacht* and
invaded Poland in 1939, precipitating the Second World War. Roosevelt,
who became a great wartime president, was confined to a wheelchair, and
there is a brief discussion in the play about whether Sylvia's paralysis was
caused by polio (it wasn't), which was the source of FDR's condition. In
this way, Sylvia too becomes a figure for America. Miller's play raises
questions about neutrality and isolationism not only in the 1930s but also
in the 1990s, when it was written, and America again debated intervention
in foreign conflicts from Iraq to Yugoslavia to Rwanda.

On 11 March 1938, the Austrian Nazi party executed a bloodless coup
d'état. On 12 March, the German army marched into Austria in what was
known as the Anschluss. It was part of Hitler's aim to restore a German-
speaking empire in lands that had been lost to Germany in the First World
War. There was virtually no opposition from France and Great Britain,
which were practising a policy known as appeasement. Eager to avoid war
with Germany, they sought to settle matters by compromise and negotiation
rather than military confrontation. Five weeks before *Kristallnacht* they
negotiated an agreement for Germany to annex the Sudetenland (the
western regions of Czechoslovakia inhabited at that time mostly by ethnic
Germans), which the British Prime Minister, Neville Chamberlain, claimed
would bring 'peace in our time'. The Allies' policy is now associated with
weakness and cowardice. In *Broken Glass*, the inability to walk, let alone
rise up and fight, hints at this failure to stand up to Nazi aggression. The
German-educated Hyman says, 'I simply can't imagine those people
marching into Austria, and now they say Czechoslovakia's next, and
Poland.' *Kristallnacht* marked the culmination of a year in which Hitler
dramatically expanded German power in Europe. It was a milestone on
the road to the Second World War. The historian Martin Gilbert notes
that 'no other event in the history of the fate of German Jews between
1933 and 1945 was so widely covered by newspapers while it was taking
place.'[3] It changed the way Nazism was perceived.

3 Martin Gilbert, *Kristallnacht* (London: Harper Press, 2006), 16.

The foreground of *Kristallnacht* began in October 1938, when Hitler ordered more than 12,000 Polish-born Jews to be expelled from Germany. Most lost everything they had earned in their decades of working and living in Germany. They were taken at gunpoint by the Gestapo to the nearest railway stations and sent to the Polish border, where the vast majority were denied entry and left in limbo. The daughter of one expelled family sent a desperate postcard to her seventeen-year-old brother Herzschel Grynszpan, who was living in Paris. The next morning Grynszpan read a vivid description of the plight of these Polish Jews in a Yiddish-language newspaper. On Sunday he bought a pistol. Monday morning he went to the German Embassy and shot the Third Secretary Ernst vom Rath. In Germany, the newspapers of 8 November denounced all Jewish people as murderers. Numerous punitive measures were put in place. Jewish periodicals were shut down. Jewish children could no longer attend 'Aryan' elementary schools and a number of demonstrations against Jews erupted throughout Germany, including vandalism of Jewish shops and synagogues.

On the evening of 9 November, news reached Berlin that vom Rath had died. German radio stations observed two minutes of silence, and crowds began to converge in thoroughfares where Jews were gathered, such as the French tourist office in Berlin, where Jews waited to get the travel details they needed in order to emigrate. The Nazi command, including Hitler and his Minister of Propaganda, Josef Goebbels, encouraged anti-Jewish demonstrations and withdrew the police, unleashing an orgy of violence against Jewish men, women and children in thousands of cities, towns and villages throughout Germany and Austria. Squads of young men roamed through Berlin's major shopping districts, breaking shop windows, looting and tossing merchandise into the streets. Thousands of storefronts were smashed, shops and houses looted, synagogues burned and holy objects desecrated. Jews, who were minding their own business, were set upon in the streets. They were chased, beaten and humiliated. Ninety-one Jews were killed. More than 30,000 Jewish men were arrested and sent to concentration camps, where they were tortured and where thousands died. In Vienna, twenty-two Jews were reported to have committed suicide. In Frankfurt, storm-troopers known as Brownshirts burned all of the synagogues, destroyed windows, goods and equipment in every Jewish shop and office, and arrested 2,000 Jews, including all rabbis, religious leaders and teachers. News spread of other indignities. In one town a Romanian Jew was forced to crawl for two and a half miles, beaten continually by hooligans. In *Broken Glass*, Sylvia reads reports of jeering crowds forcing old men with beards to crawl and scrub the pavements with toothbrushes.

Restricted to her bed or wheelchair, Sylvia's position in her Brooklyn apartment is meant to be analogous to that of incarcerated European Jews, yet it also suggests the fine aspects of her identification with those degraded and non-particularised 'others'. Rather than leading to political engagement, her identification and paralysis literalise the disempowerment she has experienced in her marriage to the tyrannical Phillip. She gave up the freedoms she had enjoyed, presumptive rights to an education and to work, when she entered into marriage, not unlike the European Jews whose relationship to the dominant German culture was often depicted as feminised. German Jews, enfranchised only in the late nineteenth century, were stripped of civil rights by the Nuremberg Laws. *Kristallnacht* proved that not only the riff-raff but also the educated German middle class that Hyman fondly remembers in the play were complicit in brutalising their Jewish fellow citizens.

Historians have debated the American response to *Kristallnacht*. Despite alarming reports in the press from the time of the German invasion of Austria in March to the pogroms in November, American anti-immigration and refugee attitudes did not substantially relax or lead to a new policy. Although the United States was officially neutral, many Americans called for the government to do something, while nativists refused to open doors to refugees and isolationists insisted that the US keep out of European conflicts. Some of this debate is reflected in *Broken Glass*. Gellburg expresses a bias against German Jews who 'won't take an ordinary good job' and 'can't even speak English'. Sylvia exclaims, '*This is an emergency!* They are beating up little children! What if they kill those children! Where is Roosevelt! Where is England! You've got to do something before they murder us all!' Negative sentiments towards Germany intensified, but American attitudes against refugees stiffened.[4] President Roosevelt denounced the attacks. He recalled the American ambassador to Berlin as a gesture of protest against the Nazi-sponsored pogrom and announced that he would extend visitors' permits for the 12,000–15,000 German refugees already in America, but other policy initiatives died in the Committee on Immigration and Naturalization in the House of Representatives. In February 1939, public opinion against admitting Jewish refugees led Congress to reject the Wagner–Rogers Bill, which would have admitted 20,000 Jewish children. American Jewish organisations, wary of inciting anti-Semitism at home, did not protest. Later in 1939 the German cruise ship *St Louis* carrying approximately 900 Jewish refugees was turned away from American shores and sent back to Europe.

4 Deborah E. Lipstadt, *Beyond Belief: the American Press and the Coming of the Holocaust, 1933–1945* (New York: Free Press, 1986), 98.

The American press gave the events of November 1938 massive coverage. Nearly every important newspaper in the country, from the *Washington Post* to the *Chicago Tribune* to the *San Francisco Chronicle*, covered the story and expressed outrage at the 'Nazi terror'. *Kristallnacht* was on the front page of the *New York Times* for more than a week. On 10 November, it ran a front-page story, 'Berlin Raids Reply to Death of Envoy: Nazis Loot Jews' Shops, Burn City's Biggest Synagogue to Avenge Paris Embassy Aide.' The next day's headlines reported that all of Vienna's twenty-one synagogues had been attacked and Jews beaten under the direction of storm-troopers and Nazi party members in uniform. Thousands of Jews were arrested, and the *New York Times* speculated on 11 November, in 'Bands Rove City', that they were being held as hostage for the 'good behavior of Jewry outside Germany'. In almost every town and city in Hitler's Reich the looting and destruction continued. On 13 November, the *New York Times* reported that Germany had issued a new series of decrees calling for the complete 'liquidation of the Jews'. These newspaper reports become Sylvia's obsession in *Broken Glass* and reflect the other characters' lack of interest in current events or their active state of denial. The wartime death of European Jews, though the numbers would soon escalate, was never again reported so prominently in the American media. Miller, who was working in the Brooklyn Navy Yard, noted 'the near absence among men I worked with [in 1942] . . . of any comprehension of what Nazism meant – we were fighting Germany essentially because she had allied herself with the Japanese who had attacked us at Pearl Harbor'[5] – not, in other words, because of the Holocaust.

Jews in America

American Jewry has never been a monolithic group. *Broken Glass* represents a microcosm of Jewish society in the late 1930s that explicitly resists homogeneity. At the end of the play, Gellburg tells Hyman, 'I wouldn't know you were Jewish except for your name.' Even the name is not a give-away. Hyman's wife Margaret has taken his last name but is not Jewish. Hyman points out that there are Chinese Jews, which prompts Gellburg to wonder what he has been looking for in the mirror over the years, as he tried to discover what made his features Jewish. As Sylvia says, 'A Jew can have a Jewish face.' But what is a Jewish face? Hyman, who is also a Jew, does not have one. For Gellburg, being a Jew is at least as much a performance as it is rooted in anything in his nature; it is, as he says, 'a full-time job'.

---

5   Quoted in Paul Fussell, *Wartime* (New York: Oxford University Press, 1990), p. 138.

Gellburg's resistance to the stereotypical model of the American Jew is indicated by the repeated mistake that Margaret Hyman makes at the beginning of the play in calling him Goldberg. 'It's Gellburg, not Goldberg,' he says. To which she replies after he painstakingly spells his name, 'It does sound like Goldberg.' *The Goldbergs* was a popular comedy-drama created by actor-writer Gertrude Berg and broadcast from 1929 to 1946 on American radio. The show featured both the Jewish ethnicity of the Goldbergs and the story of their assimilation to American life. On several occasions Berg, who wrote all the episodes until the late thirties, incorporated serious historical issues. An episode on 3 April 1939 addressed *Kristallnacht* when the family's Passover Seder was interrupted by a rock thrown through the window. Later episodes referred to friends or family members trying to escape Eastern Europe, though most avoided direct discussion of politics and focused on the family. A few other details of *The Goldbergs* illuminate aspects of *Broken Glass*. The television version, which ran on CBS from 1949 to 1951, co-starred Philip Loeb as Jake Goldberg. Loeb, who shares his first name with Miller's character Phillip Gellburg (the original title for *Broken Glass* was *Gellburg*), was blacklisted during the McCarthy period when many members of the entertainment industry were accused – often unfairly – of Communist sympathies, and NBC subsequently convinced Berg to let him go in 1950.

With the exception of Margaret Hyman and Gellburg's boss, Stanton Case, all of the characters in *Broken Glass* are Jewish. Gellburg and Hyman in particular represent contradictions of twentieth-century American Jewish experience. There does not seem to be anything essentially Jewish about Hyman. He doesn't think about being Jewish or act in a noticeably Jewish way. Aside from his name, the one sign of Hyman's Jewishness is a single spoken line of Yiddish, but it is couched in both humanist terms and an American idiom: 'I think you get further faster, sometimes, with a little common sense and some plain human sympathy. Can we talk turkey? *Tuchas offen tisch*, you know any Yiddish?' Hyman, like Arthur Miller, may know some idiomatic Yiddish, but he prefers to 'talk turkey', common sense and 'human sympathy' instead of using any tribal affiliation. Gellburg obsessively resists Jewish identification. Ironically, this resistance makes him the most ethnically marked character in the play. Although he does understand Yiddish, his allegiance is less to 'human sympathy' than it is to America. He has married a Jewish woman, Sylvia, but he hopes that his son Jerome, a West Point graduate and captain in the Army, will become the first Jewish general. (In real life, the most famous Jewish man in the military at that time was Hyman Rickover, who became a four-star Admiral and 'Father of the Nuclear Navy'.) Jerome's accomplishments and the dreams of his father seem grafted from those of Miller, who recalls in *Tmebends* that as a child he had been 'programmed to choose something other than pride in my origins' (24). His dreams too had been military rather than spiritual: 'If ever any Jews should have melted into the proverbial pot, it was our family in the twenties; indeed I would soon be dreaming of entering West Point, and in my most private reveries I was no sallow Talmud reader' but a hero of 'athletic verve and military courage' (62). Like Miller, Hyman has married a non-Jew, known often disparagingly in Yiddish as a 'shiksa', and does not make a Jewish home. He has what Gellburg considers a non-Jewish hobby: he rides horses. He is a secularist and claims that he is not afraid of anyone, but when Gellburg wonders if he married a non-Jew so that he wouldn't seem Jewish, Hyman replies 'coldly': 'I never pretended I wasn't Jewish.' In 1939, Miller himself was married to a 'shiksa' (none of his three wives were Jewish, though his second wife, Marilyn Monroe, was a convert). In *Timebends*, he comments, 'There was a deep shadow then over intermarriage between Jews and gentiles' (70). Intermarriage rates were low in the 1930s, partly because young Jews and Christians did not interact in social situations enough to fall in love. Miller's other best friends in college at the University of Michigan, Norman Rosten and Hedda Rowinski, were Jews (and later married each other). In marrying a non-Jew, Miller made a choice about which *Broken Glass* expresses sensitivity when Dr Hyman defends his decision to marry Margaret. To Miller, religion in the time of the Depression seemed absurdly irrelevant. Hyman expresses the same view.

However, Gellburg's anxieties about being Jewish are by no means unfounded. The interwar years were characterised by an upsurge of nativism, xenophobia, racism and anti-Semitism, which included growing prejudice even against Jews whose families had been in the country for generations. The Red Scare of 1919–20, which targeted suspected communists, was one source of anti-Jewish feeling, and the Great Depression made social tensions worse. Polls indicate that anti-Semitism was high in the 1930s; as late as 1940 a majority of Americans found that Jews' most objectionable quality was their supposed 'unscrupulousness'. From the 1920s to the 1930s universities from Harvard and Yale to Illinois and Kansas restricted the number of Jewish students by quotas and other means. Hotels, clubs, fraternities and resorts barred Jews, as Miller shows in his novel *Focus*. Many companies would not hire Jewish employees. Hyman interned at Mount Sinai Hospital, which was founded to address the needs of New York's Jewish immigrants, and Gellburg is proud of being the sole Jewish employee of Brooklyn Guarantee. In the 1930s 'restrictive covenants' excluded Jews from buying real estate in exclusive neighbourhoods. Physical violence against Jews also increased during the 1920s with attacks by the Ku Klux Klan and, in the 1930s, by German-Americans sympathetic to Hitler. Father Charles Coughlin, a pro-Nazi, rabid isolationist and opponent of Roosevelt's New Deal policies, had a radio programme which reached forty million listeners in the 1930s, spewing anti-Semitic vitriol. His Social Justice movement had mass appeal. For the most part, American Jews in the 1930s stayed among their own kind. That was Miller's experience growing up in Manhattan and Brooklyn, and it is the experience of the small group of characters in *Broken Glass*, except for Gellburg's interaction with Stanton Case, whom he sees only at work. American Jews of the 1930s did not need to be religious to know that they were Jews. It was not synagogue attendance, but Jewish food in the kitchen (Miller's mother made brisket, gefilte fish and *tsimmes*), Yiddish inflections in everyday conversation and close proximity to other Jews that gave a Jewish feel to a neighbourhood.

Ethnic identity often expressed itself though political affiliation. Hyman believes not in God or even religion, but, like Miller himself at the time in which the play is set, in socialism. Gellburg, trying hard to be un-Jewish, is a pro-capitalist Republican. Most American Jews fell between the two and were strong supporters of Roosevelt's New Deal. In Miller's 1992 novella *Plain Girl*, which shares many themes with *Broken Glass*, the protagonist tells her brother, 'You must be the last Republican Jew in New York.' In 1936, 85 per cent of American Jews voted against the Republicans and for Democratic President Roosevelt. By 1940 it was 90 per cent. There is some merit to the accusation that American Jews were so enamoured of the Roosevelt administration that they failed to push harder for rescue operations after *Kristallnacht*. But Jews hardly formed a single political block on this issue, and their responses to the Holocaust ranged widely, as in the play, from psychic breakdown to relative indifference. Sylvia paradoxically feels that something must be done for the victims of *Kristallnacht* and becomes paralysed, while Gellburg worries that too much sympathy for the victims might excite anti-Semitism in America.

Broken Glass also suggests a trace of Jewish divisions transplanted from the Old World to the New between more affluent, assimilated Jews of German origin and those from Eastern Europe. It represents American prejudices against recent immigrants. Miller's mother Gussie frequently voiced these prejudices. His father Isidore emigrated from Poland at the age of six, while Gussie had been born in New York, and she never let him forget it. She looked down on her husband's lack of education and, though she enjoyed the luxuries of their haute-bourgeois life before the stock-market crash of 1929, she often gave voice to anti-Semitic rhetoric about 'Jews who care for nothing but business'. Although her background was not far removed from that of the recent immigrants, she felt superior for being a native-born American and not a 'greenhorn' like those who grew up on Manhattan's Lower East Side. In the 1920s, in their posh apartment the Millers lived among the more cultured and affluent German Jews. Dr Hyman, who stays in Brooklyn because of his political ideals, would have been accepted in that company. On the other hand, orthodox Jews, though also divided into feuding camps, seem to Gellburg to be the true Jews: 'there are some days I feel like going and sitting in the Schul [synagogue] with the old men and pulling the *tallis* [prayer shawl] over my head and be a full-time Jew the rest of my life. [. . .] And other times . . . yes, I could almost kill them.' It is shocking to hear this rhetoric coming from a Jewish character in 1938. Moreover, Gellburg here seems to assume what many orthodox Jews would, that Reform or secularised Jews were not real Jews at all.

The play never represents a coherent sense of what constitutes Jewish identity, in part because there is no single way to answer this question. But its failure to resonate with American audiences in the 1990s stems in part from the fact that, while addressing contemporary concerns with identity and the Holocaust, it draws its rhetoric and its deepest preoccupations, like much of Miller's work, from the 1930s. There is no trace of the ethnic pride that characterised the most successful Jewish American playwright of the 1990s, Tony Kushner, whose exuberant two-part 'fantasia' *Angels in America* and whose adaptation of S. Anski's Yiddish play *A Dybbuk* also explicitly draw on Holocaust themes. But Kushner's work was only part of a broader theatrical investment in expressing, rather than repressing, the particularised 'traumas' that set distinctive groups of Americans apart from each other, often as defined victim communities. Important playwrights of this period include María Irene Fornés, August Wilson, David Henry Hwang, Luis Valdez and Susan-Lori Parks. Miller's 1994 play is informed by the revival of ethnic identity in American culture, yet its characters aspire to a national or humanistic rather than an ethnic source of identity. Gellburg's self-hatred and Hyman's idealism date from a more earnest time, signified by Gellburg's heart, which attacks him not once but twice. Hyman, like Miller, may not pretend not to be Jewish, but he doesn't feel much like talking about it either. His assertion that Gellburg will find the root of the problem if he looks at himself in the mirror and that *he* paralysed his wife with 'Jew, Jew, Jew' coming out of his mouth, sounds not only troublingly anti-Semitic and counter to the ethos of American drama in the 1990s, but also, and even more problematic, in aligning Gellburg with the Nazis, it suggests that the Jews themselves may be complicit in their own destruction.

Broken Glass reflects the heavy sense of culpability from the 1970s through the 1990s for American failures to rescue European Jews from the

Holocaust. The figure of the paralysed American Jew in *Broken Glass* and the rhetoric of responsibility taps into the historical soul-searching of more recent Holocaust studies, as illustrated by books with titles such as *The Abandonment of the Jews, The Failure to Rescue, While Six Million Died, No Haven for the Oppressed* and *The Jews Were Expendable*. When the paralysed Sylvia becomes transfixed by the pictures of humiliated German Jews in the newspapers, her sister says, 'What business of it is yours?' In the 1990s many believed that not only Americans but also American Jews in particular had a lot to atone for. In 1993, the chairman of the Holocaust Museum's education committee told the press that those who did nothing were 'just as guilty' as those who performed the killing.[6] Few people spoke this way in the thirties, and most Americans felt proud of the sacrifices they made to defeat Hitler. This morality-play version of history, to which Miller has been attracted in other works, such as *Incident at Vichy*, has been much disputed by historians. Invoking *Kristallnacht* and the Holocaust as the prime indicators that we are all victims, *Broken Glass* enters troubling moral waters. It exposes cowardice, timidity and self-hatred, but the characters find it difficult, if not impossible, to converse in a moderate, balanced or nuanced way. When Gellburg says, 'I wish we could talk about the Jews', Hyman becomes evasive. *Kristallnacht* heralded the Holocaust to come, but it remains unclear what, if anything, American Jews could have done to save lives in Europe. Sylvia's plight suggests a more ambiguous moral. Paralysed as she obsesses over images of old men on the pavements of Berlin, she rises to her feet in the end to reach not a distant and abstract image of a Jew but her unconscious husband, collapsed in front of her. Like most people, she becomes able to take action when presented with an immediate personal situation in which she feels that she can make a difference.

In its diverse characters, *Broken Glass* represents competing attitudes towards assimilation and anti-Semitism, yet by 1994 most American Jews were assimilated, and anti-Semitism in the United States, though still present, was on the decline. For an author feeling the sting of accusations that he had turned his back on his people, the Holocaust was the obvious theme to address feelings of guilt on both a personal and a more broadly historical level. As the stricken husband says at the end of the play, 'Why we're different I will never understand.' Gellburg's overpowering sense of his own difference makes him almost a tragic figure, though not a hero. However misguided his aspirations, he represents the failure of an

6 Helen Fagin on *ABC World News Tonight*, 21 April 1993; Peter Novick, *The Holocaust in American Life* (New York: Mariner Books, 2000), 48.

individual to liberate himself from the crushing social codes that he has internalised. Although his collapse at the end of the play is not necessarily fatal, the final tableau implies that his destruction is necessary for Sylvia to find new life.

The Great Depression

Arthur Miller was born into an upper-middle-class family. His father at one time employed 800 people in his women's coat company, and the family lived in a Manhattan apartment overlooking Central Park North. But Isidore Miller had borrowed to invest in the stock market, where people were making much more money in the 1920s. On Black Thursday, 24 October 1929, the US Stock Market collapsed and the Great Depression began. It was an economic crisis that affected nearly every country in the world. Although Isidore's business did not fail, he lost all of his savings and investments in stocks. Soon the family lost the trappings of American success: the car and chauffeur, the maid, the apartment in Manhattan. They moved to a house in Brooklyn, and the fourteen-year-old Arthur Miller had to share a bedroom with his grandfather.

Many of Miller's plays represent a weak or defeated father and a sympathetic mother, an Oedipal drama that Miller drew partly from his own experience. He was his mother's favourite, and he was deeply affected by his father's failures both in business and as a figure of authority at home. His mother verbally abused his father for his shortcomings, and Miller tended to agree with her, feeling that his father had failed the family. At the same time, he expressed contradictory emotions, and he blamed the American economic system. *Broken Glass* follows this Oedipal pattern in its sympathetic portrayal of the beautiful Sylvia, who resents giving up her education and work before her marriage, and its brutal presentation of the floundering Phillip, the weak and exhausted Jew, though Phillip seems a solid breadwinner until shortly before the end of the play. This dynamic not only characterised the Miller household but also reflected the aftermath of the Wall Street Crash, which Miller always regarded as a formative influence on his life.

In 1934, Miller moved from Brooklyn to the University of Michigan, feeling guilty about leaving his brother Kermit to prop up the family while he, the inferior student, went off to college. But the activist environment of Michigan was the making of him. He wrote for the *Michigan Daily*; he became engaged in left-wing political activities. Like Dr Hyman, he met his first wife, a non-Jew, as a student, and she became his assistant, typing his manuscripts, and sharing his socialist political convictions. It is unclear whether he joined the Communist Party, but during the 1930s he was an active sympathiser. While he was at college, his father gave up on his company and joined the ranks of the unemployed and assumed the look of defeat. Collapse of the market led to collapse of families, and the plays Miller wrote in college reflected this awareness. His 1936 play *They Too Arise* is about a Jewish family struggling to overcome a looming business failure. In addition to winning a college writing prize, the play was staged in Ann Arbor and Detroit.

To many people during the Depression, it seemed that there was a sudden inexplicable loss of coherence. *Broken Glass* represents a world falling apart, a society of scarcity, and it touches on the characters' deepest anxieties. Hyman is late for an appointment at the beginning of the play not only because his horse goes lame but also because the new union pulled a strike at the hospital. Sylvia's inexplicable paralysis evokes this historical sense of confusion and collapse. But the opening lines also shed light on the bewildering demise of Gellburg, who tries (too hard) to do everything right. He represents particular social anxieties. Gellburg is a social climber, uncertainly allied with the establishment moneyed class. He manages to hold on to a handsome pay cheque as long as he works for Stanton Case. His sister-in-law Harriet says, 'There's no Depression for Phillip.' But, in fact, Gellburg is a lightning rod of the Depression; he expresses the anti-refugee sentiment of the Republican Party, of Congress and of the vast majority of the American public. He acknowledges that his line of work has given him direct knowledge of the economic and social impact of the Depression; he personally oversaw the foreclosures 'left and right' in the severe downturns of 1932 and 1936. With high unemployment, most people, like Gellburg, were in favour of reducing quotas for new immigrants, and legislation to that effect was introduced repeatedly in the US House of Representatives. Furthermore, 1937–8 coincided with the worst phase of the 'Roosevelt Recession', when unemployment began to rise again, and Democrats suffered losses in the 1938 Congressional elections. Thus, Gellburg resents immigrants competing for American jobs when the latest official figure is twelve million unemployed, and he resents the Roosevelt administration's investment in welfare, the Works Progress Administration, designed to put people back to work at government expense, also reflecting political debates about the welfare reform of the 1990s. Hyman remarks, 'You're very unusual . . . you almost sound like a Republican.' And Gellburg replies, 'Why? – The Torah says a Jew has to be a Democrat?' Self-conscious about his difference, Gellburg evinces his own insecurity.

Miller came of age during the 1930s, and *Broken Glass* harks back to some elements of the agitprop (agitation and propaganda) theatre that influenced him then, specifically in the urgency of its central message that people should not only protest but do something about injustice. He adopted large social themes in plays throughout his career. In 1938 Miller returned to New York, where he managed briefly to gain the support of the WPA's Federal Theatre and Writers Project, at $22.77 per week. As the reverberations of *Kristallnacht* were felt in late 1938, Miller exulted that he had managed to secure a studio apartment with a desk and a rug. However, the Federal Theatre Project was targeted by a Congressional committee that aimed to ferret out every 'subversive' group in the country. The committee alleged that the Federal Theatre Project was producing communist propaganda, and discontinued its funding in 1939. 'The Depression taught us that we were all equally victims,' Miller has said.

> Suddenly we were all the victims of something unseen and unknowable, and none of us was any worse than the other guy [. . .] we were no longer individuals. And then came along psychology to tell us that we were again the victim of drives that we weren't even conscious of, so that the idea of man being willfully good or willfully bad evaporated. We are nothing but what we were born and what we were taught to be up to the age of six. And we are essentially irresponsible. I think that's the situation we're in now.[7]

These themes – universal victimisation, loss of individuality, Freudian psychology, personal responsibility and in-born guilt – inform his entire body of work, and they are central to *Broken Glass*. Although the drama taps into the 1990s obsession with identity, it retains traces of the concerns that made Miller's early plays so resonant: the instability of class, the harm of buying into conventional wisdom and the logic of capitalism, and the extension of the macroeconomic effects of the Great Depression to the microcosm of an individual family.

Holocaust plays

The problem of representing the unrepresentable is the central moral and aesthetic issue of Holocaust dramas. Should a writer attempt to bear witness by staging atrocity with scrupulous realism, or obliquely render horrors whose enormity defies conventional representation? Holocaust drama has been characterised by the tension between maintaining a reverent silence about atrocities too horrible to depict on stage and giving voice to the events that must never be forgotten. Gene A. Plunka provides a comprehensive list of representative Holocaust dramas and their respective dramatic forms: 'realism (Arthur Miller's *Incident at Vichy*), epic theatre (Tony Kushner's *A Bright Room Called Day*), surrealism (George Tabori's *The Cannibals*),

---

7   Quoted in Philip Gelb, 'Morality and Modern Drama' (1958), in Roudané, ed., *Conversations with Arthur Miller*, 49.

black comedy (Peter Barnes's *Laughter!*), verse drama (Nelly Sach's *Eli*), melodrama (Frances Goodrich and Albert Hackett's *The Diary of Anne Frank*), classical tragedy (Rolf Hochhuth's *The Deputy*) and documentary theatre (Peter Weiss's *The Investigation*)' (Plunka, 17–18).

The most famous Holocaust drama in America remains the Pulitzer Prize-winning adaptation of *The Diary of Anne Frank* by Albert Hackett and Francis Goodrich. But there were relatively few 'Holocaust plays' in America during the immediate post-war years, when few could see the value of dramatising such a horrifying subject. Most American Jews at that time wanted to be treated like other Americans, not singled out as a suffering minority. Jews were more interested in integrating into American society than in standing out. The play version of *The Diary of Anne Frank* was no exception to the tendency to treat the Holocaust not as a catastrophe particular to the Jews but as an ordeal visited upon all of humanity by the Nazis. The 1955 Broadway play, which also won the Tony for Best Play and the New York Drama Critics' Circle Award, was a box-office smash and was made into a movie four years later. By the 1990s, when attitudes about the Holocaust had changed and Miller wrote *Broken Glass*, *Anne Frank* was often condemned for its universalistic and optimistic moral, that 'in spite of everything . . . people are really good at heart'. Critics faulted the adapters for removing Anne's Jewishness from the play. But, like many Americans of her generation, the Dutch Anne Frank was an assimilated girl who expressed little awareness of specifically Jewish values or rituals.

Themes of guilt and responsibility are central to the German Protestant playwright Rolf Hochhuth's play *Der Stellvertreter* (*The Deputy*), which opened in 1964 on Broadway in its English translation. The play led to violent demonstrations, mostly between Protestants and Catholics, in Europe. Its subject was the failure of Pope Pius XII to denounce the Holocaust during the war. In the United States, Jewish leaders, who wanted good relations with Christians, were lobbied heavily by Catholics to denounce the play and to put pressure on the director and producer to cancel the production. For the most part the leaders of the Anti-Defamation League and the American Jewish Committee complied, but the play went on anyway, though it was not a success and plans for a national tour were cancelled. Nonetheless, the dispute over this play was another milestone in the evolving discourse of the Holocaust in America. Like Miller, Hochhuth emphasises the importance of the individual assuming responsibility.

Following the immediate post-war era, there was a revival or 'renaissance' in Holocaust drama, from the seventies to the nineties, which included Miller's film, later adapted as a play, *Playing for Time* (1980) and *Broken Glass* (1994). *Playing for Time* is based on the autobiography of Fania Fenelon, a Jewish musician who was imprisoned in Auschwitz. The

Israeli playwright Joshua Sobol's *Ghetto* (1984) draws on similar themes, as well as first-hand accounts and archival documents. Based on a theatre that was established in the famous Jewish ghetto in Vilna, Lithuania, *Ghetto* advocates the importance of preserving Jewish culture. By the late nineties, an estimated 150 to 250 Holocaust dramas had been produced in the US, Europe and Israel. Premiering two years after *Broken Glass*, Harold Pinter's play *Ashes to Ashes* (1996) also examines the relationship of the personal to the political. Rebecca and Devlin, like Sylvia and Phillip, undergo a wrenching form of self-analysis, which associates the husband's authoritarian personality with the Nazi regime. Devlin, Rebecca's husband (or lover), is also her therapist and potentially her murderer, while she, like Sylvia, feels a deep connection to the persecuted Jews. Miller's dramas, including *Incident at Vichy* and *After the Fall*, are frequently cited as significant contributions to Holocaust drama from the 1960s to the 1990s.

Themes

Guilt

Guilt – one of the dominant subjects of Miller's entire body of work – is central to *Broken Glass*. Each of the three central characters expresses a sense of guilt at some point in the play: Hyman for marital infidelities and for improper advances to his female patient, Gellburg for infractions at work and at home, and Sylvia for imposing her infirmity on others. Often the guilt has no clear source, and characters beg each other for forgiveness, while others reply that there is nothing to forgive. The play represents both a sense of broken faith with ethnic affiliations – Jews who turn their backs on other Jews or on aspects of themselves – and a broader notion of global culpability in the abandonment of the Nazi victims described in the newspapers. In *Broken Glass* and elsewhere, Miller implies that everyone is complicit in Nazi war crimes and the slaughter of innocents. He follows the line of a revisionist school in Holocaust history, popular in the late 1960s, which argues that Western democracies, the Pope, neutral countries and others 'became, in a sense, passive accessories to the most terrible crime in human history'.[8] In this play, *Kristallnacht* and the Holocaust more broadly symbolise the guilt of the world – not only for the Holocaust – though characters struggle to articulate precisely what they are guilty of.

---

8   Haskell Lookstein, *Were We Our Brothers' Keepers? The Public Response of American Jews to the Holocaust, 1938–1944* (New York: Hartmore House, 1985), 3.

As he acknowledged in writing *The Crucible*, Miller felt a deep affinity for the Puritans, and the guilt that pervades his plays has more in common with a Christian notion of original sin than with anything in the Jewish tradition. The title of his post-Holocaust play *After the Fall*, despite Miller's citing of Camus, refers to the story of a paradise lost – Adam and Eve's fall from innocence and expulsion from the Garden of Eden – and the notion that human nature is both inherently guilty and averse to taking responsibility. In this spirit, at the end of *Broken Glass*, Hyman urges Gellburg not only to forgive his wife but also 'to forgive yourself, I guess. And the Jews. And while you're at it, you can throw in the goyim.' In short, everybody is guilty and in need of forgiveness. But this universalising of guilt and the need for atonement runs counter to the Jewish tradition which insists on identifying and atoning for specific sins and on the obligation of those who are importuned to grant forgiveness and move on. Gellburg seems to be referring to his whole life, not a particular failing, when he finally shouts, 'God almighty, Sylvia forgive me!' And she replies, 'There's nothing to blame!' Of course, Gellburg has been to blame for compelling her to give up a job she enjoyed, for striking her on one occasion, for failing to love her as she deserved, and for other sins. In neglecting to respond substantively to his apology, she effectively dooms him. When Gellburg apologises to his boss, Stanton Case, the latter responds evasively, 'What's happening?' The inability of either Sylvia or Case to acknowledge or to forgive Gellburg when he does apologise suggests a Puritanical ethos, not a Jewish one. Both scenes end in his heart attacks, an indication, in the play's psychoanalytic vocabulary, that Gellburg is unconsciously impelled to punish his own misdeeds internally, as his conscience or super-ego inflicts him with debilitating feelings of guilt. The heart attacks symbolise this internal, self-inflicted or neurotic violence. The play posits an analogy between Gellburg's persecution of Sylvia and the Nazi persecution of the Jews, and it punishes him terribly for it.

Often Miller represents guilt as a crushing form of paralysis that must be overcome to perform moral action in the world. At the conclusion of *Incident at Vichy*, the Jewish psychiatrist Leduc tells the Austrian prince Von Berg, 'It's not your guilt I want, it's your responsibility' (289). In a 1984 interview Miller said that 'guilt is a sense of unusable responsibility; it's a responsibility that can't be expressed, that can't be utilised for one reason or another [. . .] it is a way of self-paralysis.'[9] Nonetheless, Miller's

---

9   Quoted in Steven R. Centola, 'The Will to Live: An Interview with Arthur Miller' (1984), in Roudané, ed., *Conversations with Arthur Miller*, 356.

Holocaust plays have sometimes drawn criticism for failing to acknowledge the specificity of the crimes or to delineate responsibility. In a perceptive article, Leslie Epstein faulted *Incident at Vichy* for its abstraction of individuals.[10] He cites the German philosopher Karl Jaspers's *Question of German Guilt*, which argues that to 'pronounce a group criminally, morally or metaphysically guilty is an error akin to the laziness and arrogance of average, uncritical thinking'. Leduc suggests – as Gellburg does in *Broken Glass* – that all gentiles hate the Jews. Miller has written a morality play that is perhaps more sentimental than it is pedagogical.

Miller's plays also speak to historically contingent attitudes about the role of guilt in morality. *Broken Glass* is a history play (a period piece like *The Crucible*) that enters into dialogue with a contentious debate about guilt for the Holocaust that became prevalent decades after the war. Guilt can be a productive emotion if it leads to reparation. But a pathological conscience can be tyrannical, sadistic and cruel. Sigmund Freud exercised an enormous influence on American writers of Miller's generation. He saw 'the sense of guilt as the most important problem in the development of civilization and [showed] that the price we pay for our advance in civilization is a loss of happiness through the heightening of the sense of guilt.'[11] Miller's indebtedness to Freud is particularly evident in the psychoanalytic structure of his Holocaust plays. Leduc in *Incident at Vichy*, for example, is a psychoanalyst who studied at the Psychoanalytic Institute in Vienna. In *After the Fall* the 'action takes place in the mind, thought, and memory' of the protagonist, and in *Broken Glass* the therapy is conducted by the amateur psychoanalyst, Dr Hyman. In all of these plays characters talk through memories of life-altering events and struggle with competing instincts of life and destruction, love (or sex) and death.

In *Broken Glass* Gellburg feels profoundly guilty for losing his boss a property he coveted, in spite of the fact that Gellburg did nothing wrong; on the contrary, he actively researched the site and followed a hunch conscientiously. But he made a mistake. Case's cold, unforgiving response drives the insecure Gellburg to greater and greater heights of guilt, and these feeling are coupled with his sense of real or imagined guilt for his wife's condition. Gellburg's insecurity, bound up with his sense of guilt, comes down to being fearful of the loss of love, whether of his wife or of his boss or, more broadly, of secular America; in short, his character

10   Leslie Epstein, 'The Unhappiness of Arthur Miller', *Triquarterly*, Summer 1965, pp. 172–3.

11   Sigmund Freud, *Civilization and Its Discontents*, trans. and ed. James Strachey (New York: W.W. Norton and Co., 1961), 97.

manifests a Freudian model of the sense of guilt as a social anxiety. 'Say, you're not blaming this on me, are you?' Gellburg asks Hyman; to which Hyman replies, 'What's the good of blame?' – a rhetorical question, but one the play wants us to think seriously about. What *is* the good of blame? In fact, the play *does* blame Gellburg for Sylvia's plight. As Gellburg's personal and professional lives unravel simultaneously in Case's office, like Willy Loman's in *Death of a Salesman*, all he can think of is that he has been found guilty of being a Jew. 'This is not fair!' he shouts at Case and finally collapses. But Case has said nothing and appears bewildered by Gellburg's outburst. Like Willy, Phillip has internalised the authority he attributes to his boss and the aggression that he has directed towards others. He has become the victim of his own destructive impulses, his guilty conscience. In the following scene at the Gellburgs' house, Margaret says to Sylvia, 'I hope you're not blaming yourself', and her sister Harriet insists that her husband's collapse 'could happen to anybody'. Margaret then explains her philosophy of life, which is derived from working in a pediatric ward: a person's nature is set in infancy. 'So what does that mean?' Sylvia asks. It implies that no one is responsible for his or her behaviour. 'How do you live?' Margaret responds with a fatalistic ethic: 'You draw your cards face down; you turn them over and do your best with the hand you got.'

From *All My Sons* to *Broken Glass*, Miller returns continually to the crushing force of guilt and the notion that the moral responsibility of family members must expand to include all of humanity. After the surviving son in *All My Sons*, Chris Keller, returned from fighting in the Second World War, he 'felt wrong to be alive, to open a bank-book, to drive the new car', knowing that good men had gone down sacrificing themselves for each other. In the end, he tells his father, who was guilty of selling defective parts to the Air Force, 'Once and for all you can know there's a universe of people outside and you're responsible to it, and unless you know that you threw away your son because that's why he died.' This lecture on moral responsibility, however, leads Joe Keller to commit suicide, an act of self-destruction, not reparation. Many American Jews may have felt a similar form of 'survivor guilt', and Miller acknowledged that he was the lucky beneficiary of his family's emigration from Eastern Europe. On a trip to Poland Miller realised that had his grandfathers and his father not left before the turn of the century, he would not have survived to the age of thirty. In 1947–8, Miller went to Europe. In Italy he encountered Jewish refugees waiting for a ship to what was then called Palestine: 'To this day, thinking of them there on their dark porches silently scanning the sea for their ship, unwanted by any of the civilised powers, their very presence here illegal and menaced by British diplomatic intervention, I feel myself disembodied, detached, ashamed of my stupidity, my failure to recognise myself in them' (*Timebends*, 167).

For Miller guilt was a guiding emotion. In his autobiography, he even describes feeling the 'guilt of success' after his first play, *All My Sons*, was a hit. This guilt, he believed, was reinforced by his leftist egalitarian convictions, and he says that he was unable to do much about it: 'such guilt is a protective device to conceal one's happiness at surpassing others, especially those one loves, like a brother, father, or friend. It is a kind of payment to them in the form of a pseudo-remorse' (*Timebends*, 139).

Most of Miller's plays are also steeped in sexual guilt, from the past affairs of Willy Loman in *Death of a Salesman* and John Proctor in *The Crucible* to Quentin's abandonment of Maggie in *After the Fall*. One recurring motif is the figure of the neglected or damaged woman. *Broken Glass* centres on the dysfunctional sex life of the Gellburgs, which is illuminated by the unprofessional behaviour of Dr Hyman, whose vanity prompts him to treat the beautiful Sylvia. He massages and compliments her and asks her 'to imagine that we've made love' and then reacts guiltily when Gellburg says that he doesn't understand the doctor's unprofessional display. Hyman insists to his wife that '*Nothing has happened!*' Gellburg's problems at Brooklyn Trust and Guarantee are reflected in the domestic setting, where trust and love are similarly not guaranteed. Both couples in the play struggle to achieve the basis of a true marriage and to repay emotional debts. When Gellburg expresses bewilderment at Hyman's conduct, the latter 'stands there, guilty, alarmed', as his wife enters. However, although Margaret is irritated (asking What is it – just new ass all the time?') and Hyman insists that he hasn't been unfaithful in a decade or more, she merely concludes that he 'loves the truth' too much. It is hard not to see Margaret's absolution of Hyman as an act of wish-fulfilment.

Jewish self-hatred

The disparaging term 'self-hating Jew' refers to an anti-Semitic person who is Jewish. Its use implies that a person has betrayed his or her own identity. The founder of modern Zionism, Theodor Herzl, used the term 'anti-Semite of Jewish origin' against Jews who disagreed with Jewish aspirations for nationalism. But the term 'Jewish self-hatred' gained currency in 1930 when Theodor Lessing used it for the title of his book *Der Jüdische Selbsthass*. In the United States it was introduced as a common English term by the German-Jewish immigrant Kurt Lewin, and it came to define contentious debates about Jewish American identity in the post-war decades. The most influential academic book on the subject has been

Sander Gilman's 1990 *Jewish Self-Hatred: Anti-Semitism and the Hidden Language of the Jews.*[12]

However, Jewish self-hatred' is a notion that dates back to the nineteenth century when Orthodox Jews disapproved of Reform Jews, mostly in Germany, because the latter identified more with German nationalism and Protestant social norms than with what they considered to be traditional Judaism. On the other hand, the more assimilationist German Jews regarded the Eastern Europeans as 'bad' Jews, from whom they wished to distinguish themselves. Gellburg expresses the complexity of this double-edged attitude from an American perspective in *Broken Glass* when he says, 'German Jews can be pretty . . . you know . . . (*Pushes his nose with his forefinger.*) Not that they're pushy like the ones from Poland or Russia.' He has problems with both the highly assimilated Jews of German descent and the 'bad' Jew of Eastern European descent. Gellburg reflects social divisions within the Jewish community. He both loathes and identifies with the old Eastern European figure of the Jew with the sidelocks and the black hat. Gellburg's obsession with his own otherness (e.g., his 'Jewish face') draws upon negative images of the Jew in European and American culture – books, newspapers, even medical literature – that he has internalised. The language of self-hatred in the play is reflected in the motif of the mirror.

Hyman   All right, you want the truth? Do you? Look in the mirror sometime!

Gellburg   . . . In the mirror!

Hyman   You hate yourself, that's what's scaring her [Sylvia] to death. That's my opinion. How's it possible I don't know, but I think you helped paralyze her with this 'Jew, Jew, Jew' coming out of your mouth and the same time she reads it in the paper and it's coming out of the radio day and night? (82–3)

This revealing passage, which lays the central problem of the play (Sylvia's paralysis) at the feet of Jewish self-hatred, implies that Gellburg's problem with Jews does not come out of nowhere, or at least not only from himself; it also comes from the images and language of the media at home and abroad. Furthermore, in this dialogue between two Jewish men, it

---

12 Herzl used the phrase 'anti-Semite of Jewish origin' in his 1896 book *Der Judenstaat* (*The Jewish State*), which launched political Zionism. See Paul Reitter, 'Zionism and the Rhetoric of Jewish Self-Hatred', *Germanic Review*, vol. 83, no. 4, Fall 2008, pp. 343–64, and Susan A. Glenn, The Vogue of Jewish Self-Hatred in Post-World War II America', *Jewish Social Studies*, vol. 12, no. 3, Spring/Summer 2006, pp. 95–136.

represents the tradition of the self-critical Jew and the paradoxical logic that Hyman, the one who accuses the other of being a self-hating Jew, may himself be a self-hating Jew, as Gellburg hints later when he wonders why the atheistic, horseback-riding doctor married a non-Jewish woman. As Sander Gilman writes, 'The language of the other, the mirror of the world it perceives about it, is permeated with the rhetoric of self-hatred. It takes its discourse, its mode of self-description, from the world about it, and that language is saturated with the imagined projection of the Other' (Gilman, 13). Gellburg and Sylvia discover images of themselves in the newspapers of 1938, in bearded Jews crawling the streets and being jeered at by others. It is in these images that they discover their 'Jewishness' – though they respond differently – and in the Jewish/Nazi relationship they find an ugly analogy for their own marriage.

In Gellburg's character, the play traffics in stereotypes of the feminised and sexually impotent Jewish man. In Miller's own terms of contrast, he imagined himself when a boy as 'no sallow Talmud scholar', the weak or emasculate Jew, but as one of numerous American heroes of 'athletic verve and military courage' (*Timebends*, 62). Jews were commonly depicted as bookish, urban and hysterical. In this respect, Gellburg follows the characters portrayed by Woody Allen, Saul Bellow, Phillip Roth and their precursors dating back to the early nineteenth century. But Gellburg must also be understood in relation to the stereotypical 'good Jew' of Holocaust literature, Anne Frank, the image of the Jew as 'positive' victim, the Jew who deserved to be saved because she didn't seem too 'Jewish'. Of course, Anne Frank became the good Jew by becoming first a dead Jew. *Broken Glass* deploys the polar definition of the 'self-hating' Jew – good Jew versus bad Jew – as Gellburg veers between his desire to pull a *tallis* over his head and his desire to become an assimilated American (as Anne Frank was assimilated Dutch). He internalises the charges of anti-Semitic rhetoric and projects these charges on to others labelled as Jews. Ironically, Hyman accuses Gellburg of self-hatred for continually drawing attention to the fact that he is a Jew.

Fragmentation

The title *Broken Glass* indicates not only the historical event, *Kristallnacht*, that is central to the play, but also a broader theme of brokenness or fragmentation, starting with the Gellburgs' fragmented or broken marriage, broken trusts at work, and the fragmentation of individual lives and social structures in the historical events of the late 1930s, from the Depression to the Spanish Civil War and the breaking up of Europe in the face of Nazi aggression. The 'broken glass' of the title, suggested by the director David Thacker, also evokes an important metaphor of the Jewish mystical tradition involving the shattering of cosmic vessels and the scattering of shards of evil throughout the world. The related notion of *tikkun olam* involves the repairing of those vessels by righteous acts. It is unlikely that Miller had this specific expression in mind – he was not a practising Jew – but many Jews, who turned from their religious traditions to socialism or communism, may have redirected those traditional obligations. The phrase *tikkun olam*, which literally means to repair or perfect the world, found its way into secular forms of expression that didn't seem religious at all.

Beyond the smashing of Jewish storefronts in Hitler's Reich, the 'broken glass' of the title also refers to the breaking of the glass under the *chupah*, the wedding canopy, at the conclusion of the Jewish marriage ceremony, linking marriage, by some accounts, to the destruction of the Temple in Jerusalem. In this sense, breaking the glass identifies the married couple with the history and destiny of the Jewish people. In doing so, it relates the private, domestic covenant of marriage to a national tragedy, as Miller does in his play. Insofar as it is the groom who breaks the glass, it also suggests a moment of, perhaps, transitory or illusory male power (he gets to 'put his foot down' at least this once). Some have even linked it to the bride's loss of virginity, the breaking of the hymen. But the meaning of the ritual is disputed. Another interpretation holds that people need to remember those who are suffering in their moments of greatest joy, and this reading hints at a historical allegory especially for American Jews, wedded for the most part in peace, prosperity and security to a new homeland, not to forget their less fortunate cousins in faraway countries. Broken glass might also suggest, more simply, the wreckage following a domestic squabble. Although it is impossible to say whether Miller had any of these traditions or interpretations in mind, the evocative title of a play about a marriage suggests that the play, like the broken glass, is open to multiple interpretations.

The theme of fragmentation is also reflected in the form of the drama. Rather than unfolding like a 'well-made' play in a pattern of exposition, complication, crisis and denouement, *Broken Glass* is episodic, made up of eleven short scenes or conversations that often seem disjointed or directionless, as the speakers probe each other's hidden motivations. The conversations do not proceed in a linear or cause-and-effect pattern, and characters become confused as they trigger emotional reactions in each other by twists and turns in the dialogue. For instance, after Gellburg and the supposedly scientific Dr Hyman provoke each other, Hyman ends up complaining, 'What are you driving at, I don't understand this conversation.' The 'determined scientific idealist' finds his diagnostic powers thwarted by deep and unconscious impulses, his own included. The episodic form reflects the associative structure of memory explored by psychoanalysis, which digs into the patient's past in order to understand a present malady.

Genre

Miller's method for addressing social issues in *Broken Glass* draws on a tradition of drama that goes back to the mid-nineteenth century. At the University of Michigan he studied drama with Kenneth T. Rowe, who taught playwriting with an emphasis on form that influenced Miller's work. In his Michigan seminars and in his influential book *Write That Play!* Rowe devoted considerable attention to an analysis of Ibsen's *A Doll's House* and to Greek tragedy. During that same period Miller saw a production of *A Doll's House* on Broadway that affected him deeply, and his indebtedness to Ibsen has been widely noted. (He also wrote an adaptation of Ibsen's *An Enemy of the People*, which centres on the need for individuals to take social responsibility.) A crucial aspect of Ibsen's dramatic method that informs *Broken Glass* is the way he uses material that happened before the play began not simply to introduce a new conflict but as the play's main subject. Bringing the past to life or showing how it bears on the present is the essence of the play. This technique goes back to Sophocles' *Oedipus*, but Ibsen used it in slowly unfolding the past to tell a story about the hidden realities of everyday, middle-class life. Those realities are interpersonal.

Like *A Doll's House*, *Broken Glass* is a play about a woman trapped in an unhappy marriage, though she does not at first seem to realise that she is trapped. Both plays involve a love triangle which includes husband, wife and family doctor. Both show how people internalise the rhetoric and assumptions of their social world: what it means to be a 'good' wife and mother or husband and provider. Ibsen, too, is preoccupied with the tension between free will and determinism, the way people are shaped by a genetic inheritance or identity or whether they can assert their own selfhood in the present. In *Broken Glass*, Miller employs psychoanalysis as a way of unpacking the past in the present, but his use of the doctor as the central figure to do so is highly conventional. Furthermore, it manifests the anti-theatrical prejudice of dramatic realism: the idea that people should stop playing roles and discover the truth about themselves. Sylvia literally embodies this anti-theatrical logic in her refusal or inability to act as her husband or doctor desire, and the play punishes Gellburg's theatrical conceptions of identity – whether it means acting the Jew or the Republican or anything that seems false to the 'human'.

The thesis play developed in the nineteenth century to deal with controversial social concerns in a realistic manner. Thesis plays commonly required a character to serve as presenter and preacher and to function as the author's mouthpiece. Known in French as the *raisonneur*, many modern plays have given this role to a doctor, who generally brings a scientific approach to problems yet also has a personal involvement with the characters which suggests the limits of rationality. While in some ways doctors such as those in Ibsen's *A Doll's House* and Chekhov's *Ivanov* serve as precursors for Dr Hyman in *Broken Glass*, Miller's play differs in its treatment. Instead of being a marginal character, Dr Hyman is central to the play's action and is its key moraliser, and though Hyman's wife Margaret seems occasionally bemused, the play does not deflate or question his self-importance and 'scientific idealism'.

Characters

Phillip Gellburg

A 'self-hating Jew' in his late forties, Phillip Gellburg is head of the Mortgage Department at the Brooklyn Guarantee and Trust Company and answerable only to the WASP (White Anglo-Saxon Protestant) owner. He is the only Jew ever to have been hired by the company and proud of it. Gellburg evaluates properties and establishes the terms of mortgages. The ideas of 'guarantee' and 'trust' resonate at a deeper level, as Gellburg loses the trust of his boss and, he fears, the guarantee of his status in America. He has internalised the mirage of the 'typical Jew' as a reality. His anxieties are self-fulfilling and represent a double-bind: he makes a mistake at work by trying to be too clever. He overreacts to slights and anticipates prejudice, which only antagonises his prejudiced boss and alienates his wife. He wants to erase his origins but succeeds only in drawing attention to them. He is a Republican (most Jews were and are Democrats) and prejudiced against immigrants, but his politics draw attention to his difference. Gellburg's inability to 'be a man' in the bedroom reinforces the stereotype of Jews as physically weak and, given the practice of circumcision, not quite 'whole' men. As the theatre critic Vincent Canby writes, Gellburg 'is a small man but he's a gigantic mess. Half of him is as anti-Semitic as [his boss] Stanton Case . . . The other, only vaguely recognised half is the bewildered son of immigrants, a first-generation Jewish American trying to assimilate' (*New York Times*, 1 May 1994).

Sylvia Gellburg

The wife of Phillip, Sylvia Gellburg, is a beautiful and talented woman, paralysed from the waist down. Intellectually curious but with little formal education, she is a constant reader of books and newspapers, and 'remarkably well informed'. Before her marriage, she was head bookkeeper for a company in Long Island City. She loved work and having people depend on her. Her husband says that if she were a man she could have run the Federal Reserve and that he can talk to her as to a man. These comments reinforce a sense of gender confusion and sexual dysfunction in the Gellburg home; Sylvia's temporary inability to use her legs is parallel to Phillip's inability to use his penis. Both suggest castration anxieties. Her husband compelled her to give up her job, and Sylvia represents the frustrations of a generation of women who came of age between first – and second-wave feminism. She is both a comfortable American housewife and a victim of domestic abuse. She was paralysed and confined, figuratively, long before her legs gave out. Her predicament resembles that of many frustrated women. Miller claimed that he knew an actual woman who suffered 'hysterical paralysis' and whose husband dressed in black (like Gellburg), but Sylvia is an emblematic figure, less realistic than allegorical.

Through her the play brings together public and private concerns. Her paralysis also suggests the failures of American Jews in the face of the European Holocaust, Western appeasement and American neutrality, as German forces penetrated Europe in the late thirties. Although her condition represents American inaction, she is also a figure for the victims of an oppressive anti-Semitic regime (in her case represented by her husband). In Sylvia, we see how an inner life reflects larger social and historical events. The married couple is a microcosm that channels larger social pathologies.

Dr Harry Hyman

Hyman is a 'determined scientific idealist', implying a capacity to regard his existence from two standpoints and, thus, to perfect the baser material reality by reference to the higher, idealistic one. Hyman's name (pronounced high-man) indicates that he is the opposite of Miller's best-known character, Willy Loman; this sense of opposition is enhanced by the fact that Gellburg – Hyman's opposite in the play – resembles Willy Loman. A successful physician and Casanova, Hyman's high opinion of himself is shared by most of the other characters in the play, though he lacks the ambition that his wife Margaret believes would land him a practice on Park Avenue. But Hyman is a socialist, and he explains at one point that he likes to think carefully before he speaks, comparing himself to the literary doctors Somerset Maugham and Anton Chekhov.

In Greek mythology, Hymen was a god of marriage and attended every wedding (Shakespeare employs the figure in *As You Like It*). If the god Hymen wasn't present, legend had it, the marriage would prove disastrous. (Hyman's references to the Ancient Greek god of medicine and to the Greek etymology of 'hysteria' invite the reader to make similar inferences about his name.) The hymen is also the mucous membrane on a woman's vagina, which has a long history in medicine and the popular imagination, including the myth that examining the hymen could prove a woman's virginity or that damage to it could cause 'hysteria' (Dr Hyman claims that Sylvia suffers a 'hysterical paralysis'). The name also has a Jewish provenance. Miller's uncle was named Hymie, a name that remains a classic anti-Semitic epithet. In short, Hyman's overdetermined masculinity in the play is balanced by a name that was not only common among Jews but that also evokes mythic aspects of female anatomy, suggesting the complex interplay between the masculine/feminine terms in the play. There is a long tradition of depicting Jewish men as impaired, limping and feminised, not completely male. Yet all of the women in the play, from Sylvia and her sister Harriet to Hyman's wife Margaret, refer to his sexual potency, and he gives evidence of seductive power on stage with both Margaret and Sylvia. Hyman's assertion of both his masculinity and his secular humanism are related to what he is asserting it against: a figure embodied by Gellburg but also latent in himself.

Margaret Hyman

Margaret is the 'shiksa' or non-Jewish wife and medical assistant of Dr Hyman. A vivacious Midwesterner who came east, she met Hyman when he was an intern at Mount Sinai Hospital. Margaret is a limited character, but she offers a complicated, even contradictory, comment on the sources of identity. On the one hand, in her marriage she represents the idea that identity can be freely chosen, a matter of consent rather than descent. Intermarriage between Jews and gentiles was frowned upon (and rare) in the 1930s, as Miller has noted regarding his own first marriage to non-Jewish Mary Grace Slattery. In choosing Hyman, Margaret indicates that identity is not fixed. When Gellburg pretentiously and improbably claims that his family was 'originally' from Finland, where few Jews ever lived, Margaret casually answers that hers, equally improbably, came from Lithuania; it is a way of bursting Gellburg's bubble and of hinting that it doesn't matter where one's family came from. On the other hand, in the penultimate scene of the play, attempting to absolve Sylvia's feelings of guilt, Margaret says that people's characters are determined before birth: 'each one has twenty thousand years of the human race backed up behind him . . . and you expect to change him?' This remark, suggesting that character is formed totally by descent rather than consent, baffles Sylvia.

Harriet

Sylvia's sister Harriet is younger by a couple of years. She helps to look after Sylvia, taking care of her housework and shopping. Much less intense and thoughtful than her sister, she is a conventional housewife. Another limited character, her main function is to set off Sylvia's qualities of intellectual curiosity, frustration with her lot, political engagement and empathy for strangers. She provides additional evidence that women in general are attracted to Hyman.

Stanton Wylie Case

Mr Case is Gellburg's boss and the President of Brooklyn Guarantee. Case represents the American WASP establishment. His yacht won the America's Cup. He wants to purchase an annexe for the Harvard Club, implying that as a member of the Northeastern elite he went to Harvard, which restricted the number of Jewish students admitted to the university from the 1920s to the late 1930s. Case's fifty-year-old company, however, depends on its key Jewish employee, Gellburg. He is a two-dimensional character without psychological depth. He comes close to being a standard capitalist villain. His main purpose in the play is to serve as an occasion for Gellburg's Jewish self-hatred. He appears oblivious to his own prejudices when Gellburg finally becomes exercised at his unconscious but deep-seeded bigotry.

Key Productions

Broken Glass premiered at the Long Wharf Theatre in New Haven, Connecticut, on 1 March 1994, with Amy Irving as Sylvia, Ron Rifkin as Gellburg and Ron Silver as Hyman, before moving to Broadway, where Silver was replaced by David Dukes. Miller's producer Robert Whitehead insisted on doing the play in New York rather than London because he was concerned that if the production turned out badly or was poorly reviewed in Britain, he would have difficulty raising money to do it in New York. The opening on 24 April 1994 at the Booth Theatre marked Miller's return to Broadway after an absence of fourteen years, but the play ran only two months and opened to mixed reviews. Although Amy Irving was acclaimed for her performance as Sylvia, the critic David Richards complained in the *New York Times* that the play was predictable, 'all talk and fumbling confession'. The set was designed by Santo Loquasto on a sleek turntable (doctor's office, bedroom, board room), with a shared visual motif of white tiles. Original cello music was composed for the production by William Bolcom.

The Royal National Theatre in London scheduled *Broken Glass* for its Lyttleton Theatre under the precise direction of David Thacker, who enhanced the drama's general atmosphere of foreboding. Miller revised the play immediately after it closed in New York; so the text of the final script was very different from the one used in the American production. Considerably strengthened, the play won the Olivier Award as the Best New Play of the year for the 1994–5 London season. British theatre critics argued that the New York failure had been that of American audiences rather than of Miller's play. The Royal National Theatre production featured Margot Leicester as limpid-eyed Sylvia, Henry Goodman as a prickly, impatient Phillip and Ken Stott as a rumpled, chain-smoking Hyman. The play was staged in a dreamlike set designed by Shelagh Keegan that suggested the fragility of the characters' safety in New York. The triangular stage tapered sharply towards the back, where the cellist played mournfully between scenes, and the walls were sheets of glass. After its sell-out run at the Royal National Theatre, *Broken Glass* transferred to the West End for a ten-week season. Thacker also went on to direct a film version in 1996, which was produced by the BBC and aired in America on 'Masterpiece Theatre'. The film employed a strong cast, with Leicester and Goodman again as the struggling Gellburgs, and Mandy Patinkin as a burly Hyman, and it 'opened out' the action by showing events which are only reported in the original dialogue, such as Hyman riding on horseback on the beach, Gellburg foreclosing an apartment and dark, haunting images of Nazi violence blended with Sylvia's dreams. It also introduced new minor characters, such as the Gellburgs' nephew David.

Shortly after the London triumph, the play returned to the United States, where it was produced outside Washington, DC, at the Olney Theatre Center, in a co-production with the Rep Stage Company. In this production James Kronzer's revolving set, lit in evocative shadows, was composed of dark wood and panes of broken glass. The co-directors Jim Petosa and Halo Wines created an intensely acted show with Ed Gero playing Phillip as 'a black hole of angst', in the words of the *Washington Times*. Subsequently, the play has had a long and varied production history, from a 1998 production in Australia, to Joseph Chaikin's elegantly directed production in Atlanta, Georgia, to productions at Burbank's Victory

Theatre in Los Angeles and the Winnipeg Jewish Theatre in Canada in 2006. In 2009 a spare production was put on at the Blackwood Little Theatre in South Wales, and it was staged several times in 2010, including one version at the Walnut Street Theatre in Philadelphia, and another in London at the Tricycle Theatre, starring Antony Sher. In October 2010, the *New York Times* described the Tricycle Theatre production, directed by Iqbal Khan and intended for a commercial transfer to the West End, as the 'best yet'. Tara Fitzgerald replaced Lucy Cohu when the production moved to the Vaudeville Theatre a short time later. With a super essemble around Sher and a mood-setting onstage cellist, this staging sharpened the drama's focus and did 'nothing less than put the Jewish psyche on trial'. Though critics have sometimes found the symbolism heavy-handed and the tone moralistic, most have generally agreed that in performance it conveys impressive moral power.

Notes

The notes below explain words and phrases from the play, with page
numbers referencing the Student Editions published by Bloomsbury
Methuen Drama.

page

5   *that new union's pulled a strike:* in the United States, in the
       1930s, high unemployment led to labour unrest. Workers
       attempted to organise unions and exercise the right to collective
       bargaining, which led to numerous bitter strikes and demands for
       changes to labour legislation.

5   *Ocean Parkway:* Ocean Parkway, a wide street that extends from
       Prospect Park to Coney Island and Brighton Beach, and is also a
       neighborhood located in Brooklyn. New York.

5   *Mount Sinai:* founded in 1852 by a group of Jewish charities and
       originally named the 'Jew's Hospital'. Mount Sinai served the
       Jewish population of New York City.

5   *Minnesota:* a state located in the Midwest of the USA.

6   *Lithuania . . . Kazauskis:* the town has been spelled in many
       ways – Kazhiskis, Kasauskis, Kasauskas, Kazusk. etc. – from
       the time when Lithuania was Polish, German or Soviet (each
       rule would change the spelling). To downplay his Jewishness,
       Gellburg says that his family was 'originally' from Finland,
       where there were few Jews. Margaret, who is not Jewish,
       asserts that her family is from Lithuania, home to a large Jewish
       population before the Second World War, later wiped out during
       the Holocaust. Her point is to 'put down' Gellburg.

7   *polio:* poliomyelitis, a viral infectious disease that often leads
       to paralysis, especially affected children. Numerous polio
       epidemics occurred during the 1930s in the United States.
       Franklin D. Roosevelt, President of the United States during that
       time, was crippled by polio.

7   *Park Avenue:* originally named 'Fourth Avenue', Park Avenue is
       one of the main streets running north – south in Manhattan, New
       York. It is synonymous with wealth.

8   *scientific idealist:* pursuing or forming ideas based on a scientific
       method of hypothesis, deduction and controlled experiment, in
       short the exercise of reason while assuming an ultimate reality
       based in ideas. For the doctor and socialist, Hyman, this seemingly

contradictory phrase suggests a way of regarding the world from two standpoints, a material world and an imagined or ideal world from which present existence can be judged and improved.

8   *Moxie:* gutsy, feisty.

9   *Aesculapius . . . Anton Chekhov:* Aesculapins was the god of medicine and healing in Ancient Greek mythology. W. Somerset Maugham (1874 – 1965), the British writer of plays, novels and short stories, was very popular during the 1930s; he studied medicine in London before becoming a writer. Anton Pavlovich Chekhov (1860 – 1904), the Russian writer of plays and short stories. He studied medicine and practised as a physician throughout his literary career.

10   *They've been smashing the Jewish stores in Berlin all week:* This refers to *Kristallnacht* or the 'Night of Broken Glass', two days of anti-Jewish violence that took place in Berlin, Germany, on 9 and 10 November 1938. Nazis targeted and damaged or destroyed Jewish properties, businesses and synagogues.

11   *Kurfurstendamm:* a famous boulevard in Berlin.

11   *refugees:* many German Jews fled Germany because of Nazi persecution. From the 1880s the United States had been a refuge for European Jews fleeing persecution.

11   *Roosevelt:* Franklin D. Roosevelt (1882–1945) was the thirty-second president of the United States. He was in office throughout the Great Depression and the Second World War, from 1933–45. The WPA (Works Progress Administration) was established by President Roosevelt's administration to create employment through public works projects.

11   *mishugas:* derived from the Yiddish word *mishegas.* meaning 'crazy' or 'craziness'.

11   *Republican:* a member of the Republican Party, one of the two dominant political parties in the United States, together with the Democratic Party. A Republican is generally viewed as conservative, or right of centre, while a Democrat is left of centre and generally progressive.

11   *the Torah:* the first five books of the Bible and the books of Jewish laws.

11   *Heidelberg:* a city in Germany, home to the University of Heidelberg, which was known for educating famous physicians. (MD, Doctor of Medicine).

11   *I simply can't imagine . . . Poland. . .:* this refers to Nazi Germany's territorial acquisitions, which culminated in the invasion of Poland, precipitating the Second World War.

12   *Especially for this neighborhood:* few Jewish women had educational opportunities at this time.

12   *Federal Reserve:* the Federal Reserve is the central banking system of the United States.

12   *Congressman:* a member of the United States House of Representatives. A member of Congress is elected by voters in an electoral district to represent their interests. During President Roosevelt's time in office, the Democratic Party dominated the House of Representatives.

13   *hysterical paralysis:* a form of 'conversion disorder', a medical condition in which a person's mental state manifests itself in a physical disorder or disease.

13   *shell-shock during the War:* the reaction of soldiers to the stress and horrors of warfare. From the time of the First World War, it was considered a psychiatric illness which primarily affected the nervous system.

14   *Mortgage Department of Brooklyn Guarantee and Trust:* the department where loans are obtained in order to finance buying property. A bank called the Brooklyn Trust Company (founded in 1866) was located in Brooklyn Heights. Before the Depression, many people took out mortgages but after the economic crash they could not afford to keep up their payments. Lenders took possession of the mortgaged properties and as a result many people lost their homes.

14   *Tuchas qffen tisch:* a Yiddish figurative saying: 'arse on the table'. This common idiomatic expression was heard frequently in card games, often to mean: 'Put up or shut up!' or 'your cards face up' in poker games, political arguments and other such festive occasions. Yiddish is a language spoken by Ashkenazi Jews, of central or eastern European descent which is based on a German dialect, though written in Hebrew letters.

15   *Rudolph Valentino:* Rudolf Valentino (1895–1926) was an Italian-American screen star and a sex symbol. He was a screen idol in the 1920s.

16   *anti-Semites:* people who are hostile to or prejudiced against Jews.

16   *the Depression:* the economic crash that began in 1929 and continued until the outbreak of the Second World War.

16   *foreclosing:* the act of taking possession of mortgaged property when a client has been unable to make mortgage payments.

17   *only Jew:* anti-Semitism was common in the United States during the inter-war period. It affected employment and educational and social opportunities for Jewish-American citizens.

19   *old country . . . Russia:* the native country of an immigrant.
        Gellburg represents one of the thousands of Jews who
        immigrated to the United States from Central or Eastern Europe.
        He is referring to the Pale of Settlement, a region of Imperial
        Russia, in which permanent residency by Jews was allowed and
        beyond which they were largely prohibited. This region included
        much of present-day Lithuania, Belarus, Poland, Moldova,
        Ukraine and parts of western Russia.

19   *dybbuk:* according to Jewish folklore, the disturbed ghost or
        spirit of a dead person. There is a famous 1914 Yiddish play
        called *The Dybbuk, or Between Two Worlds* by S. Ansky which
        relates the story of a young bride possessed by a dybbuk. It was
        made into a film in 1937.

19   *Rabbi:* in Judaism, a religious teacher and leader.

20   *the Beverly . . . the Rialto:* in the 1930s the Beverly was a
        second-run movie theatre in Brooklyn, while the Rialto was a
        first-run movie theatre, also in Brooklyn, in the neighbourhood
        of Flatbush. Ginger Rogers (1911 – 95) and Fred Astaire (1899 –
        1987) were a famous American film duo, popular actors, singers
        and dancers. James Francis Gagney (1899 – 1986), an American
        actor known for his portrayal of tough characters, was a popular
        film star in the 1930s.

23   *he says college wouldn't help him get a job anyway:* during the
        Depression, unemployment was so severe that a university or
        college education did not necessarily lead to a job. As a result,
        secondary school and college enrolment dropped significantly.

24   *it must have been cold: Kristallnacht* took place in November of
        1938.

25   *Greenbergs:* a fictional deli (delicatessen) in the neighbourhood
        of Flatbush in Brooklyn, which had a sizable Jewish population
        during the 1930s.

25   *A&S:* Abraham and Straus, two Jewish entrepreneurs,
        established a department store chain which had a branch on
        Fulton Street in Brooklyn, New York, in the 1930s. The store is
        now owned by Macy's.

25   *General MacArthur:* Douglas MacArthur (1880–1964) was
        the Chief of Staff of the United States Army during the 1930s.
        Fort Sill is a United States Army post located near Lawton,
        Oklahoma, which was home to the United States Army Field
        Artillery School.

26   *Men who can't do anything else:* many men who were desperate
        for employment during the Depression joined the army.

26   *West Point:* a United States military academy established in 1802 and located in New York State.

26   *First Jewish General:* Jews held the rank of general in the United States Army before 1938, but this was not well known.

27   *Dodge:* an American brand of cars manufactured by the Chrysler Corporation.

29   *That doesn't matter anymore, Philip:* his sexual impotence.

32   *NYU:* founded in 1831, New York University is a private university in Greenwich Village in Manhattan, New York.

32   *Coney Island:* a residential area, beach, resort and amusement park on the southern shore of Long Island, located in Brooklyn, New York.

33   *Long Island City:* formerly a city, now a neighbourhood, in the west part of Queens, New York. Empire Street is a fictional company. A bookkeeper keeps the financial records.

36   *foulard:* a scarf or necktie made of a lightweight fabric.

37   *Crown Heights:* a neighborhood in the centre of Brooklyn. It hosted a Jewish community during the 1930s.

37   *Narrows:* a tidal strait that separates Staten Island and Brooklyn. It is the primary access to the New York Port and was popular for sailing.

37   *the Harvard Club:* a private club reserved for students and affiliates of Harvard University, the Ivy League university in Cambridge, Massachusetts.

37   *you people:* this distancing and anti-Semitic comment suggests that all Jews have the same (negative) characteristics.

38   *Mr Liebfreund:* a Jewish name that also implies collusion, being German for 'dear friend'.

38   *Wanamaker's:* one of the first department stores in the United States. At the height of its popularity, there were branches in New York and Philadelphia.

39   *Title Guarantee:* Title Guarantee and Trust was a bank in New York City

39   *defensive price:* a purchase price that protects a property investor from a financial loss if the value of the building decreases.

40   *Brighton Beach:* a community in Brooklyn, New York, near Coney Island.

40   *Ocean Parkway . . . poetry:* the tree-lined boulevard had a bridle path during the 1930s and for many years after that.

43   *Anthony Adverse:* published in 1933, a bestselling American romance written by Hervey Allen. The film version was released in 1936.

43   *Womrath's:* a rental library. Rental libraries flourished in the
        United States in the 1920s and 1930s, transforming American
        book-buying and reading habits. Libraries were often adjuncts to
        bookshops, but many operated as independent businesses. Arthur
        R. Womrath developed one of the most significant chains of
        libraries, charging fees of twenty-five cents a week or more. By
        1930 Womrath had seventy-two branches in fourteen cities.

45   *The American medical schools . . . maybe never get in:* after
        the First World War and into the 1950s many private American
        universities and medical schools had quotas on the number of
        Jewish students who could be admitted.

45   *These Nazis can't possibly last:* this represents a common
        (paralytic) North American attitude towards the Nazis. It
        suggests that the German people (and the world) couldn't
        possibly tolerate a Nazi government for long.

45   *picture in the Times:* there was substantial coverage of
        Kristallnacht in the *New York Times* in November 1938. The
        New York Times is a daily American newspaper published
        in New York City On 11 November 1938 the front page was
        devoted to the events.

45   *But nobody really wants to talk about it:* in 1938, many
        Americans did not want to acknowledge the persecution of the
        Jews in Germany.

49   *Jersey:* New Jersey is a north-eastern state that borders on New
        York State.

51   *bigyen:* slang (probably of Chinese origin) for craving: here,
        sexual desire.

55   *psychiatry:* the study and treatment of mental illness, emotional
        disturbance and abnormal behaviour. Progressive reformers
        in America in this period believed that mental illness was the
        product of environmental factors and that it was both preventable
        and progressively serious. Sigmund Freud, the father of
        psychoanalysis, also exercised enormous influence in New York
        in the first half of the twentieth century, but popular prejudices
        against psychiatry persisted.

58   *Eddie Cantor. . . Suzie:* Eddie Cantor (1892 – 1964) was a
        Jewish-American singer, songwriter, actor, dancer and comedian
        who was popular in the 1920s and 1930s. 'If you knew Suzie
        like I know Suzie' was one of his hit songs.

58   *Crosby's:* Bing Crosby (1903 – 77) was an American singer and
        film actor who was hugely popular. He was one of the bestselling
        recording artists from the 1930s up until the 1950s.

58   *they're making ten . . . opera man:* some crooners, like Bing
        Crosby, were highly paid artists during the Depression era.
        Here Hyman makes a distinction between the popular musical
        entertainment that Crosby represents and his own taste for opera,
        which is typically considered a higher form of music and another
        signifier of Hyman's link to European culture rather than to the
        American popular culture in which Jews played a major role.

59   *zoning meeting:* a land-use planning meeting.

59–   *You know, as a child. . . mother:* Sylvia refers to
60   Brooklyn in the early part of the twentieth century before large-
        scale urbanisation took place. Parts of Brooklyn remained rural
        until the 1930s.

59   *I've learned. . . That's not my training:* during the nineteenth
        and twentieth century the study of dreams was popularised by
        advocates of psychoanalysis such as Carl Jung and Sigmund
        Freud. Freud published *The Interpretation of Dreams* in 1899.

62   *relations:* sexual intercourse.

64   *I finally got him to go with me to see Rabbi Steiner:* rabbis, as
        religious authorities in the Jewish community, also gave advice
        in matters related to marriage.

65   *German music . . . like this:* this comment refers to many
        people's disbelief when they became aware in the 1930s that
        Germany, historically a country of sophistication and culture,
        had been taken over by Nazis who burned books and committed
        atrocities.

66   *What is going to become of us?:* Sylvia's statement can be
        interpreted on a number of levels. She might be referring to her
        relationship with Phillip or their future as American Jews in the
        light of the Holocaust. Or she might be speaking of the fate of
        Jews globally.

66   *I don't know . . . and I'm . . . :* Sylvia's comment draws a link
        between her concern about what Hyman will decide about her
        fate and the uncertain fate of Jews in Europe.

67   *This is an emergency . . . before they murder us all!:* Sylvia
        conflates the realities of life in Brooklyn and the violence against
        Jews in Europe. She calls upon President Roosevelt and England
        to intervene. But the US was maintaining a policy of neutrality
        and England had adopted a policy of appeasement towards Hitler.

69   *Don't sleep with me again:* here, share a bed.

71   *You didn't want me to go back to business:* before the second
        wave of feminism, women were expected to remain in the
        domestic sphere.

71   *A Jew can have a Jewish face:* Sylvia challenges Gellburg's
      denial of his Jewish identity by stating that there is no logical
      reason for a Jewish person to be embarrassed of looking Jewish.

73   *New York taxes:* property rates paid to the city of New York.

73   *just because he is also a Jew?:* anti-Semites frequently assume
      that Jews conspire with other Jews to achieve their own ends.

74   *The heart is a muscle; muscles can recover sometimes:* This
      statement refers directly to Gellburg's heart attack. It implies too
      that the muscles in Sylvia's legs, which have failed her, might
      recover. It may also suggest, less directly, that her heart and
      Gellburg's, or their feelings for one another, might be healed.

75   *Rock of Gibraltar:* the rocky promontory on the southernmost
      tip of the Iberian peninsula, thought to be indestructible, which
      inspired the saying 'solid as the Rock of Gibraltar'.

76   *pediatric ward:* area of a hospital devoted to the treatment of
      children.

76   *You draw jour cards face down:* card players do not know the
      hand they are dealt; they must make the best of it. similar to our
      lives.

78   *the Yid:* an offensive term for a Jew.

78   *That's the system:* the informal 'system' of discrimination against
      Jews in the United States in the 1930s.

71   *the Philippines:* The United States army occupied the
      Philippines until the mid-1980s. By 1938, the United States
      was in the process of assisting the Philippines to achieve their
      independence.

71   *Schrafft's:* Schrafft's was an American candy and chocolate
      company with a number of locations, including one in
      Manhattan, New York City. Abraham & Straus was also known
      as A&S (see note to p. 25).

79   *Orchard Street:* a street in the centre of the Lower East Side
      in Manhattan, New York City which was home to many first-
      generation Jewish immigrants who lived in tenement housing. It
      was also known for discount shopping.

79   *one Moses after the other:* Moses is a common Jewish name, or
      a manner of referring to Jews.

79   *Odessa:* a major city in the Crimea, a region in southern Ukraine.

80   *shiksa:* a Yiddish word (which can be pejorative) for a non-
      Jewish woman.

80   *I never pretended I wasn't Jewish:* here Hyman accuses Gellburg
      of often masking his Jewish identity, but his attitude also hints at
      defensiveness, implying ambivalence about his own affiliations.

80	*goyim:* a Yiddish word (which can be pejorative) for non- Jews.
81	*Socialist. . . Religion:* a socialist believes in the collective ownership of the means of production and that history can be understood on the basis of scientific laws. It is not necessary for a socialist to believe in God. The Socialist Party of America grew considerably in the early twentieth century.
83	*You hate yourself, that's what's scaring you to death:* this refers to the damage that self-hatred can cause. Gellburg is a 'self-hating Jew' in that he hates himself for his Jewishness and has internalised the anti-Semitism of the world around him.
83	*Schul:* a word for synagogue, a Jewish house of worship.
83	*tallis:* a Jewish prayer shawl. With the sidelocks and the black hat describes the distinctive appearance of ultra-Orthodox Jewish men.
83	*kvetches:* Yiddish word for 'complaining'; *'pecker'* is slang for penis.

Questions for Further Study

1 Does characterising Miller as a 'Jewish writer' enhance or diminish our understanding of his work? Is it important to identify the author or the play in this way? If so, why? Draw on the text for examples of how identifying someone as Jewish is either useful or counterproductive.

2 What is the significance of Harry Hyman's horse-riding and of his riding costume?

3 When Dr Hyman says that he 'never pretended [he] wasn't Jewish', he implies that being jewish is what he *really* is; it is not pretence. But where does Jewishness come from? Is it something in the blood? Does it come from a set of beliefs or from practices? If Jewishness comes from what one *does* rather than what one *is,* how is that different from pretending? What answers does the play offer to these questions?

4 How does the play reflect on its own theatricality? In what sense does the play suggest that Jewishness is a construct? Consider Phillip Gellburg, in his suit of solemn black and his obsession with his image in the mirror, both of which evoke the theatrical character of Hamlet, who has 'that within which passes show'.

5 The play concludes with an ambivalent image, as Sylvia rises above her prostrate husband, 'charged with hope yet with a certain inward-seeing alarm'. What is the ethical significance of this conclusion? Does it imply that free will triumphs over determinism in the end?

6 Does the play suggest that guilt is a productive or a destructive emotion?

7 What are the underlying problems of the Gellburg marriage, and how are these problems related to large social questions of how people should treat one another? Gellburg complains that Stanton Case treats him unfairly. Does his wife also treat him unfairly?

8 Does the play treat Gellburg unfairly by virtually killing him in the end?

9 As a moral allegory, how does *Broken Glass* speak to social and political problems today?

10 How does thinking about issues of Jewish identity and prejudice affect the play's representation of capitalism and the Great Depression?

11 Some critics find key scenes in the plays to be melodramatic. What scenes would you identify as melodramatic and why?

12 Gellburg says that when the last Jew dies the light of the world will go out, but Hyman believes that all religions will be subsumed by consumerism and that people are basically the same. Does the play give more weight to one view or the other?

13 The play portrays paralysis as a physical and metaphorical pathology and seems to advocate some form of political action in the world. What kind of action does it suggest is possible and what is needed to bring it about?

14 What is the importance of absent characters, such as the Gellburgs' son Jerome and their nephew David?

15 How does the play illuminate the tension between the personal and the professional? Consider the particular occupations involved. What is the significance of crossing, or not crossing, the line between the personal and the professional in particular instances?

16 How does the play reflect on anti-Semitism and other forms of prejudice that still exist today?

17 What is unique about the anti-Semitism that Miller presents in *Broken Glass?* How do you think it differs from other forms of prejudice?

18 To what extent is the female figure in this play always in the object position? Does this change at the end of the play?

19 Why does Gellburg always wear black?

20 What are the historical, metaphorical and psychological resonances built into the title for this play?

21 *Broken Glass* has been called a morality play. Do you agree with this assessment and does it prevent it being a moving portrayal of a marriage?

22 Does Arthur Miller see this marriage from a woman's point of view?

Further Questions on Miller's Plays

1   What significance should be assigned to the titles of Miller's plays? How do the changes from *Gellberg* to *Broken Glass*, from *The Sign of the Archer* to *All My Sons*, from *These Familiar Spirits* to *The Crucible*, and from *The Inside of His Head* or *Free and Clear* affect the meaning and central focus of these dramas?

2   To what extent is ethnicity a useful entry point for the experience of reading and seeing Miller's plays? What are its limitations as well as its possibilities for understanding the themes he explores with his audience in his ongoing repertory?

3   Discuss the changing role of women as we encounter the series of female characters established in Miller's drama from *All My Sons* to *Broken Glass*. To what extent are they assigned a satellite role? To what extent do they succeed in out-sizing their uneasy assignment to a secondary part? How might they do so in performance?

4   What role do music and other sound elements play in creating the atmosphere of a Miller play?

5   In these plays do you think Miller has put to rest the question of writing an effective and evocative 'tragedy' for 'the common man'? What dramatic techniques has he explored in his attempt to deal with this question?

6   Based on your study of these plays, what aspects of marriage emerge and develop from one work to the next? In what ways are these marriages similar, and in what ways are they different? Are all of these marriages equally doomed?

7   What symbolic elements does Miller use to enhance the meaning and range of the thematic elements in his plays?

8   Is the drama Miller portrays in his theatre uniquely American? If so, in what specific ways? Do you think his drama also succeeds in encompassing a more universal frame of reference?

9   In what ways does Miller's drama serve as a moral allegory for our own time?

10   Are there melodramatic elements at work in Miller's plays? If so, what part do they play in bringing his stories to their conclusion? Do you think this is a weakness in his writing? Or is some other strategy at work here?

11   To what extent are these works determined and inspired by history and historical events? How does Miller transform these elements into convincing interpersonal relationships among his characters on stage?

12 If you were directing these plays, what qualities would you look for in casting the major protagonists in these dramas?

13 Discuss the ways in which the plays make use of visual and other non-verbal elements to sustain an audience's interest with the plays in performance. What use do they make of stage props to advance the story Miller tells on stage?

14 Do you think it is necessary for productions of these plays to adhere to the strict and specific stage directions specified by the playwright? What do you think might happen to these plays when a production takes dramatic license and departs from them?

15 Discuss the ways in which these plays make use of absent and non-appearing characters.

16 In what ways are Miller's characters obsessed with materialism, consumerism and a reliance on material objects for their sense of themselves and their sense of their world?

17 To what extent can we understand Miller's characters as products of their political, economic and social realities? Do his characters seem to be aware of these realities? Do they strive to confront them? If so, are they successful?

18 Is Miller a playwright of dramatic realism? Do the changing forms of these plays challenge or undermine this definition in any way?

19 How does Miller base a secure dramatic situation on the choices and decisions characters make before the curtain rises? What power do such back-stories have as each drama unfolds?

20 Discuss the role Miller assigns to Fate as each drama moves forward to its conclusion. What other classical elements of drama seem to be in play here?

21 Miller has often been praised for his ability to transform questions of moral ambiguity into convincing dramatic conflict. Which scenes from the works you have studied display this dynamics most efficiently and impress you most?

Further Reading

Works by Miller

Arthur Miller Plays, 6 vols, with introductions by Arthur Miller, vols 1–5, and
Enoch Brater, vol. 6: (vol. 1: *All My Sons, Death of a Salesman, The Crucible,
A Memory of Two Mondays, A View from the Bridge*; vol. 2: *The Misfits, After
the Fall, Incident at Vichy, The Price, The Creation of the World and Other
Business, Playing for Time*; vol. 3: *The American Clock, The Archbishop's
Ceiling, Two-Way Mirror*; vol. 4: *The Golden Years, The Man Who Had All
the Luck, I Can't Remember Anything, Clara*; vol. 5: *The Last Yankee, The
Ride Down Mount Morgan, Almost Everybody Wins*; vol. 6: *Broken Glass,
Mr Peters' Connections, Resurrection Blues, Finishing the Picture*). London:
Methuen, 1988–2009.
All My Sons, with notes and commentary by Toby Zinman. London: Methuen
Drama, 2010.
Broken Glass, with notes and commentary by Alan Ackerman. London: Methuen
Drama, 2011.
The Crucible, with notes and commentary by Susan C. W. Abbotson. London:
Methuen Drama, 2010.
Death of a Salesman, with notes and commentary by Enoch Brater. London:
Methuen Drama, 2010.
Echoes Down the Corridor: Collected Essays, 1944–2000, ed. Steven R. Centola.
London: Methuen, 2000.
'Salesman' in Beijing. London: Methuen, 1984.
The Theatre Essays of Arthur Miller, ed. Robert A. Martin. London: Methuen,
1994.
Timebends: A Life. London: Methuen, 1987.
A View from the Bridge, with notes and commentary by Stephen Marino. London:
Methuen Drama, 2010.

Secondary reading

Bigsby, Christopher. *Arthur Miller: 1915–1962*. London: Weidenfeld &
Nicolson, 2008.
—. *Arthur Miller: 1962–2005*. Ann Arbor: University of Michigan Press, 2011.
—. *Arthur Miller: A Critical Study*. Cambridge: Cambridge University Press,
2004.
—, ed. *The Cambridge Companion to Arthur Miller*. Cambridge: Cambridge
University Press, 1997.

Brater, Enoch. *Arthur Miller: A Playwright's Life and Works*. London: Thames and Hudson, 2005.

—, ed. *Arthur Miller's America: Theater and Culture in a Century of Change*. Ann Arbor: University of Michigan Press, 2005.

—, ed. *Arthur Miller's Global Theater: How an American Playwright Is Performed on Stages around the World*. Ann Arbor: University of Michigan Press, 2007.

Gottfried, Martin. *Arthur Miller: His Life and Work*. Cambridge, MA: Da Capo Press, 2003.

Gussow, Mel. *Conversations with Miller*. New York: Applause Theatre & Cinema Books, 2002.

Martin, Robert A., ed. *Arthur Miller: New Perspectives*. Englewood Cliffs, NJ: Prentice-Hall, 1982.

Mason, Jeffrey. *Stone Tower: The Political Theater of Arthur Miller*. Ann Arbor: University of Michigan Press, 2008.

Roudané, Matthew C., ed. *Conversations with Arthur Miller*. Jackson: University Press of Mississippi Press, 1987.

Savran, David. *Communists, Cowboys and Queers: The Politics of Masculinity in the Plays of Arthur Miller and Tennessee Williams*. Minneapolis: University of Minnesota Press, 1992.

Notes on Contributors

SUSAN C. W. ABBOTSON is Professor of Modern and Contemporary Drama at Rhode Island College and author of *Masterpieces of 20th-Century American Drama*, *Thematic Guide to Modern Drama*, *Student Companion to Arthur Miller* and *Critical Companion to Arthur Miller*, as well as *Understanding Death of a Salesman* (co-authored with Brenda Murphy). A specialist on Arthur Miller, she is currently the Performance Editor for the *Arthur Miller Journal*.

ALAN ACKERMAN is Professor of English at the University of Toronto. His books include *Just Words: Lillian Hellman, Mary McCarthy, and the Failure of Public Conversation in America* and *Seeing Things, from Shakespeare to Pixar*.

ENOCH BRATER is the Kenneth T. Rowe Collegiate Professor of Dramatic Literature at the University of Michigan. He has published widely in the field of modern drama, and is an internationally renowned expert on such figures as Samuel Beckett and Arthur Miller. His recent books include *Arthur Miller: A Playwright's Life and Works*, *Arthur Miller's America: Theater and Culture in a Time of Change*, *Arthur Miller's Global Theater: How an American Playwright Is Performed on Stages around the World* and *Ten Ways of Thinking About Samuel Beckett: The Falsetto of Reason*.

STEPHEN MARINO is founding editor of the *Arthur Miller Journal* and adjunct professor of English at St Francis College, Brooklyn Heights, New York. He is former president of the Arthur Miller Society. His work on Arthur Miller has appeared in *Modern Drama*, the *South Atlantic Review*, the *Nevada Historical Quarterly* and the *Dictionary of Literary Biography*. He is editor of *The Salesman Has a Birthday: Essays Celebrating the Fiftieth Anniversary of Arthur Miller's 'Death of a Salesman'* (University Press of America, 2000) and author of *A Language Study of Arthur Miller's Plays: The Poetic in the Colloquial* (Edwin Mellen Press, 2002). He has also contributed an essay on Miller's poetic language to a collection of essays about Arthur Miller, *Critical Insights* (Salem Press, 2010).

TOBY ZINMAN is Professor of English at the University of the Arts in Philadelphia, where she was awarded the prize for Distinguished Teaching. She has lectured internationally on contemporary American drama, including a semester as Fulbright professor in Israel and another as a visiting lecturer in China. Her third book, *Edward Albee*, was published in 2008. She is also the theatre critic for Philadelphia's major daily newspaper, *The Inquirer*, and a frequent contributor to a variety of arts magazines. Forthcoming book from Methuen includes *Replay: Classic Modern Drama Re-imagined*.